Praise for 'Living with Purpose'

'*Living with Purpose* is a profound and thought-provoking work, a magical outcome of over three years that delves into the essence of moral and civic education, offering a holistic approach to intellectual and personal development. This book stands out for its ability to seamlessly integrate emotional intelligence, motivation and ethical reasoning into the learning process, fostering an educational experience that is both meaningful and transformative.

'At its core, the book highlights the importance of cultivating the whole person – one whose intellectual growth is grounded in a shared framework of moral, emotional and intellectual values. Through insightful discussions and practical applications, it underscores the role of value-based education in shaping responsible, compassionate and socially conscious individuals.

'A key strength of Values Education is its ability to bridge theoretical concepts with real-world implications, making it an indispensable resource for educators, students and policymakers alike. Its emphasis on personal meaning and motivation encourages readers to actively engage with their own ethical perspectives, creating a profound connection between knowledge and action.

'Well-researched, eloquently written and deeply impactful, this book is a must-read for anyone invested in the future of education and human development. It is not just an academic guide but a powerful testament to the transformative potential of values-based learning.'

—**Professor (Dr) Anoop Swarup**
Chair, Centre for Global Nonkilling (In Consultative Status of the UN)
Secretary General of the Association of Universities of Asia and the Pacific

'This book provides valuable insight into fostering holistic development in moral and civic education by integrating intellectual growth with personal meaning, emotions and motivation. This approach cultivates the whole person, grounding learning in a shared framework of moral, emotional and intellectual values.'

—**Professor Terence J Lovat**
Honorary Research Fellow – The University of Oxford, UK
Emeritus Professor – The University of Newcastle, Australia
Distinguished Visiting Professor – The University of Johannesburg, South Africa
Chief investigator of several Australian Values Education Program projects 2004–2010

'I am so delighted to endorse this transformative book, which will enable young people to understand, recognise the importance of, and most importantly, live by a set of enhancing human values. The world desperately needs ethical leaders at all levels of society. The wisdom contained in this book, through its narrative and activities, will help students to be in the vanguard of an ethical renaissance.'

—**Dr Neil Hawkes**
Founder IVET Foundation and Values-based Education (VbE), UK

'In an era marked by uncertainty and rapid change, *Living with Purpose* emerges as a beacon of wisdom, guiding us towards a life of deeper meaning, stronger relationships and a more sustainable world. With an insightful exploration of the three foundational pillars – personal wellbeing, positive relationships and environmental stewardship – this book offers a comprehensive roadmap for anyone seeking to lead a fulfilling and responsible life.

'Drawing from philosophy, psychology and global perspectives, the authors masterfully weave together research, practical wisdom and personal reflections to illuminate the path to self-actualisation and conscious living. From the pursuit of purpose and emotional intelligence to the importance of love, family and ethical environmental responsibility, this book provides invaluable insights into cultivating a life aligned with core human values.'

—**Professor Rania Lampou**
Multi-awarded STEM Instructor & Researcher Greek Ministry of Education, Religious Affairs and Sports, Greece

'Knowing and living according to our true values is such an essential element of a life of flow, contribution and alignment, yet so little of this is taught in schools. This is a great resource to those wanting to explore this important area with greater focus and an invaluable resource to those responsible for teaching it to young people. When we know our true values, every aspect of our journey in this life is enriched and brought into sharp focus, so we truly get to live the difference we are born to make.'

—**Heather Yelland**
Founder and Director, The Elevation Company

'It is an absolute pleasure that I write this as an Australian Aboriginal woman, of the Gudang Aboriginal Clan in far northern Cape York, Queensland. As well, with current knowledge and pride of my ancestral connection with Scotland, Ireland and Asia. This book affirms the teachings and learnings of my formative years, growing up on Thursday Island in the Torres Strait Islands and the Western Far Northern Cape York Peninsula in Queensland. These ways were learned from the faith groups and the multicultural community who were peoples of goodwill. Enhancement of these teachings were gained in my interactions over many years with diverse cultural groups since those formative years. The rules of my Gudang Clan Lore, the Torres Strait Islander Lore and John Wesley's Poem, 'Do All the Good', are the reasons why in my 80th year, I am still of a sound mind. Your book, in my opinion, has the potential to restore and re-create empathy and mutually respectful relationships with each other as human beings, throughout the world. This will bring love, joy and peace to all peoples, of all ways of life, in all homelands on Earth, our Mother Planet.'

—***Pearl McLaren Wymarra***
Dip. Primary School Ed. NSW (1981), Master of Health Science Primary Health Care
Dip. Theology 2025, Honorary Fellow, University of Western Sydney (2000)
National Inaugural Award for University Teaching of Indigenous Studies Recipient (1997)

Living with Purpose

3 Pillars of Wellbeing, Positive Relationships, and a Sustainable and Peaceful Future

Dr John Bellavance • Dr Tuong Thi Phan
• Dr Rafia Naz

Three Pillars Framework: a comprehensive approach to education, nurturing ethical individuals and relationships, responsible businesses, effective governance and engaged global citizens.

Title: Living with Purpose – *The Three Pillars of Wellbeing, Positive Relationships, and a Sustainable and Peaceful Future*

Volume One of *Six Pillars Framework for Wellbeing, Positive Relationships, and a Sustainable and Peaceful Future*

Published by South North Group for the Universal Peace Federation Australia and the International Association of Academicians for Peace Oceania, Melbourne, Australia

Editor: Wendy Millgate-Stuart, Wendy & Words

Copyright © 2025 South North Group

All right reserved.

No part of this publication may be reproduced, stored in a retrieval system, or transmitted in any form or by any means—electronic, mechanical, photocopying, recording, or otherwise—without the prior written permission of the publisher, except in the case of brief quotations embodied in critical articles or reviews.

Although the publisher and the author have made every effort to ensure that the information in this book was correct at press time and while this publication is designed to provide accurate information in regard to the subject matter covered, the publisher and the author assume no responsibility for errors, inaccuracies, omissions, or any other inconsistencies herein and hereby disclaim any liability to any party for any loss, damage, or disruption caused by errors or omissions, whether such errors or omissions result from negligence, accident, or any other cause.

This publication is meant as a source of valuable information for the reader; however, it is not meant as a substitute for direct expert assistance. If such level of assistance is required, the services of a competent professional should be sought.

Paperback ISBN: 978-1-7640746-0-5

Acknowledgments

This book would not have become such a valuable resource without its editor, Wendy Millgate-Stuart. She brought not only her editorial skills but also her life experience and wisdom to important topics. We are thankful for her attention to detail and her patience. I am also sincerely grateful to the other contributing authors, Dr Tuong Thi Phan and Dr Rafia Naz, who so generously shared their time and expertise, for free. Clearly their contributions to values education are deeply appreciated.

—Dr John Bellavance

About the Authors

Dr John Bellavance is a distinguished academic and community leader with extensive experience in international peacebuilding and education. He currently serves as a Global Vice-President at Sun Moon University, South Korea and is the Oceania Coordinator for the International Association of Academicians for Peace (IAAP). Additionally, he holds the position of Vice-President of the Universal Peace Federation (UPF) Australia. He holds a Doctor of Philosophy from Monash University, Australia in values education and the use of Information and Communication Technology and has been teaching Information Technology in high schools for 20 years.

Dr Tuong Thi Phan (PhD) has been working in the higher education sector in Sydney University and New Zealand over the past 35 years. Her PhD was on *Western-Based Approaches to Assessing Psychiatric Symptoms in Vietnamese*. By invitation, she has engaged in teaching, supervising and curriculum development at several other overseas universities as a visiting professor. Her academic achievement has been centred on preventing and enhancing health and diagnosing mental illness, particularly among underprivileged groups and communities. She developed a culturally sensitive instrument to identify four major scopes of mental health, which has been widely utilised in Australia and abroad. She is a Member of the Oceania International Association of Academicians for Peace (IAAP) and Ambassador for Peace Universal Peace Federation (UPF).

 Dr Rafia Naz is a notable academic and has local, regional and international experience in Management and Public Administration. She is presently Professor and Head of MBA at the University of Fiji. She has been an active member of Universal Peace Federation (UPF) and Oceania International Association of Academicians for Peace (IAAP) and has been a Consultant at the Graduate School of Business, the University of the South Pacific. Dr Naz has held the position of the Dean for the Faculty of Business and Entrepreneurship (FoBE) and the Deputy Vice Chancellor for Research and Innovation at the National University of Samoa. She holds a Doctor of Philosophy from the University of the South Pacific, Fiji in Management and Public Administration.

CONTENTS

Introduction 2
Making Sense of Your World 4
Happiness Beyond Material Pursuits 9
The Great Human Contradiction 10
Six Pillars Framework 15
Book Structure 19

PILLAR 1: Managing Ourselves and Self-Actualisation 21

1: Finding Meaning and Purpose 24
Frankl's Levels of Meaning 26
Joy and Meaning 27
Meaning, Identity and Morality 29
Purpose of the Whole and Purpose of the Individual 34

2: Living Conscientiously – Know Yourself 37
The Comparison Trap 37
Self-Inquiry – Fostering Your Conscience 39
Self-Awareness and Self-Evaluation 40
How to Become Self-Aware 45
Mental Prisons – Free Your Mind 49

3: Personal Responsibility 55
Human Responsibility 55
Responsibility and Self-Esteem 58
Challenging Our Demons: The Hero's Journey 65

4: Understanding Mind and Body Relations 78
Mind–Body, Subject–Object, Giving–Receiving 79

Holism: An Integrative Explanation of Purpose 81
Are We Our Mind or Our Body? 84
Mind–Body Conflict and Inner Conflict 95

5: Managing Mind and Body Well 101
Love's Role in Mind–Body Unity... 102
Self-Control and Mind–Body Unity 105
Setting Goals and Mind–Body Unity 110

6: Mindfulness and Mind–Body Unity..121
Mindfulness, Attention and Flow... 122
Mindfulness, Meditation and Wellbeing... 123
Mindfulness, Brainwaves and Practising Mindfulness............................... 124
A Teacher's Reflection on Mindfulness, Meditation and
Wellbeing During COVID 130

7: Emotional and Spiritual Intelligence and Mind–Body Unity..........134
Four Features of Emotional Intelligence 135
Spiritual Intelligence 142
Emotional Intelligence for Enhanced Leader Relations............................. 145
Emotional Intelligence for Enhanced Relations and
Conflict Management 148

8: Cultural Impacts on Self-Actualisation and Self-Development 153
Challenges of Low Assertiveness in Southeast Asian Communities........... 156
The Importance of Acculturation.. 158
Cultural Aspects of Self-Management.. 159
Assertiveness and Self-Actualisation 160
Self-Cultivation and Self-Actualisation 162
Acculturation and Transculturation 163
Wellbeing and Acculturation 165

PILLAR 2: Managing Our Relationships and Self-Actualisation.......169

9: Love Is the Central Value of Life 173
Love Gives Life Meaning 175
Joy is an Outcome of Love.. 176
Systems and Connections... 178

Giving and Receiving 180

10: Values and Practices that Underpin Good Relationships 184
Living for the Sake of Others 184
The Importance of Shared Values.. 191
Communication.. 193

11: Families As Schools of Values and Love..198
Families as Foundations for Moral and Emotional Development............... 199
The Family as a School of Love 200
Social Challenges to Family Life... 202
Economic Challenges to Family Life 204
The Source of Morality is the Family 206
The Family is an Integrative Whole 207
Extended Family and Spheres of Support 209
Dysfunctional Families... 212

12: Conjugal Love (Sphere 1) 217
The Benefits of Marriage.. 218
Core Values and Qualities of a Good Marriage.. 220
The Impact of Respectful Communication on Spouse Relations and
Marriage Satisfaction 232
Fostering Sexual Ethics and Healthy Sexual Development 237
Sexual Ethics Guidance 248

13: The Need for Sexual Ethics in Sexual Education (Sphere 1) 256
Assessing High-Quality Sexual Education.. 257
Conclusion 262

14: Parental Love, Attachment and Effective Parenting
Styles (Sphere 2)...265
Parental Attachment and Personality Development.. 266
Parental Attachment and Social Development... 267
Parenting Styles and Their Influence 269
Authoritative Parenting and Inductive Discipline 273
The Benefit of Authoritative Parents: A Personal Reflection 276

15: Sibling Love and Children's Love for Parents (Spheres 3 & 4) 283
Sibling Love 283

PILLAR 3: Managing Our Natural Environment and
               Sustainable Development 290

16: Managing and Caring for Our Natural Environment 294
Paradigms for a Technological Society 295
Managing Science, Technology, Economics and the Environment 300
The Separation of Values from Development 301
The Need for Transdisciplinary Research 306
Implementation and Governance Challenges 308
Sustainable Practices and Policies of Organisations and Individuals 310

17: Conclusion 319

— COMING SOON — 323
Three Pillars of Global Citizenship:
Universal Values, Interdependence and Mutual Prosperity 323

References 326

Table of Figures

Figure 1 Meaning and connection 14
Figure 2 Six Pillars Framework for Wellbeing, Positive Relationships,
    and a Sustainable and Peaceful Future 15
Figure 3 The United Nations (UN) Sustainable Development
    Goals (SDGs) 16
Figure 4 Three life goals 17
Figure 5 Maslow's Hierarchy of Needs This file is licensed under the
    Creative Commons Attribution-Share Alike 3.0 25
Figure 6 Frank's Levels of Meaning 27
Figure 7 Plato's Cave 42
Figure 8 The Heroes Journey (2009) 66
Figure 9 Mind and body positive and negative feedback 80
Figure 10 The reciprocal and interchanging nature of subject
    and object 81
Figure 11 An individual as a self-actualised integrative whole 82
Figure 12 A loving family as an integrative whole 82
Figure 13 A theory of consciousness woven into the evolutionary story 95
Figure 14 Managing self-gratification 97
Figure 15 Managing mind and body and self-actualisation 102
Figure 16 Love and mind/body unity 103
Figure 17 Outcomes of self-control 108
Figure 18 Self-control concept map 109
Figure 19 Managing mind/body and setting goals 116
Figure 20 Three types of intelligence 135

Figure 21 Reciprocity between reason and emotion 136
Figure 22 12 Spiritual intelligences (Blackbyrn 2022) 144
Figure 23 Joy is an outcome of relationships 177
Figure 24 Feedback loop between humans and their natural environment 179
Figure 25 Giving and receiving feedback loop 181
Figure 26 Outcomes based on shared values 192
Figure 28 Four expressions of love 208
Figure 29 Spheres of Love and Developmental Assets 210
Figure 30 The global layers of support 211
Photograph By Raja (Khalsa Studio) Own work, CC BY-SA 4.0, ... 224
Figure 31 A holistic sexual education program 242
Figure 32 Feedback loop between humans and their natural environments 298
Figure 33 Values and sustainable development 305
Figure 34 Circular Economy 312

'The most important human endeavour is the striving for morality in our actions. Our inner balance and even our very existence depend on it. Only morality in our actions can give beauty and dignity to life.'

—***Albert Einstein***

Introduction
Dr John Bellavance

The values education and personal development program presented in this book cultivates lifelong values and skills that empower you to effectively manage yourself, your relationships and your interactions with your environment. It equips young people and adults with a moral framework to navigate and understand the world around them.

This program encourages a mature approach to self-awareness and personal growth, starting with the fundamental realisation that you are inherently a good person engaged in a shared human journey. Begin from the position of your intrinsic worth and approach reflection on improvement without self-criticism or undue stress.

The program also involves character education, which helps individuals become not just academically capable ('smart') but also morally sound and virtuous ('good'). A virtue is a deeply ingrained quality of a person's character that is considered morally good and is developed over time through practice. The essence of a good society is based on the virtue of its citizens and leaders. Societies benefit when virtue is cultivated as the basis for wellbeing. Virtue involves developing the 'whole person' and equipping them with the values and skills needed to navigate life's challenges, make responsible decisions, and contribute positively to their families, schools, communities and the wider world. This is one of the goals of this program.

This program is intended for senior **high school students** (ages 15–18), **university students, adults** looking to enhance personal development and relationships, and **civil society, government** and **business organisations** aiming to foster a moral, thriving and sustainable society through value-based programs.

Teachers using this program in the classroom are encouraged to introduce and clarify key terms and concepts to support students' understanding and engagement. Lesson plans and activity sheets that go along with this program can be provided. *Please contact Dr John Bellavance – bellavanceja@gmail.com.*

This *Living on Purpose* program incorporates the *Six Pillars Framework for Wellbeing, Positive Relationships, and a Sustainable and Peaceful Future*, with this text focusing on the first three pillars: **Managing Ourselves**, **Managing Relationships** and **Managing Environments**. We believe the Six Pillars Framework offers a comprehensive approach to education, nurturing ethical individuals and relationships, responsible businesses, effective governance and engaged global citizens.

Education is never truly value neutral. It moulds individuals into a particular kind of person with a particular type of character. Educators, parents, business leaders and government officials agree on the importance of a holistic approach to education that fosters self-esteem, tolerance and respect for others, a willingness to take responsibility, integrity, pride in achievements and self-motivation. The role of values in developing confident, ethical, resilient and successful learners has long underpinned national education goals around the world.

Other worthwhile qualities include resilience in the face of criticism, the capacity to be both loving and lovable, a readiness to pursue meaningful and challenging goals, and the ability to take responsibility for one's own life.

To achieve this vision, the cognitive and intellectual aspects of education must be integrated with moral and civic education – embracing personal meaning, emotions and motivation. Such an approach nurtures the whole person, grounding learning in a shared set of moral, emotional and intellectual values.[6]

The proceedings of a series of Values Education Summits held in 2021 and 2022 organised by the Universal Peace Federation consistently found that values education is important for the wellbeing of children, social and emotional development, healthy and respectful relationships, student engagement with learning, reduced behavioural problems, better learning outcomes and community harmony.[7]

A holistic values-based education needs to foster:

- moral values and practices
- intellectual and creative abilities
- emotional and social abilities that underpin wellbeing and connection with others
- service learning through community or public service that supports personal development and the common good.

These are the vision and goals of this program.

Making Sense of Your World

This program focuses on achieving success in the things that truly matter in life. It encourages you to reflect on what matters to you, understand your purpose and identify your core values, so that these meaningfully shape your personal worldview – rather than leaving you with the sense that that something essential is missing.

Every experience is shaped by a particular perspective. Your worldview and values are guiding principles that help you navigate life and make sense of both you and the world around you. A worldview seeks to answer fundamental questions such as:

- *Who am I?*
- *What is important to me?*
- *What is the nature of the world and universe I live in?*

Ultimately, such key questions revolve around identifying the values, skills and behaviours that will lead to your happiness, benefit both yourself and others, and sustain your life and relationships.

Without these answers, as American philosopher and psychologist William James famously put it, the world becomes nothing more than 'a blooming, buzzing confusion'. The rise of online engagement has broadened our exposure to diverse values and ideas from different cultures. However, hyper-connectivity does not necessarily lead to a deeper understanding of ourselves or others.

We urgently need to make sense of ourselves and the world around us. One of the greatest challenges societies face today is how to integrate new values while preserving the wisdom and nourishing the traditions that have sustained past civilisations. Sometimes in our pursuit of new ways of seeing the world, it's easy to overlook that humanity has progressed thanks to the wisdom of the past.

> We urgently need to make sense of ourselves and the world around us.

How might we embrace change while still honouring history's lessons?

Can we move beyond the 'us versus them' mentality and the polarisation often amplified by social media – divisions that separate us, distort our perceptions and prevent us from seeing the best in others?

We live in an age where dehumanisation is prevalent and many struggle to recognise the humanity in others or respond with compassion. We have now reached a critical point where we must rethink both our understanding of the world and our role within it.

One of the key challenges of our times is the tendency to equate human success in manipulating the world through science and technology with having the right values to guide such power.

While advancements in science, economics, education and society have been remarkable, they have also led to unintended, and often damaging, consequences. Our capacity to shape the world does not guarantee that we fully understand its complexity or the full impact of our actions. Consequently, alongside great progress, we have caused significant harm to the natural environment and the delicate balance of our planet.

The need for values education, as individuals and as a society, is evident. Trust in political institutions is declining and pessimism about the future is growing.[8]

Could this be in part due to a decrease in values-driven beliefs and behaviours?

Perhaps it is time to reassess who we are, 'who I am' and how we see the world.

Our worldviews and focus

The self can be understood through three fundamental orientations towards the world:

a) As an **individual,** existing independently and distinct from others.

b) As a **connected being**, forming emotional bonds with family, community and nation.

c) As a **universal identity**, shaped by a deep connection to humanity, culture, spirituality and nature, internally guided by values.

Each of these orientations possess both an internal dimension – for example, our values and morals that shape who we are – and an external expression of our values such as how we run our businesses.[9]

As Albert Einstein wisely observed, 'When you change the way you look at things, the things you look at change.' This insight highlights how the way we perceive the world – our worldview – fundamentally shapes our reality and our sense of self.

This leads us to a crucial question:

Where should we focus our attention when we look at the world and ourselves?

What values drive us, and how do they shape our identity – our sense of self and the way we engage with the world around us?

Attention is not merely an intellectual process but a disposition – an approach shaped by our consciousness – a continuous flow of conscious and unconscious experience filtered by the brain – and by our worldview.(10) So, the way you choose to see others depends on your values and the focus of your attention.

For instance, in a workplace, you can perceive a co-worker as merely part of a system governed by policies and procedures. Or you can see them as a whole person, engaging with them in a more empathetic and human-centred way.

A useful analogy is tuning a radio. Initially, we scan different stations, but over time we settle on one. The other stations still exist, but we no longer hear them because our attention is directed towards a specific station.

Albert Einstein once noted that the most fundamental decisions in life involve how we perceive the world: *Do we see the universe as friendly or hostile? Is the world filled with anger, conflict and people driven by hate and violence?* Is that the reality you choose to perceive? Or do we see the world with great potential for love and harmony?

Our values and perspective shape how we experience the world. When we view the world as hostile, we unconsciously contribute to creating that reality in our own lives. Conversely, when we view it as a place of possibility, kindness and connection, we cultivate a more positive and fulfilling existence.(11)

I remember walking around a cruise ship recently, observing fellow holiday makers. Many had their heads down, not really engaging with anyone. I reflected on how some people can be surrounded by others and still feel alone. Yet others walk with their heads lifted, smiling and engaging with those around them. I said to myself, *John, look up and engage. Don't walk through life seeing others as passersby or even nuisances.* The simple act of looking up – of meeting people's eyes – helps us see the world as less hostile and more human.

Adopting a detached view can distance us from the struggles of others, making us less likely to see their problems as our own. Whether we are present or disengaged, connected or alienated,

> ...the way we direct our attention has the power to transform whatever it encounters.

empathetic or indifferent, the way we direct our attention has the power to transform whatever it encounters.(10)

Since our consciousness influences what comes into being, where we place our attention holds the power to create or destroy, to engage or ignore – but never to leave the world unchanged. We can't detach ourselves from this reality, for we are both part of it and shaped by our relationship to it.

The way you direct your attention matters. By focusing a certain way, you can either humanise or dehumanise, cherish or diminish value. A fragmented, polarised and alienating perspective can reduce both humanity and the natural world to mere utility(10) – objects to use. This distances you from the very world you are inherently connected to. The more you see the world in a dehumanising, mechanical way, the more that becomes your reality.

Your worldview can set you free

Your worldview can either open doors to new possibilities or limit your ability to see things differently. As the saying goes, 'You can't put new wine into old wineskins', meaning sometimes we need to let go of outdated or unhelpful beliefs to open ourselves up to new ideas or methods. For example, a report found that many people don't pursue their dreams because of how they see themselves and their low self-esteem.(12)

When a new worldview challenges our existing beliefs, we often resist it until we realise that our current understanding no longer aligns with reality. A clear example of this is seen in scientific progress. When new discoveries challenge established theories, at first scientists often push back. However, over time, as evidence accumulates, their understanding must adapt, reshaping their perception of the world. We also often push back when we are confronted with new ideas or perspectives.

As an idealist, I believe in the goodness of people and the potential for positive change. I have spent 40 years working for peace. Yet, when a friend gave me a book about the possibility of creating a non-violent world, my first reaction was, *Is this really possible?* We hope for the best, yet deep down we often doubt whether a world of peace, prosperity and happiness can truly exist.

Cynicism can often seem like the smarter choice compared to believing in the goodness of others. Politicians disappoint, and trusted institutions sometimes prove self-serving. This scepticism reflects a common mindset – doubting both people and the potential for positive change. Yet it also underscores the importance of recognising the power that values and ideals have in transforming ourselves and the world around us. Nelson Mandela profoundly believed in the power of ideals. His entire life was a testament to his unwavering commitment to a set of core values and principles, even in the face of immense personal hardship and decades of imprisonment.

Looking at the violence throughout history, and today, it can be difficult to remain idealistic. Some anthropologists argue that humans are biologically wired for aggression. However, there is reason for optimism. Historical records show that, over the centuries, less than 5% of all humans have killed others.[13] Since this evidence suggests that peaceful societies have been more common than violent ones, it is inaccurate to claim that human nature is inherently non-peaceful.[14]

A key message of this book is the importance of opening your mind to the possibilities of what you can achieve – both in your own life and in society – through the values and practices you embrace. Your happiness, wellbeing and sense of peace are shaped by these choices.

This book encourages you to prioritise the pursuit of meaning, connection and service to others over external measures of success like wealth and power.

Happiness Beyond Material Pursuits

While happiness is often regarded as the truest measure of social progress and a central goal of public policy, much of society remains focused on economic growth. Material wellbeing matters, but prioritising meaning, connection and service is essential for fostering a culture of love, prosperity and peace – both in our own lives and in the lives of others.

We seem to have become consumed by the external world – appearance, status and wealth – while losing sight of our internal world of love, meaning and connection. A fulfilling and happy life are about far more than accumulating possessions or pursuing self-gratification. You can eat well, exercise and live in comfort yet still feel unfulfilled. You can even be travelling on a cruise ship yet still feel disconnected.

Why is this?

External success alone can't satisfy our deep need for connection, purpose and self-transcendence. Even with wealth, education and social status, we may still experience anxiety if our lives lack meaning, genuine relationships and a sense of purpose beyond ourselves.

We can observe today that despite the deep-seated craving for love, almost everything – like success, prestige, wealth – is considered more important than love. As a result, almost all our energy is used to learn how to achieve these aims and almost none to learn to love.[12] How often do we sacrifice more meaningful pursuits and relations because we find our value in careers, external accomplishments and the approval of others?

The prevalence of mental health issues, injustice and conflict suggests that we need to pay more attention to the social foundations of happiness, namely love, values, meaning, and our connection with others and the natural environment. Research shows that love, freedom, altruism, honesty, health, income and good governance are the main factors that support happiness and social wellbeing.[15]

To truly experience wellbeing and happiness, we need a sense of meaning, purpose and connection with others. Psychologists Sigmund Freud and Carl Jung emphasised that love is at the heart of mental wellbeing.[12]

The Great Human Contradiction

> *'We become what we love and who we love shapes what we become.'*
> —*Clare of Assisi*

Happiness arises when our values, ideals and desires are fulfilled. Each of us has goals and aspirations shaped by what we value and the ideals we pursue. While some desires and associated actions can be positive, others may be harmful or dysfunctional. When our desires lead to unethical or unproductive choices, they can create unhappiness – not just for ourselves but also for those around us.

Human history and countless texts are full of stories of people recognising divisions within themselves and in their relationships with others. Collectively, we often produce outcomes that nobody truly wants. We have all witnessed moments of ethical and effective behaviour in ourselves and others – but also moments of failure, selfishness or harm. Sometimes, these contradictions coexist within the same individual. We can be both good and unethical, effective and ineffective, at different moments in our lives.

In this text, goodness is defined as actions that benefit both the individual and the greater whole, while unethical behaviour serves the self at the expense of others. At the heart of this contradiction lies selfishness, which often drives the tension between doing what is right and acting in our own interest.

> Goodness – actions that benefit both the individual and the greater whole

Otto Scharmer[16] uses the analogy of a farmer's field to illustrate the Great Human Contradiction. While the farmer plants seeds, it is the quality of the soil that determines what will grow. Similarly, society's 'social field' represents what is visible on the surface, while beneath it lies the foundation that shapes what we create. The richness of this foundation depends on how we relate to ourselves, to one another and to the natural world. In other words, the values we embrace, the consciousness we cultivate, and the choices we make form the soil in which the seeds of our collective future either thrive or wither.

Where does this human contradiction stem from?

According to Scharmer and Kaufer[16], it arises from three key divides:

1. **Spiritual divide** – a disconnection from our true selves
2. **Social divide** – separates us from others
3. **Ecological divide** – reflects humanity's disconnection from nature.

Changing our mindset and heartset

The spiritual divide is often the least recognised. It refers to the gap between who we are now and who we have the potential to become – our greatest, most fully self-actualised selves. Its effects are profound. Feelings of anxiety, depression and even suicidal thoughts can sometimes reflect this inner disconnect.

This divide can be also understood as the tension between our mind, which holds our cherished values, and the body, which may act in ways that conflict with them. This is a struggle that most, if not all, humans can relate to at some point in their lives.

According to the World Health Organization, in the year 2000, more than twice as many people died from suicide as from war. Why is this happening? And what can we do?

- How can we shift our mindset to transform ourselves and society?

The key to bridging this divide lies in changing our **mindset** and our **heartset** – our capacity to love and care. Otto Scharmer[16] advocates for a shift from an **ego-centred** (me-focused) mindset to an **eco-centred** (we-focused) awareness – one that prioritises personal wellbeing as well as the wellbeing of the whole, such as the whole family, the whole organisation, the whole society. This requires a way of thinking and acting that considers the welfare of others.

To truly transform systems, we need to change how we focus our attention and engage with the world, both individually and collectively (Scharmer and Kaufer, 2013). How do we achieve that? We need an **open mind**, an **open heart** and an **open will** – a new framework for learning, leading and innovating. The quality of outcomes in any system is directly linked to the level of awareness of those operating within it. Our success as changemakers depends on the inner state from which we act.

The first step towards being both effective and good – thinking and acting for the benefit or the whole, not just yourself – is aligning with the highest values and focusing on what truly matters. This is crucial because strong beliefs in misaligned values or goals can lead to unhappiness. Understanding values, skills and behaviours can reshape how you see the world, helping you adopt a new perspective and positively change your actions.

This book and program propose that **love is the central value of life** – the connecting force that binds humans together and to the natural world. It allows us to transcend ourselves and achieve unity through our actions of love.

However, as discussed, we humans have become divided within ourselves and from others. Some psychologists maintain that this sense of separateness is the fatal flaw and central pathology of the human condition. Psychologists such as Eric Fromm and Otto Rank identified it as the root problem of human existence, the source of all suffering, and the cause of human destructiveness. Our deepest need is to overcome this separateness.[16]

A key question arises:

- What is the **root cause** of this dysfunction – this departure from what is considered healthy?

Unification Thought suggests that while love is the force that connects us to each other and the natural world, when it becomes self-serving, relationships break down, leading to division, conflict and chaos.[17]

Know yourself, live responsibly and lovingly

'To exist is to change, to change is to mature, to mature is to go on creating oneself endlessly.' —**Henri Bergson**

As we grow from infancy to childhood and into adulthood, our understanding of the world evolves, as do our relationships with others and our communities. Development requires building on foundational concepts to grasp more complex ideas and explore new possibilities. However, many adults struggle to develop advanced cognitive, interpersonal, emotional and moral skills due to challenges such as a difficult upbringings or limited education. Happiness and wellbeing seem unattainable dreams for many.

- How can we achieve happiness?

Across generations, people have shared wisdom and cultural traditions that form the foundation for how we develop as humans. Drawing on this collective wisdom can help us understand what supports happiness and wellbeing.

Research and experience highlight three key aspects of happiness: **self-awareness** (knowing yourself and your purpose), **inner and outer peace** (harmony within yourself and with others), and **living responsibly** and **lovingly** (building meaningful connections).

Some psychologists maintain that wellbeing and happiness are more than the absence of negative psychological states, but rather rely on a life of love, values and ideals that provide meaning and purpose, connection and belonging (see Figure 1).[18, 19]

- What drives meaning and connection?

It is the values, love and ideals that you pursue. Getting your values right is the first step on the journey. *I need to figure out what I want to pursue, who I want to become, and what kind of love and relationships I want to build.* One of the purposes of this book is to assist you to do just that.

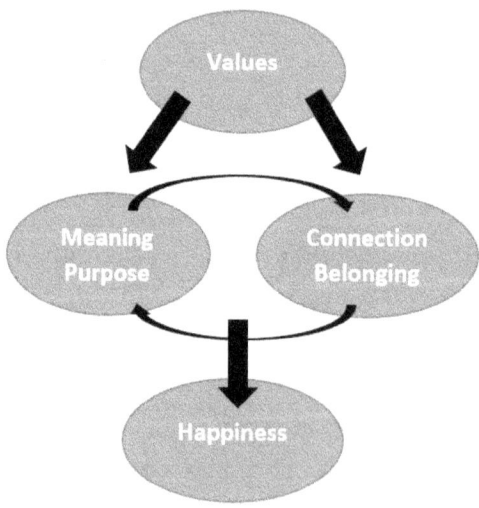

Figure 1 Meaning and connection

Six Pillars Framework

The values and skills explored in this book draw from moral and developmental psychology, social and emotional learning (SEL), values education and philosophy. Additionally, personal development skills frameworks are included, as they highlight essential priorities for education – helping schools integrate values, SEL and key life skills into teaching and learning to support personal and social development.

This book focuses on the first three pillars of the *Six Pillars Framework for Wellbeing, Positive Relationships and a Sustainable and Peaceful Future* – Managing Ourselves, Managing Relationships and Managing Environments. The remaining three pillars – Universal Values, Interdependence and Mutual Prosperity – are explored in a separate volume.

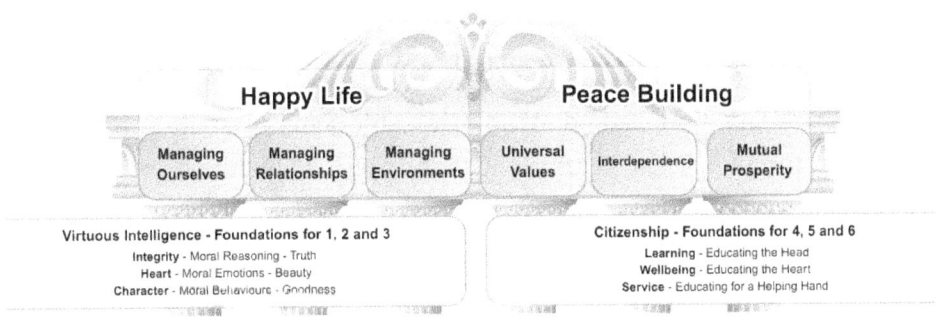

Figure 2 Six Pillars Framework for Wellbeing, Positive Relationships, and a Sustainable and Peaceful Future

The Six Pillars Framework is drawn from Unification Thought,[17, 20] values education literature, psychology and other academic sources. (See Figure 2) Contributors to this work come from diverse academic disciplines, education sectors and professional backgrounds.

Whenever relevant, we align the topics in this book with the United Nations (UN) 17 Sustainable Development Goals (SDGs), which are supported by 168 targets and 330 indicators. (See Figure 3) The SDGs serve as a blueprint for peace, wellbeing and prosperity – both for humanity and the planet. They are referenced throughout this text as businesses and civil society organisations increasingly recognise the importance of their integration into operations.

Figure 3 The United Nations (UN) Sustainable Development Goals (SDGs)

The UN Sustainable Development Goals can be explored in detail at https://sdgs.un.org/. The 2030 Agenda for Sustainable Development outlines clear objectives for industries to drive economic growth while ensuring social wellbeing and ecological sustainability.

The Six Foundations

The six pillars are supported by the core values and abilities known as the Six Foundations, which will be outlined in a third volume (See Figure 2).

Pillars 1, 2 and 3: Three life goals

The first three pillars focus on three essential life goals that form the foundation of values education and social-emotional learning. These goals emphasise developing the values and skills necessary to:

- manage ourselves effectively
- build and maintain healthy relationships
- care for and sustain our natural environment.

While humans strive to create comfortable living conditions, it is essential to do so responsibly, with respect for other people and nature. These three life goals empower individuals to reach their full potential (self-actualisation), cultivate loving relationships, and contribute meaningfully to both society and the environment (see Figure 4).

Education aimed at these goals includes fostering virtuous and excellent individuals capable of positively contributing to society and building good families, where parental love, conjugal (spousal) love, siblings love and children's love are fully realised. Being educated to love and care for the natural environment is also paramount.

To cultivate such individuals, education of the **heart** (focusing on love and moral values) is needed. To build strong families and societies, education of social norms – covering parental values and practices, conjugal love, siblings love and children's love for parents – is needed. True, genuine care for the natural environment depends on fostering a caring heart alongside sustainable practices.

The journey from an ego-centred ('me') mindset to an eco-centred ('we') awareness unfolds in three key dimensions[16]:

1. A deeper connection with ourselves.
2. Stronger, more meaningful relationships with others.
3. A greater sense of responsibility towards the world and the natural environment.

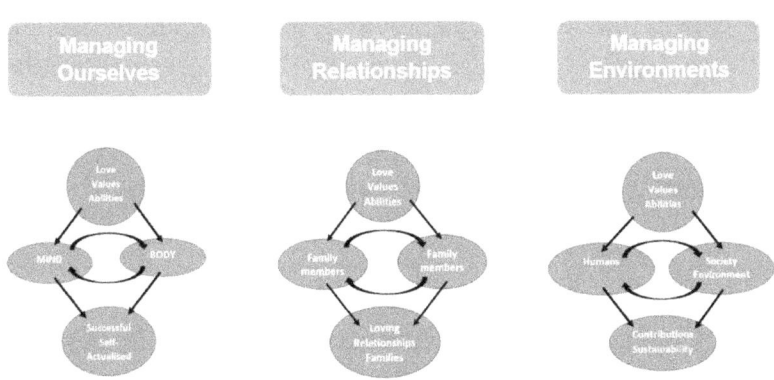

Figure 4 Three life goals

Pillars 3, 4 and 5: Three global citizen mindsets and practices

The second set of pillars consists of three global mindsets and practices that support a vision for peace and sustainable development:

1. Shared universal values
2. Mutual interdependence
3. Mutual prosperity

These principles cultivate national and global citizens who seek to embrace our common humanity and shared values.

A global citizen understands the deep interconnectedness between individuals, communities and the natural environment.[21] This sense of interdependence and shared identity forms the foundation for social justice and meaningful relationships. Furthermore, global citizens recognise that mutual prosperity – at local, national and international levels – is essential for a thriving and just society.[22]

Foundation 1, 2 and 3: Three moral and psychological domains

The three life goals are supported by three key moral and psychological domains,[23] which are represented by three inner qualities:

1. Moral reasoning → Integrity
2. Moral emotion → Heart (empathy and love)
3. Moral behaviour → Character

Integrity reflects the values and abilities tied to moral reasoning. Heart represents the depth of our moral emotions. Character embodies the actions that align with ethical principles.

Foundations 4, 5 and 6: Three teaching and learning domains

Three teaching and learning domains support the global citizen mindsets and practices:

1. Learning – Developing intellectual and creative abilities.

2. **Wellbeing** – Cultivating emotional and social skills for personal and interpersonal growth.

3. **Service** – Engaging in public service and service learning to promote both personal development and the common good.

The moral and psychological domains, along with these teaching and learning domains, will be explored in a separate volume.

In today's world, education must go beyond marketplace skills to nurture inner growth and balanced development.[24] To meet modern challenges, we need to cultivate the mindsets and skillsets that support both personal wellbeing and the ability to contribute meaningfully to society.

Book Structure

This book is divided into three parts:

Pillar 1. Managing Ourselves and Self-Actualisation

Pillar 2. Managing Our Relationships and Self-Actualisation

Pillar 3. Managing our Natural Environment and Sustainable Development.

The values and abilities discussed throughout this book use the following structure to facilitate teaching and learning:

1. **Key Topics** – Essential knowledge about values and abilities.
2. **Critical Questions** – Opportunities to reflect on the relevant topics and to encourage critical thinking.
3. **Abilities** – Guidelines to help foster values and abilities.
4. **Activities** – Practical exercises and questions to develop and strengthen values and abilities.

The activities are suitable for individual reflection and for educators to incorporate into values education programs. Skills can be developed through tutorials, group discussions or seminars, role-plays (both in person and online), and online blogs, fostering both understanding and practical application. For some activities, readers are invited to reflect, write and share their thoughts with another person or small group, if they feel comfortable. Through such sharing, understanding and growth can be consolidated.

We invite you now to embark on a journey of discovery, unlocking new potential and joy.

PILLAR 1:

Managing Ourselves and Self-Actualisation

Pillar 1 focuses on personal self-management, self-actualisation and mental wellbeing, all of which contribute to better health and educational outcomes. Self-actualisation is a core concept in humanistic psychology, most famously associated with Abraham Maslow. It represents the highest level of psychological development, where an individual realises and fulfils their full potential.

Self-actualisation is a lifelong journey towards a meaningful and enriched life, which involves transcending the limiting beliefs we have set for ourselves and the world around us. When you go on this journey, you will most likely build a better version of yourself – and perhaps the world around you. This process requires committing to core values and ongoing personal growth.

A key part of self-actualisation is self-awareness – understanding who you are and who you aspire to be. Self-actualised individuals:

- seek authenticity and honesty
- have a desire for self-improvement
- show humility and respect for others
- consider the common good and act with compassion
- possess a strong moral sense
- view life with a sense of wonder, embracing creativity, inventiveness and originality.

Related UN Sustainable Development Goals (SDGs)
Goal 3: Good Health and Wellbeing

- **Target 3.4:** Reduce premature mortality from non-communicable diseases by one-third through prevention and treatment and promoting mental health and wellbeing. Indicators that this goal is met are lower suicide mortality rate and coverage of treatment interventions (pharmacological, psychosocial and rehabilitation, and aftercare services) for substance use disorders.

- **Target 16.1:** Significantly reduce all forms of violence and related death rates everywhere. One of the indicators, **16.1.3**, is proportion of population subjected to physical, psychological or sexual violence in the previous 12 months is reduced. See https://ourworldindata.org/sdgs

Goal 4: Quality Education

Goal 16: Peace, Justice and Strong Institutions

Goal 17: Partnerships for the Goals (revitalised global partnerships)

'Many persons have the wrong idea of what constitutes true happiness. It is not attained through self-gratification but through fidelity to a worthy purpose.'

—***Helen Keller***

1

Finding Meaning and Purpose
Dr John Bellavance

Helen Keller, disability rights advocate and American author, inspires us to seek meaning and purpose in life when she says true happiness is attained through fidelity to a worthy purpose –the focus of this chapter. Purpose, meaning, connection (love) and fulfilling our potential are key to achieving self-actualisation and overall wellbeing. According to Maslow's hierarchy of needs, people are motivated to fulfill physical needs such as shelter and food, and safety before they can progress to more advanced ones. We need to feel secure before progressing towards higher ideals such as love and esteem (see Figure 5).

Self-actualisation represents the highest level of psychological development – where individuals fully realise their potential after meeting their physical and ego needs. (Ego is our sense of a separate self; it is the 'me', 'myself' and 'I' – the part of the personality that is conscious and interacts with the outside world.)

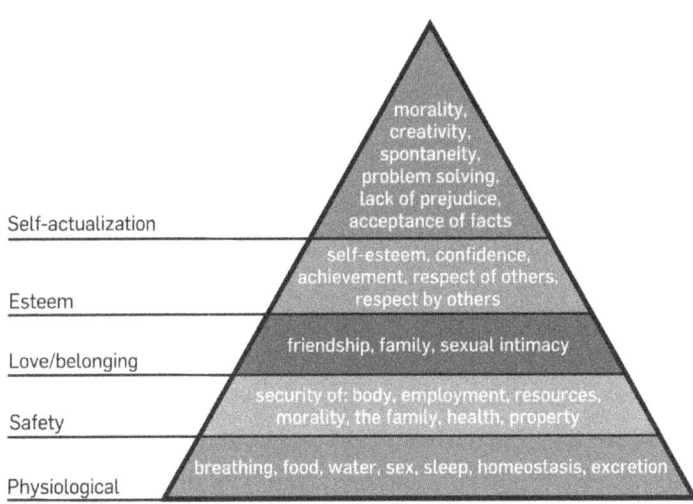

Figure 5 Maslow's Hierarchy of Needs
This file is licensed under the Creative Commons Attribution-Share Alike 3.0

Becoming self-actualised is a conscious journey that requires awareness of our current state and a commitment to pursuing higher ideals, meaning and love. Many us go through life on a straight path from birth to death, rarely pausing to reflect or question their choices. We tend to focus on immediate responsibilities, such as careers and family needs, which are important but may not necessarily lead to a life of deep meaning and self-fulfilment. Not so, Victor Frankl, who wrote:

> *'When we engage in self-reflection, we become aware of both our potential and shortcomings, allowing us to see what truly matters. In my own life, self-reflection helped me realise that my deepest priorities were inner peace, meaning rooted in authentic values, and genuine connections (love). Ever more people today have the means to live, but no meaning to live for.'* —***Viktor Frankl***

This sense of searching for meaning resonates with many, including a young woman who once posted on Facebook: 'Has anyone seen the plot? I've f**** lost it somewhere.' Her candid expression of confusion and subsequent post about getting drunk over the weekend reflect a deeper struggle. At some point, we've all asked ourselves, 'What is the purpose of my life?' We've wondered what 'the plot' is. It's a question that demands an answer. We need to know our 'why'. Without it, we risk feeling anxious, lost or as if we are merely going through the motions.

At our core, most of us don't just want to exist; we want to be part of something bigger than ourselves. Yet, when we ask, 'How do I find my purpose?', it often masks deeper fears: 'What if I have no purpose?' or that devastating thought, 'What if I have no value? – I am worthless'.[12]

Research from BlueZones.com suggests that having a strong sense of purpose can add up to seven years to our life expectancy. Meanwhile, the World Health Organization reports that more than 800,000 people die by suicide each year – more than the combined deaths from conflicts, wars and natural disasters.[25]

This stark contrast highlights a crucial truth: **Finding meaning and connection is essential to mental wellbeing.**

Frankl's Levels of Meaning

According to Viktor Frankl's psychotherapy called 'logotherapy', humans have a profound desire to find and experience meaning in life – what he called the 'will to meaning'. Logotherapy's goal is to help individuals orient their lives around meaning rather than external desires. Frankl argued that this 'will to meaning' is more primary than Freud's 'will for pleasure' and Nietzsche's 'will to power'. Through pursuing meaning, we are able to develop into larger, more evolved versions of ourselves.[12]

Frankl's concept of meaning, as illustrated in Figure 6, outlines three levels of meaning:

> **Level 1, individual meaning** – focuses on finding a unique and specific purpose that only we can fulfil. This satisfies our personal need for meaning.
>
> **Level 2, shared meaning** – allows us to connect with others, as meaning is an essential component of any meaningful relationship. This connection

expands as we engage with those close to us such as our family (explored in Pillar Two – Managing Our Relationships and Self-Actualisation).

Level 3, super meaning – By working through Levels 1 and 2, we begin to catch a glimpse of the super meaning, explored in Level 3. Super meaning links individuals to a broader, universal purpose. This meaning transcends logic, connecting us to universal values, spirituality and love.

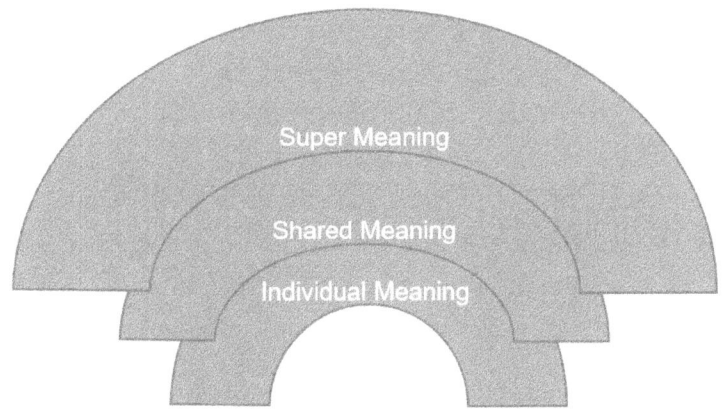

Figure 6 Frank's Levels of Meaning

Joy and Meaning

Many would argue that joy is our ultimate purpose, and it is through joy that we find meaning. But what exactly is joy?

Joy is one of the three types of happiness, alongside pleasure and satisfaction. Joy is different to happiness or satisfaction. Pleasure is happiness felt through your senses and satisfaction is happiness we feel when something meaningful to you is achieved: 'I am happy because of __.' Joy, however, is intrinsic to you. Humans are born with the capacity for joy. And infants express joy before language or social conditioning. If you have spent any time with a baby or an infant, you have seen this truth in action.

Joy is a vital life force. Many psychologists and wellbeing practitioners suggest that joy can act as a kind of inner signal, helping us recognise what feels meaningful and life-giving. Following what brings us genuine joy can help us feel more connected – both to others and to a deeper sense of purpose. (12)

Where do you find joy and meaning?

First, on a personal level, they arise from living your purpose, cultivating your skills and talents, and striving towards self-actualisation – reaching your full potential.

Second, you discover joy and meaning through your relationships. It's within these connections that your life takes on deeper significance, as you begin to live for something greater than yourself. Love is at the heart of this pursuit.(12) Without love, happiness and success feel hollow. Holden suggests that if our definition of success doesn't include love, we need to rethink it. Too often, our definitions of success are narrow, egocentric and self-serving, keeping us confined to our smaller selves.

> Without love, happiness and success feel hollow.

Love and service to others can provide a deep source of meaning and purpose in your life. When you're in love, you don't need to ponder the meaning of your existence; you are living it, and happiness naturally flows. Life feels whole. If you're seeking true love, you already sense its deep potential to bring meaning, joy and fulfilment.

On a broader level, beyond the individual, purpose enables you to transcend feelings of separateness and become an instrument of a greater good, dedicated to serving others. Embracing love as a shared purpose is key to unlocking this deeper sense of connection.(12)

Activity #1: Discovering what matters

Ponder. Write. Share with another person or small group:

Write down in your journal the things that make your life feel purposeful, bring you joy or reflect what matters most to you. Share your thoughts with a partner or small group.

Finish the sentence:

- I feel on purpose in my life when…
- I feel joy in my life when…
- If I had to choose between money, fame or love, I would….

Debrief:

- Which values or activities give you the greatest sense of purpose?
- How do these insights help you make decisions or set goals?

Meaning, Identity and Morality

The identity you form is essential to your sense of meaning and wellbeing. Identity is the self-constructed understanding of who you are and how you define yourself, which is important for all of us. Identity is vital for self-esteem. You can become distressed, even depressed, when you feel your identity is built on unstable foundations.

There are many types of identities – academic, sports, arts and more. For instance, the goal of higher education has often been to foster an academic identity. However, this focus may encourage students to apply their analytical skills and professional expertise for personal gain, without necessarily fostering personal growth or contribution to the welfare of society.

Research indicates that during adolescence, personal and social development help shape moral identity – the understanding of oneself as a person who acts according to moral values, such as fairness, care and justice. Moral identity involves a commitment to behave in ways that support the wellbeing of others, in alignment with one's sense of who they are. A person with a strong moral identity identifies their self-interest in terms of the moral values they consider important.

Moral values are not personal preferences. Personal preferences include things like favourite music, hobbies or food. Moral values, by contrast, concern how we treat others – values such as justice and respect that contribute to the public good. Morality involves the vast realm of social intentions, emotions, actions and judgements aimed at benefiting others, society and the world beyond the self.[26]

For me, being a good dad is part of my moral identity because I place importance on the care I show my kids. This personal commitment reflects a value that shapes how I understand myself and how I choose to act. The concept of moral identity implies knowing what is morally important and actively nurturing those values in one's life.

Adolescents are at a point when they can begin to think about their responsibility towards others when it comes to self-control and social values. Many studies have confirmed that both exemplary and antisocial behaviour can be predicted by the way adolescents integrate moral concerns into their descriptions of self. In other words, how they see themselves is how they will act out.[6]

To the extent that moral identity helps support such actions, it is society's responsibility to foster moral identities.[27] Helping every person acquire a moral identity helps them find a moral sense and purpose in any situation. Helping young people become aware of moral values and ideals facilitates their development of a moral identity.[6]

Activity #2: What do you identify with?

Examine the qualities and roles that shape your sense of identity and influence how you see yourself.

1. Consider the following examples and the qualities behind them:

    Academic identity: 'I'm smart.'

    Athletic identity: 'I'm good at sport.'

    Artistic identity: 'I'm a good dancer.'

    Moral identity: 'I'm a good person.'

2. Write a statement in your journal about your own identity:

My identity is _____ because _____.

Reflection:

- Which aspects of your identity feel most central to who you are?
- How do these identities influence your choices, actions or relationships?

Purpose

Mary Oliver's poem *Sometimes* invites us to truly pay attention – not merely to pass through the world, but to live meaningfully and authentically. (Check it out online. It's a great poem!) Our purposes offer us a clear system of values that guide how we measure our lives and shape our life vision. A strong vision is ambitious and rooted in big ideals. For example, it could be about finding inner peace, freeing yourself from anxiety and doubt, living consciously, staying true to who you are with others, being the best spouse and parent, making a positive impact in the community, or striving to be the best version of yourself in education and at work.

Living consciously and finding meaning are important for mental wellbeing, while a diminished sense of meaning and purpose undermines it. Some psychiatrists suggest that as many as one-third of patients seeking help from mental health professionals do so not because of chronic anxiety of depression, but because they lack a sense of meaning and purpose in their lives. Widespread problems such as depression, aggression and addiction become more understandable when we recognise the vacuum of meaning and connection in many people's lives.[28]

Young people today are generally less resilient and more anxious than previous generations. Perhaps what is missing is a sense of clear purpose and connection. With respect to self-actualisation, a clear purpose in life helps people believe in their ability to reach their goals and offers protection against depression.[29] When we think about young people, we often envisage friendships, possibility and

> Perhaps what is missing is a sense of clear purpose and connection.

hope. Yet increasingly, they report feeling isolated and lacking direction. Low connection with parents and friends, limited community participation and insufficient physical activity are among the factors contributing to loneliness.[30]

Young people long to be seen, to belong and to connect – underscoring the importance of purpose in life. The search for values, meaning and purpose starts with 'me', yet it can also be found in the longstanding wisdom and experience of human history. Even the smallest tasks, when approached with mindfulness, care and creativity, contribute meaningfully to our wellbeing, homes, work places, communities and the wider world.[31]

The journey begins with identifying the authentic values and purposes that resonate deeply with us. The development of morality can offer valuable insights here.

During adolescence, there is a shift from simply conforming to adult values towards developing a more sophisticated understanding of morality – the formation of one's own moral framework. At this stage, young people come to believe in moral standards they have personally adopted. These standards provide a sense that their values are not merely personal options but moral values that impact others and are non-negotiable.

Adolescents often feel there must be an ultimate answer to every moral question. However, adults who retain this absolute way of thinking may become rigid or fundamentalist.[32] This highlights the importance of deeply reflecting on our values and worldviews. For example, we may unintentionally dehumanise those who do not share our beliefs.

Many adolescents also experience an internal tension between the need for peer acceptance and the desire to remain true to themselves and their values. In this context, the still-developing ego reflects the inner voices and unconscious processes that influence their actions and how they wish to be perceived by others. When the ego is overactive or insecure, it can keep us within our comfort zones – relying on familiar patterns that feel safe – and prevent us from stepping into our deep values or authentic selves.[33] It is crucial not to lose sight of who we truly are. Supporting adolescents in strengthening their sense of self helps them navigate these pressures without losing sight of what matters to them.

Abilities: Acting with purpose

To achieve what truly matters in your life, you need to think deeply about what you want to accomplish, understand your purpose and persevere in pursuing what you believe is important. You may have a project or vision you want to bring to life, but you can't expect to be immediate success or a challenge-free path. Nor can you expect people to instantly see the value of your work or support it. So don't stop. To stop is to fail; to persevere is to succeed.

Success requires quiet endurance – working steadily to build your foundation without seeking recognition. Act out of purpose, not for approval. In time, your accomplishments, both internal and external, will give you the authority speak with integrity and influence.

Those who succeed are often the ones who persevere quietly and think deeply. In life, the loudest voice isn't always the most successful. When change occurs, it is the person who reflects carefully on their goals and steadily builds their foundation, without acting impulsively, who endures. They will resolve to start acting and only speak when the foundation is built. It may feel good to speak out constantly, but in the long run, it is not wise.[34]

Activity #3: What's holding you back

In your journal, write down what stops you from achieving what you want – achieving your purposes or goals. Examples might include worrying about what others think, doubting your abilities or fearing failures.

Reflection:

1. What patterns do you notice in the barriers you've written down?

2. How might these limitations be influencing your choices or confidence?
3. What steps could help you move beyond these barriers?

Purpose of the Whole and Purpose of the Individual

The question 'What is my purpose?' can be limiting because the word 'my' narrows our focus too soon. Our purpose isn't solely 'ours' as it doesn't exist in isolation. Instead, it is interconnected and woven into the larger web of life. What we often call our *personal* purpose is, in fact, a *shared* purpose that extends beyond ourselves.

For example, the liver serves its specific function within the body, but it also contributes to the wellbeing of the whole organism. Similarly, the bee has its individual role in tending the queen and producing honey for the hive, yet it also contributes to pollinating plants and crops, serving a greater, collective purpose.[12]

We cannot fully understand our personal purpose without considering humanity's broader purpose. When we do this, we no longer experience ourselves as separate entities – 'me', 'myself' and 'I' – but as expressions of a greater whole and purpose. Guided by the ego-self – the narrow self of 'I' – we find ourselves pursuing ideals and achievements in isolation, independently of others. But our lives hold both an individual, personal purpose and a shared purpose with others and with all of creation – a purpose that reaches far beyond the ego.

Understanding our individual purpose involves recognising how it connects to this larger shared purpose – the bigger picture. The two are inseparable: the individual purpose sustains and develops the self, while the shared purpose calls us to live in ways that nurture the greater community and the world.[20]

It is important not to try to figure out your purpose by yourself, but to seek guidance from others and explore it through your relationships.

Activity #4: Mapping your purpose and connections

Explore the intricate connections between the purpose of the individual and the purpose of the whole and clarify your own role within the larger picture.

1. Write down in your journal or the table below the values and purposes that give your life meaning and direction.
2. Consider how these connect (or don't) with others such as your family, community or country. How clearly do you see the connection between your personal goals and the needs or values of others?
3. Define your individual purpose and how this does or does not connect to a bigger purpose – your family, community and country.

My Purpose	How this Connects	A Bigger Purpose

Debrief:

- In what ways can understanding these connections give your life deeper meaning or direction?
- What insights did you gain about your sense of belonging and contribution?

'Be at least as interested in what is going on inside you as what happens outside. If you get the inside right, the outside will fall into place.'

—*Ekhart Tolle*

2

Living Conscientiously – Know Yourself
Dr John Bellavance

Living conscientiously means being motivated and behaving by one's moral sense of right and wrong. This influences how we define and manage ourselves, how we develop our relationships, and how we act in the world and treat others with care and love. Emotional intelligence (EI) is an important part of this. EI involves consciously choosing how to think, feel and behave. We can begin developing EI by becoming aware of our thoughts and emotions and noticing how they shape our actions.

...self-reflection is crucial in living an intentional and fulfilling life

Throughout history, the great psychological, philosophical and spiritual teachings have reminded us that we are often not who we think we are, and that we have not yet become the best of ourselves. We must uncover our true selves. As Socrates said, 'To know thyself is the beginning of wisdom.' We can't overcome our biases and limitations unless we first recognise them. Self-awareness involves clarifying our values and preparing ourselves to face life's challenges.[35]

The Comparison Trap

Knowing who we are and what is vital for us is crucial when constantly flooded with news, social media and commercial interests that urge us to compare ourselves with those portrayed as more beautiful, youthful, rich, famous, successful or smart. Too often, we seek external approval rather than looking inward to discover the personal qualities that foster happiness and self-actualisation.

It's important not to get stuck in the comparison trap. However, such reflections can push us to self-enquiry, where we question who we are, what truly matters and our shortcomings so that we can improve ourselves. By recognising our strengths, biases and weaknesses, we move closer to becoming our best selves and experiencing wellbeing.

However noble our purpose or intentions, we all still make mistakes, even with the best of intentions. What matters is our willingness to learn from them and continue the journey towards self-understanding. This is where self-enquiry is valuable.

Activity #5: The Comparison Trap

This activity invites you to examine how comparing yourself to others might affect your self-esteem, motivation and overall wellbeing.

1. Write your name in the middle of the spiderweb.
2. In the surrounding web sections, write down your comparison traps – the areas where you compare yourself with others (e.g. looks, friends, talents, success).

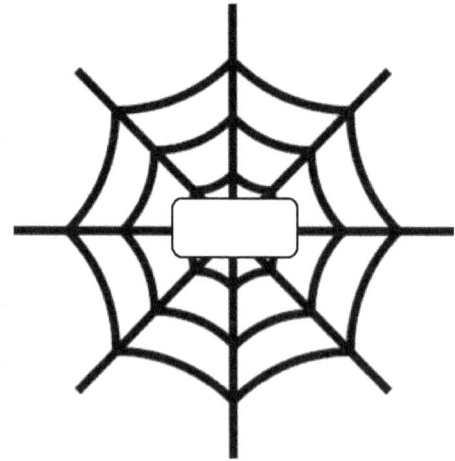

Reflection:

- Are these comparisons causing you to devalue yourself?
- What strengths or qualities do you have that are uniquely yours?
- How can focusing on your own qualities and accomplishments help you reduce the impact of these comparisons?

Self-Inquiry – Fostering Your Conscience

'All human beings are born free and equal in dignity and rights. They are endowed with reason and conscience and should act towards one another in a spirit of brotherhood.'
—**Article 1, Universal Declaration of Human Rights**

One of the key purposes of self-inquiry is to help you recognise higher values, meaning and purpose in your life, which in turn nurtures your conscience – your inner guide that distinguishes right from wrong. By listening to your conscience (your moral compass), you can become more aware of your actions, allowing you to acknowledge your mistakes and learn from them. Too often, we hurt others or fail to be authentic simply because we ignore this inner voice.

Personal integrity is essential for wellbeing, as most people wish to see themselves as good and consistent with their values and take pride in their character. In a study on 14-year-olds' use of social media, participants reflected on remorse for past online actions. Tyrone admitted, 'A lot of people look back at what they've said on Facebook and think, *Why was I such an idiot?*

Some students described how their conscience motivated them to stand up for peers facing online bullying. Shouja expressed, '... it's that feeling of just going for it, getting pumped up and knowing you'll feel better after doing it.'

Their teacher Dee emphasised the importance of conscience. 'It sets the foundation of your reasoning... children with a stronger moral compass are more likely to behave ethically online.'

Additionally, some young people demonstrated a sense of responsibility by holding themselves accountable for their actions on social media, suggesting a connection between their conscience and the remorse they felt for the wrong they did. This finding is significant, as it indicates that some youth have internalised their values and experience genuine remorse when their actions conflict with those values.[23]

The conscience develops as children learn to see situations from others' perspectives and realise that harmful behaviour has real negative consequences on others.[36] Discussing conflict situations and how they make others feel can therefore help foster children's moral sensitivity with respect to others.[36] Some data suggest that emotional learning can occur from mistakes made while using social media.[23]

Self-Awareness and Self-Evaluation

Self-awareness and self-evaluating our values, thoughts, emotions and behaviours are essential for personal growth and wellbeing. They help us understand what truly matters to us and what drives our actions. This generates self-honesty that is needed to meet our fears and demons head on and to discover our creative potential.[12]

How many times do we hurt others because we aren't aware of how our shortcomings and views affect others, or how group norms shape our judgements? Many of us go through life unconsciously, unaware of who we truly are, the origins of our judgements and biases, or our strengths and weaknesses.

For instance, our value judgements are often shaped by group consensus without us even realising it, such as when we dehumanise others who don't meet the views of our group. We strip them of their individuality, dignity and moral worth. This process makes it easier to justify mistreatment, discrimination or even violence against them. This highlights that self-reflection is crucial in living an intentional and fulfilling life.

There are many ways to understand ourselves and the world around us, as outlined by Combs[32]:

- **Thinking** – developing awareness of reality and confidence in our reasoning
- **Values** – recognising what is best and what matters most to us
- **Emotional awareness** – understanding our own emotions and those of others
- **Relationships** – knowing how to relate to others in a meaningful way
- **Needs** – identifying our physiological, safety, love and belonging, esteem and self-actualisation needs
- **Self-identity** – answering the question, 'Who am I?'
- **Self-expression** – exploring creativity and the arts to express ourselves
- **Spirituality** – understanding what we consider most important in life
- **Self-acceptance** – feeling comfortable in our own skin
- **Resilience** – developing the inner resources to manage psychological challenges and stress effectively.

This understanding becomes more meaningful when we apply it to our own lives. The following reflection invites you to explore your own experiences with self-awareness and your inner conscience.

Activity #6: Listening to your conscience

Often people hurt others because they are not aware of how their shortcomings and problems affect them. What about you?

1. Think of a time when your emotions or words unintentionally hurt someone. What did you learn from that experience?
2. Recall a moment when your conscience urged you to act, or to stay silent. What did you do, and how did it feel?
3. How do group norms or social expectations influence your behaviour or moral choices?
4. Complete these sentences...

   I sometimes feel my conscience telling me...

I feel uneasy when I don't...

When I do the right thing, even when it's hard, I feel...

Reflection:

- Do you believe your conscience is your friend? If so, why?
- What did you discover about the relationship between self-awareness and conscience?
- How might listening more closely to your inner voice affect your relationships or choices?

Plato's Cave

Plato's Cave, an allegory presented by the Greek philosopher Plato in his work *Republic*, provides a compelling analogy for understanding self-awareness (Figure 7). In this allegory, a group of people has spent their entire lives chained inside a cave, facing a blank wall. They perceive reality only through the shadows cast by objects passing in front of a fire behind them. To them, these shadows represent the real world, even though they are merely distortions of true forms.

Socrates explains that philosophers and the self-aware are like prisoners who break free from the cave, stepping into the sunlight and realising that the shadows were only illusions. This journey symbolises the transition from ignorance to enlightenment, highlighting the importance of self-awareness in perceiving reality beyond surface-level appearances.[37]

Figure 7 Plato's Cave

Departure from the cave

When a prisoner is freed and steps outside the cave, the bright sunlight overwhelms him, making it difficult to see the world as it truly is. Accustomed to the shadows on the cave wall, he struggles to believe that what he now sees is reality. The light is painful, and his instinct is to turn away and retreat to the familiar darkness of the cave.

If someone were to forcibly drag him into the sunlight, he initially resists, feeling anger and discomfort. But over time, as his eyes adjust, he gradually perceives people and objects in their true form. This transformation represents the challenge of confronting new truths and breaking free from deeply ingrained illusions. Our ego must dissolve before we can truly see the world with fresh eyes.[12]

Leaving the cave is akin to a kind of death – a letting go of the familiar and the limited perceptions we cling to. We often resist releasing our narrow views of ourselves and the world, yet this surrender is essential for embracing a greater sense of self and the vast reality that exists beyond 'the cave'.

Return to the cave

Plato proposed that the freed prisoner would come to see the world outside the cave as far superior to the shadowed reality he once knew. Eager to share this truth, he would attempt to convince the others trapped inside to embark on the journey beyond the cave. However, upon returning, his eyes – now accustomed to the light – would struggle to adjust to the darkness, making him appear blind. The remaining prisoners, seeing his impaired vision, would assume that leaving the cave had harmed him. Rather than embracing the opportunity for enlightenment, they would resist any attempts to free them, fearing the same fate.

Griffith[38] argued that Plato's analogy of the cave reflects the human condition. Those living in the cave represent people who exist in a state of denial, unaware of their true nature. The individual who escapes into the light (one willing to see a new point of view) perceives reality for the first time: both the world and themselves as they truly are. Upon returning, the freed prisoner (transformed thinker) tries to explain to the others that they have only been seeing shadows – distorted reflections of the real world (reality) and themselves. He urges them to free themselves and step into the light, symbolising the journey towards truth and self-awareness.

However, the cave dwellers resist, unwilling to confront the reality of their condition. This reluctance represents our tendency to avoid uncomfortable truths and to resist change. Those of us trapped in the cave often excel at critiquing others and meddling in others' affairs but struggle to reflect on and change ourselves. We may believe that our circumstances are the problem when it is often our own perceptions and reactions that shape our experience.

Leaving the cave

As people who leave the cave – our 'prison' of long-held beliefs, illusions and our fears – we need to focus our energies on seeking truth and changing ourselves and the world. On the hero's journey, we dedicate our life to something bigger than ourselves. The hero begins the journey with a narrow self, but embarks on a journey that fosters transformation and allows new consciousness to emerge.[12]

Recognising my shortcomings – such as not truly listening to others – motivated me to become a better listener. Becoming aware of my judgemental tendencies, much like stepping out of the cave, helped me judge less and appreciate the good in people. Leaving the cave allowed me to see the world from a new, more enlightened perspective.

Self-awareness – stepping out of the cave – is particularly challenging when it comes to emotions, which can bring discomfort, much like the sunlight hurting the eyes. Emotions often arise before we become conscious of them. Research shows that the amygdala, the part of the brain responsible for processing emotions, reacts more quickly than the rational, thinking brain – the neocortex. While this rapid response is essential in dangerous situations, it can also lead to emotional overreactions or impulsive actions based on faulty mindsets.[39] These may include seeking attention, making snap judgements, assuming others dislike us or engaging in constant worry.

Another common distraction within the 'cave' is the tendency to centre events around oneself. Some individuals turn ordinary situations into personal crises, shifting the focus onto themselves – a pattern I call 'seeking attention by crisis'. While this behaviour may be expected from teenagers, it is less appropriate for adults.

Activity #7: Stepping out of the cave

Plato's allegory of the cave challenges us to recognise how our perceptions can be shaped by illusions and limited beliefs. The journey from darkness to light symbolises awakening to truth and self-awareness – a process that can be both uncomfortable and transformative.

Ponder. Write. Share with a partner or small group:

1. In what ways does Plato's allegory reflect human attitudes today?
2. Do you relate more to those who resist leaving the cave or to the one who seeks the light? Why?
3. Think of a time when you stepped out of your own 'cave' – when you confronted old rigid beliefs or saw something in a new way:
   - What challenged you the most?
   - What changed in your outlook, behaviour or understanding?
4. How does this experience help you understand yourself and others differently?

How to Become Self-Aware

How do we leave our 'cave' and discover our strengths and weaknesses? There are several ways. First, we can start by paying close attention to our actions and how we treat others.[40] Our thoughts, words and actions reflect our values and aspirations. By using the 'sunlight' of self-awareness, we can renew ourselves and break free from dysfunctional mental patterns and behaviours.

Personally, I have learned a great deal about myself by observing my thoughts and actions, as well as by openly expressing what truly matters to me. When you honestly share your views, you gain insight into both your strengths and areas for growth. There is where psychotherapy can provide useful techniques for such exploration.

Cognitive Behavioural Therapy

Psychotherapy aims to enhance self-awareness. One way is through Cognitive Behavioural Therapy (CBT). CBT helps individuals recognise and change harmful thought and behaviour patterns by replacing them with more accurate and constructive alternatives. It is based on the idea that our emotions and behaviours are shaped by how we perceive events. Charles R Swindoll said:

> 'Life is 10% what happens to you and 90% how you react to it.'

For example, individuals struggling with depression often interpret situations in an excessively negative way. Through collaboration between a therapist and patient, CBT helps patients identify maladaptive thinking, test its accuracy against reality and make necessary adjustments for healthier mental patterns.[41]

A key practice in CBT is 'guided discovery', which involves exploring a patient's perspective and helping them expand their thinking. It allows individuals to recognise their underlying assumptions, consider alternative perspectives and discover new solutions. Therapists facilitate this process by asking open, reflective questions that invite curiosity rather than judgement. Examples include:

> 'What else could we assume?'
>
> 'What do you think causes this?'
>
> 'What alternative ways of looking at this are there?'
>
> 'Why is this important?'

These questions encourage critical thinking and self-reflection, helping individuals to critically evaluate their thoughts and develop more balanced, constructive thinking patterns.[41]

Rewriting rigid rules about living

Many rigid beliefs quietly shape how we think, feel and behave. Many of these arise from persistent, perfectionist and often irrational demands we place on ourselves, others and the world such as[42]:

- 'I must achieve perfect results.'
- 'I should always be successful.'
- 'Other people should show me respect.'
- 'People ought to know better.'
- 'I must be liked by everyone I meet.'
- 'Other people should see things from my point of view.'
- 'Life should not be difficult or frustrating.'

These 'musts' and 'shoulds' often operate beneath our awareness, influencing our emotions and reactions. Through self-awareness, we can begin to recognise when these rigid rules are at play and how they create pressure, frustration or disappointment.

To cultivate greater flexibility in thinking, and thus inner freedom, you can replace these rigid, absolute demands with flexible, realistic preferences. By doing so, you can reduce frustration, improve relationships and develop a more balanced perspective on life. For example:

- Instead of *'I must succeed,'* think *'I'd like to do well, but I can learn even if I don't.'*
- Instead of *'People should always treat me fairly'* try *'I prefer fairness, but I can handle it if others fall short.'*

This process allows you to disengage from unrealistic standards and embrace a mindset that fosters growth, resilience and understanding.

The following activity guides you to identify a rigid belief you may hold, examine its emotional impact, and reframe it into a more balanced alternative. This reflective process is central to building ongoing self-awareness.

Activity #8: Identify and replace rigid beliefs

1. ***Identify*** – Take time to reflect on your beliefs that come from inner demands or expectations about yourself, others or the world around you (refer to the list above).

   Write down one rigid belief that often influences your thoughts, emotions or behaviour.

2. ***Reflect*** – How does this rigid belief make you feel? What unrealistic demands does it create for you or others?

3. ***Replace*** – Use your self-awareness to reframe the belief into a more flexible, balanced statement. Instead of focusing on what *must* or *should* happen, consider what you would *prefer* to happen – and what choices or opportunities remain open to you.

- For example: 'I would prefer to be successful and respected, but I understand that perfection is impossible. Not everyone will always like or respect me, and that's okay. I can focus on doing my best and valuing those who appreciate me.'

- This shift allows you to embrace life with more flexibility, reducing unnecessary stress and creating space for growth and fulfilment.

So, how would you prefer things to be? I would prefer / I would like..........

4. ***Reflect again*** –

- How does this new belief make you feel?

- What changes do you notice in your expectations, sense of control or openness to possibilities?

- How might constant self-awareness help you maintain this flexibility in daily life?

Abilities: Using humour to challenge negative thoughts

A technique for challenging unrealistic or anxious thoughts is to practise hearing them in a funny voice, such as Daffy Duck, SpongeBob SquarePants or even Siri. While it may seem silly, this approach can help turn an anxious or upsetting moment into a humorous one. By doing this, you distance yourself from the intensity of the thought, making it easier to recognise its irrationality and lessen its emotional impact. Humour can be a powerful tool for breaking the cycle of negative thinking and reducing anxiety.

Mental Prisons – Free Your Mind

> *'That you may retain yourself respect, it is better to displease the people by doing what you know is right, than to temporarily please them by doing what you know is wrong.'*
> —**William J. H. Boetcker**

Self-esteem has to do with what we think of ourselves, not what others think of us. We need to live consciously, responsibly and with integrity. If we silence our own judgements in order to win the approval of others, we may win that approval, but our self-esteem will suffer.[43]

One way to understand ourselves and what truly matters is by becoming aware that we have created mental prisons for ourselves. We build walls within our minds that limit who we believe we are and what we can become. We also put up mental walls *between* others and ourselves, shaped by assumptions about how we think others see us. These prisons are constructed from deeply engrained patterns of thought and behaviour that shape and govern our lives. Becoming aware of these prisons is the first step towards freeing ourselves from them.

Carl Jung, the founder of analytical psychology, saw the struggle with seeking approval as a roadblock on the journey of self-actualisation. The person who lives for the approval of others is not living their own life; they are living the life others expect of them. True psychological freedom comes from aligning our actions with our inner truth, not with how we imagine others perceive us.

By prioritising inner development over external validation, we can cultivate a sense of self-worth that is resilient to the shifting opinions of others.

Becoming aware of my personal need for the approval of others and learning to let go of it was a crucial turning point for me. My desire for validation led me away from being true to myself, causing unnecessary suffering. Recognising this allowed me to break free from the mental prison I had unknowingly built – the 'approval of others prison'. I refused to live in a prison of my own making.

Many of us are trapped by our own concepts, judgements, insecurities, anger and anxiety – often without even realising it. We simply feel anxious, dissatisfied or frustrated, yet struggle to understand why. A rude comment, a traffic jam or a job rejection might set us off and shatter our confidence. Yet much of our suffering doesn't come directly from what happens to us. Instead, it arises from our attachment to outcomes, people and expectations.

We build new prisons through the stories we tell ourselves. For example, you might think about doing public speaking or starting a project and immediately become self-conscious or anxious about what others might think, or you worry that you may not be good enough. Our prisons can also take the form of possessions we don't need or work we don't want to do, among many others. True freedom begins with self-awareness – recognising these internal barriers and choosing to let them go.

> True freedom begins with self-awareness – recognising these internal barriers and choosing to let them go.

Watching the thinker

We are more prone to stress when we don't listen to our inner voice.[12] Holden recommends that we become curious about our anxiety and stress to discover the message behind them. Another mental prison is the constant racing of our minds – dwelling on the past, worrying about the future and failing to live in the present moment. Much of our suffering stems from these dysfunctional mental patterns.

We are not our compulsive thoughts; in fact, compulsive thinking is a kind of addiction.[44] Try to stop it, and you'll quickly realise how difficult it is to break free from negative thought loops or persistent worries about things beyond our control. Often, these thoughts have little connection to reality, yet they consume our energy and peace of mind. True freedom begins when we recognise this pattern and learn to disengage from it.

Holding inaccurate concepts, labels and judgements distorts our perceptions of reality and interferes with our relationships. Clarity comes from freeing ourselves from involuntary internal dialogues. The moment that we observe our own thoughts, we begin the journey towards liberating our minds from unhelpful, distorted patterns of thinking.

Tolle[44] referred to this practice as 'watching the thinker'. We often remain unaware of both our authentic and dysfunctional selves, preventing true freedom. Our lack of self-awareness makes it difficult to manage our minds effectively, which in turn affects our behaviours. This disconnect separates us from our true selves, with our minds and bodies misaligned and not focused on genuine values.

I once watched a movie about the life of Dr Martin Luther King Jr, the civil rights leader. While I can't say for certain that the film accurately portrayed events, it conveyed a powerful lesson. In one scene, Dr King entered a courtroom to demand basic human rights but realised he carried a 'slave mentality' – a mindset of pleading for dignity rather than asserting it. Upon leaving, he resolved never to enter a courtroom in that way again. He understood that before he could change the world, he first had to free his own mind.

In a 1954 sermon, Dr King expressed a similar idea:

> *'Here is another type of slavery which is probably more prevalent and certainly more injurious than physical bondage, namely mental slavery. This is slavery that the individual inflicts upon himself.'*[45]

We create so many inner dialogues and stories in our minds that sometimes they can consume us. We must free our minds, free ourselves and be ourselves. Recognising and challenging the thoughts and emotions that limit us is an essential step towards greater self-awareness and growth.

An important part of my journey has been setting myself free from the mental prisons that I unknowingly created for myself – but I had to first become aware of these. I had to acknowledge my emotional desire for approval, my anger and my insecurities before I could start managing my thinking, emotions and behaviours, and be true to myself and at peace.

Activity #9: Emotional self-awareness and mental freedom

An important ability is identifying and describing the factors that influence our thinking and emotional responses. A good method to achieve this is to list the inappropriate thinking and emotions that have guided your actions in the past.

1. In the first column in the table below, list any fixations you have with the past or future, fears or rigid thoughts and insecurities that influence your thinking or emotions. These may include beliefs like 'I'm not good enough' 'Things must always go my way', or 'If I fail, I'm worthless'.

2. In the second column, describe how you can use this awareness to monitor your thoughts and emotions, and to guide your decisions and actions more intentionally.

Limited beliefs, fixations or insecurities	How you can use this awareness to guide your thoughts, emotions and actions more intentionally
e.g. I often replay past mistakes in my mind	*When I notice this, I can remind myself that the past can't be changed, but I can learn from it and move forward*
e.g. I believe I must please everyone	*I can recognise this as a form of fear and practise setting healthy boundaries with kindness.*

Reflection:

- Which of your fixations or insecurities affect you the most?
- How does noticing them change how you see yourself or your reactions?
- How could this awareness help you respond differently in the future?
- What new opportunities for growth or connection might open as you release these mental prisons?

'Becoming conscious of [shadow] involves recognising the dark aspects of the personality as present and real. This act is the essential condition for any kind of self-knowledge.'

—Carl Jung

3

Personal Responsibility
Dr John Bellavance

Personal responsibility is the cornerstone of personal growth, self-esteem and meaningful living. It is the recognition that, although we cannot always control what happens to us, we are always responsible for how we respond. It is living 'consciously' and recognising that we are not merely driven by habit, emotion or circumstance, but by how we choose to respond to them.

> True self-esteem arises from discovering meaningful pursuits that promote personal growth...

According to Jung's psychology, the goal is to become a whole, unique and integrated person. Psychological problems are seen as obstacles or challenges on this path. Happiness can't be pursued; it ensues from how we live our lives and the actualisation of a potential meaning or purpose.[28] Self-actualisation and our search for meaning and happiness start when we realise that life doesn't owe us happiness and that human responsibility can never be avoided. Taking responsibility is the opposite of having a victim mentality. There truly is freedom in taking responsibility for how we respond to what happens to us in life. Being responsible puts us in charge of our lives and having a strong self-esteem plays a vital role in this.

Human Responsibility

Greaney[46] argues that human beings are responsible for their actions, making us, in a sense, 'self-made people'. This responsibility stems from our nature as rational beings who, when properly educated, can discern truth from falsehood and distinguish between good (serving the public good) and harmful (serving self-interests at the expense of others).

Complaining is the opposite of taking responsibility. Research suggests that complaining or venting won't make you feel better. You'll feel worse and, in the process, alter the way your brain functions. The pattern is easy to fall into:

- Something bad happens to you or around you. ⇨ You vent.
- Something else bad happens to or around you. ⇨ You complain.
- Soon you become good at complaining!

The way the brain functions reveals the importance of human responsibility. Our thoughts and actions generate myelin in the brain. Myelin is a microscopic neural substance that enhances the speed and accuracy of both cognition and movement. It strengthens neural pathways related to specific skills, but these pathways themselves don't make value judgements.

- Repeated positive actions reinforce beneficial skills and habits.
- Repeated negative actions strengthen destructive ones.

The key takeaway is that when something goes wrong, instead of complaining, we can choose to redirect our energy towards improving the situation. By consistently practising this approach, we train our brain to response constructively, build neural pathways that make constructive responses increasingly natural and easier, eventually becoming our default mode.[47]

Building resilience through responsibility

The pursuit of happiness can sometimes lead to negative outcomes, as not all approaches to happiness are effective or fulfilling. True wellbeing is often found in developing resilience and taking responsibility for life's challenges, not in avoiding difficulties. If you accept negative emotions as a natural part of life, you will tend to experience greater overall happiness. In contrast, if you try to suppress or avoid negative emotions, you will often experience higher levels of anxiety and depression.[48]

The quality of your life largely depends on how much you take responsibility for yourself and strive towards self-actualisation. When you feel unhappy or unfulfilled, the crucial question to ask is, 'What do I need to change or do differently?' Erich Fromm (cited in [32]) argued that avoiding individuality – and the choices and responsibilities that come with it – can lead to significant personal and societal issues. His analysis of Germany during the Third Reich highlighted how the tendency to escape personal responsibility can have serious consequences, both for individuals and for society.

Freedom without responsibility is an unsustainable concept because it inevitably leads to a loss of freedom for individuals and society. When people exercise their freedom without considering the consequences of their actions, it often infringes upon the rights and freedoms of others, leading to a need for stricter rules and regulations to restore order and protect the greater good. This increase in regulation, in turn, curtails the very freedoms that were initially enjoyed.

> *You don't need more time, you need less distractions.*
> *You don't need motivation, you need self-control.*
> *You don't need more resources, you need resourcefulness.*
> *You don't need luck, you need preparation.*
> *You don't need to be busy, you need to be focused.*
> *You don't need to know everything, you just need to start.*
> *You have everything you need.*
> *—**Stoicism** (Ancient Greek philosophy)*

The Chinese philosopher Confucius used archery as a metaphor for personal responsibility. When an archer misses the target, they don't blame external factors but instead look to themselves to find the cause of the failure. Psychology supports this idea, showing that individuals who embrace personal responsibility are better equipped to:

- overcome fears
- align with their values
- experience positive emotions

- help others
- seek solutions rather than avoid problems
- turn setbacks into opportunities
- achieve goals
- accept challenges
- learn from difficulties
- work hard
- manage stress effectively.

Taking responsibility empowers you to navigate life's challenges with resilience and purpose.[49]

Frankl[28] suggested that meaning and growth can be found even in struggle, hardship and suffering. Life inevitably presents challenges and worries, but those who seek to understand the deeper lessons within their difficulties can grow through their experiences. For many of us, our struggles have been opportunities for learning, self-discovery and personal development.

Responsibility and Self-Esteem

> *'Most feel that a sense of competence is strengthened through realistic and accurate self-appraisal, meaningful accomplishments, overcoming adversities, bouncing back from failures, and adopting such practices as assuming self-responsibility and maintaining integrity, which engender one's sense of competence and self-worth.'*
> —***Robert Reasoner***

Self-esteem to key to our capability to take responsibility. Our ability to think, to learn and to respond to change is our basic means of survival and development. Self-esteem – a belief in ourselves as competent – allows us to deal with changes confidently. The right understanding of self-esteem and the role it plays in values education is important for this endeavour.

There are celebrities who have physical beauty and millions of fans and dollars, yet they still can't get through a day without drugs and alcohol, living with severe anxiety or depression. Good looks, popularity and wealth are clearly not a guarantee of healthy self-esteem. External approval can never replace self-approval. Ultimately, the foundation of self-worth lies in how we appraise ourselves. Of all the judgements we pass in life, none is more important than how we judge ourselves.

Authentic versus false self-esteem

'Self-esteem is the disposition to experience oneself as being competent to cope with the basic challenges of life and of being worthy of happiness' (Nathaniel Branden). It a result of how we live our lives. The National Association for Self-Esteem (NASE) defined it as, 'the experience of being capable of meeting life's challenges and being worthy of happiness.'

NASE also states, 'We believe in personal responsibility and accountability. This implies not only being worthy of respect but also as having the basic skills and competencies required to be successful in life.'[50]

This definition of self-esteem is based on the idea that it is deeply connected to both competence and worthiness. The worthiness aspect is often mistaken for merely feeling good about oneself, but it is linked to living in alignment with fundamental human values. True self-esteem arises from discovering meaningful pursuits that promote personal growth and making commitments that foster integrity and a deep sense of fulfillment.

Responsibility and self-esteem also rely on self-evaluation – consciously recognising the gap between what you wish to be and the realistic appraisal of how you see yourself. The emotional aspect refers to your feelings when considering that gap. Self-esteem can only be healthy when you experience and embody the qualities of a self-actualised individual.

However, false self-esteem arises when we rely on external validation or defensive strategies to feel worthy, rather than cultivating genuine competence and integrity. It can even manifest as conceit, narcissism or a sense of superiority.[51] In some cases, people derive self-esteem from external factors such as peer popularity, sexual conquests or even bullying.[52] Yet, these aren't indicators of authentic and healthy self-esteem; rather, they are defensive responses to its absence.

Individuals with low self-esteem may deflect blame onto others and avoid taking accountability for their actions.[1]

Fostering authentic self-esteem

A primary source of self-esteem lies in how we control our thoughts, emotions and actions. Self-esteem doesn't just appear spontaneously. It is developed intentionally by individuals and nurtured by families and the community.[53]

Educators, parents and leaders across all sectors agree that fostering healthy self-esteem is essential for personal and social wellbeing. Authentic, healthy self-esteem is characterised by:

- respect for others
- responsibility for one's actions
- integrity
- pride in accomplishments
- self-motivation
- ability to accept and learn from criticism
- compassion
- willingness to pursue challenging and worthwhile goals.

In other words, we need to help foster the development of people who have healthy or authentic self-esteem because they trust themselves to be constructive, responsible and trustworthy.

Setting high expectations for people helps them build character and self-esteem. When we expect more from them, they begin to set higher expectations for themselves. If we fail to set expectations, we send the message that we believe they are incapable of achieving more. This shows a lack of respect for their potential.

...if you set high expectations for yourself, you are telling yourself that you believe you can achieve more...

Similarly, if you set high expectations for *yourself,* you are telling yourself that you believe you can achieve more – and you are respecting yourself. It is up to you to nurture your self-esteem.

Six pillars of self-esteem

Branden[1] identified six essential practices for nurturing and maintaining healthy self-esteem, which he called *The Six Pillars of Self-Esteem*. Each pillar represents an essential aspect of living consciously and building a foundation of healthy self-esteem.

Pillar 1: Living consciously – facing uncomfortable truths about yourself, being fully aware of your actions as you perform them, and actively seeking truth, knowledge and feedback to foster personal growth. Developing authentic self-esteem requires defining your values and embodying them with integrity. A fundamental aspect of this process is your commitment to self-honesty – being willing to critically evaluate your own values and actions without avoidance or justification.[6]

When you live consciously and learn from your mistakes, you gain a greater sense of control over your life. Through this self-reflection and willingness to acknowledge your shortcomings, personal growth and self-esteem can truly develop.

Pillar 2. Self-acceptance and worthiness – facing your thoughts, feelings and actions honestly, and embracing yourself without denial or self-deception. Recognising your inherent value allows you to treat yourself with respect and build emotional resilience.

Pillar 3. Self-responsibility – taking responsibility for your life. Self-esteem is cultivated through the way you live. It requires a conscious effort to act with responsibility and integrity. When you make good choices and witness the resultant positive outcomes, your sense of self-worth is reinforced. Taking responsibility for your life fosters empowerment, providing a sense of control and freedom. By acting responsibly, you promote your personal growth, which in turn strengthens your self-esteem and self-respect. Through this process, you take ownership of your character development.[52]

Therefore, responsibility plays a crucial role in self-esteem. Research shows that when young people are given a lot of freedom without clear boundaries or expectations, they often feel unsupported and uncared for. Teaching young people to live within appropriate behavioural boundaries is essential for their emotional wellbeing.

> ...responsibility plays a crucial role in self-esteem.

Studies have documented a strong correlation between low self-esteem and various social and personal issues, including violence, substance abuse, eating disorders, school dropouts, teenage pregnancy, suicide and low academic performance.[51]

Pillar 4. Self-assertiveness – expressing your thoughts, feelings and values openly and appropriately, and standing up for yourself while respecting others. Being authentic and clear about your needs strengthens self-respect and reinforces healthy self-esteem.

Pillar 5. Living purposefully and competently – setting goals and working to achieve them, rather than living at the mercy of chance and outside forces. Competence is the behavioural aspect of self-esteem. It is concerned with achieving a sense of effectiveness in achieving the results you desire in life, as well as confidence in your ability to make good decisions. Competence is strengthened through realistic and accurate self-appraisal, meaningful accomplishments, overcoming adversities and bouncing back from failures. Adopting practices such as self-responsibility and maintaining integrity engenders your sense of competence and self-worth.[51]

Pillar 6. Integrity – walking the talk, where your words, convictions and actions align. Integrity means speaking and acting from your deepest convictions. It also means being authentic in your dealings with others, without hiding or distorting who you are or what you value to gain approval or avoid disapproval.

Integrity is acting according to what you believe is right, telling the truth and honouring your commitments. You can't experience self-respect if you betray your conscience, knowledge and conviction.

People can be inspired and guided to live more consciously, embrace self-acceptance, take responsibility for their actions, assert themselves, live with purpose and uphold personal integrity. However, the responsibility for *cultivating* and *maintaining* these practices rests with each individual. Self-esteem is developed from within; it can't be given by others.[1]

> Self-esteem is developed from within; it can't be given by others.[1]

Activity #10: Habits of the mind and self-esteem

In the spaces provided in the table below, write your self-reflections on your mindset – how your thinking affects your behaviours in different situations. Some examples of mindsets and behaviours are provided to guide you. Reflecting on these mindsets and behaviours will help you recognise which pillars of self-esteem you are already practising, and which ones could use more attention.

Unaccountability – not feeling responsible for my thinking, feelings and actions.	
Mindset	**Behaviours**
People protect themselves from feeling hurt, ashamed or angry when they perceive criticism or do something wrong. They are emotionally defensive.	When dealing with a problem in my life I tend to … • *not relate well to others* • *not accept responsibility for my actions* • • • When I make a mistake, I tend to… • *try to prove myself or impress others* • *not handle criticism well* • *blame others for my mistakes* • • When I disagree with others, how do I react to their response and what they say about me? • *I am angry, frustrated, which leads to heated arguments rather than productive dialogue.* • •

Self-assertiveness – to speak and act from your deepest convictions is to have integrity. If you silence your own voice, others won't know what you want or need.	Do I speak and act from my deepest convictions? • *I am not willing to express my thoughts, values and feelings and to stand up for myself.* • *I fake who I am to avoid disapproval. I pretend to agree through my silence or even white lies.* • • • If my wants and needs are different from those of others' I am likely to… • •

Feeling responsible for my thinking, feelings and actions.	
Mindset	**Behaviours**
Living consciously – being aware of your thoughts and actions, and their impact on yourself and others.	Do I face up to facts about myself? • *I am realistic and accurate with my self-appraisal….* • *I do speak and act from my deepest convictions when…* • •
Self-acceptance – facing your mistakes and learning from them.	Am I willing to admit my mistakes and learn from them? • *I can handle criticism…* • •

Challenging Our Demons: The Hero's Journey

'One does not become enlightened by imagining figures of light, but by making the darkness conscious. The latter procedure, however, is disagreeable and therefore not popular.' —**Carl Jung**

Just as developing self-esteem involves facing uncomfortable truths and taking responsibility for our actions, personal growth often requires confronting our inner challenges and transforming them into opportunities. This process of transformation is well captured in the work of Carl Jung. Jung described the hero's journey as a transformative process in which an individual leaves the comfort of their familiar world to confront their inner demons and overcome personal struggles. They experience a call to change their life.

This journey is not only about self-discovery, but also about pursuing higher ideals or a greater cause. Along the way, the hero faces resistance both internally and externally, including from others who oppose their path. Ultimately, they emerge stronger, wiser and more self-aware, embodying the growth that comes from embracing challenge and change.

This journey is a universal narrative pattern found in myths, legends and stories across cultures. American writer Joseph Campbell, influenced by Jung's analytical psychology, popularised the study of this mythic structure and coined the term, 'The Hero's Journey'. In these stories heroes embark on quests, confront their 'dragons' – both real-life challenges and metaphorical tests – and uncover hidden treasures of wisdom and growth.

At its core, the hero's journey mirrors the human experience. Each of us has the potential to be the hero of our own story. Heroes aren't born extraordinary; they are ordinary people who embrace an extraordinary path. They are you and me. Inside each of us is an inner voice that whispers we are meant for something greater. True heroism lies in listening to that voice, pursuing a dream despite challenges and continuing forward with courage even when doubt arises, whether within or from others.

The hero's journey unfolds in three stages – the Departure (the call to adventure), the Initiation (transformation) and the Return (see Figure 8). These stages offer a powerful framework for understanding the human experience and personal development to achieve our highest, unique potential.⁽⁵⁴⁾

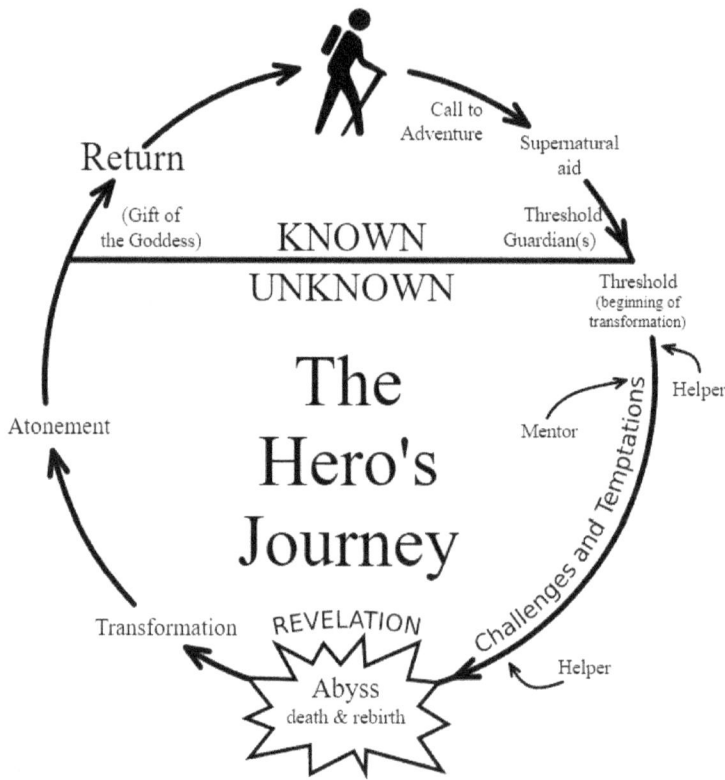

Figure 8 The Heroes Journey (2009)

The Departure – the call to change your life

The hero's journey begins with a call to adventure, to change your life, prompting the hero to leave the familiarity of their ordinary world. This 'ordinary world' represents the environment where most people live – a place of comfort shaped by personal and societal expectations. While it may feel safe, it can also be stifling, draining dreams and leaving us feeling stuck or stagnant.

Yet, the hero refuses to remain confined. At some point, they encounter a pivotal challenge or crisis – 'the innermost cave' – marking the true beginning of their journey. This moment of realisation often becomes the turning point where the hero decides it's time to take that first bold step towards transformation.

Like the hero, you have the choice to accept or refuse this call to adventure. This decision significantly shapes your character. Often, heroes resist initially, held back by duty, fear, insecurity or self-doubt – reasons that anchor them to their current circumstances. Refusing the call means surrendering control over your own destiny, allowing external forces to dictate the course of your life. True growth begins only when you overcome hesitation and step forward into the unknown to begin your adventure.

Crossing the first threshold

Accepting the call means leaving the predictable, comfortable world behind and crossing the first threshold into an unfamiliar realm filled with challenges and possibilities. Often, this transition is triggered by a significant life event – illness, suffering, a transformative encounter or a sudden realisation – that disrupts the ordinary and demands change. Sometimes, we are pushed rather than stepping willingly, jolted awake by an event that compels us to act. At this point, we have truly left behind the world we knew. 'Toto, I've a feeling we are not in Kansas anymore.'

Many of us have had extraordinary life experiences that shook us up. For example, when I was 19 years old, my girlfriend broke up with me, and a disagreement with my father led me to leave home. Within the space of a few weeks, I found myself embarking on a journey into the unknown, travelling from Montreal, Canada to British Columbia with nothing but a backpack. This was my 'hero persona' responding to a call to change.

After the departure, the hero recognises that they can't return to the world they knew, and they don't know what lies ahead. Once we awaken from the ordinary thinking of the ordinary world, we must prepare for the challenges ahead. Our yearning for something greater sparks the beginning of our transformation, setting us on a path of discovery that separates us from the familiar. Discovering new truths and levels of consciousness creates portals to 'crossing over' where we learn to pay close attention to clues left by other truth seekers and begin to trust our own inner guidance.[54]

The Initiation

Along the journey, the hero confronts outdated beliefs, assumptions and immature behaviours formed since childhood. On the journey, tests arise – whether psychological, physical, emotional, mental or spiritual – that challenge the hero in various ways. However, we aren't alone in this journey. Events, people and experiences along the way provide valuable support, guidance and sometimes even unexpected solutions. Those who are open to accepting help and wisdom from others often discover creative ways to overcome the challenges they face. As we continue to pass these tests, we are rewarded with new possibilities, wisdom, authenticity, and ultimately a sense of joy and peace.

In *The Wizard of Oz*, the Scarecrow, Cowardly Lion and Tin Man each believed they lacked something essential. Yet, through their journey, they demonstrated that they already possessed the qualities they sought: intelligence, courage and heart. Only by facing challenges and recognising their inner strengths could they truly believe in themselves and claim those qualities. **The journey itself was the key to unlocking their potential and self-belief.**[54]

The hero's goal is to find the treasure – the highest expression of self, wisdom and joy. Yet sometimes the hero becomes tempted to keep it for themselves. This self-serving choice often leads to misery and ruin, as we lose sight of the true purpose of the journey. Most of us, however, wish to share our newfound wisdom and joy with loved ones and community.

This altruistic intention can bring its own trials; family or friends may not be ready for these insights, leaving the hero feeling misunderstood or alone. These final trials, however, help us solidify our growth and demonstrate the true value of our journey – transformation not only for oneself but to benefit others.[54]

The Return

The conclusion of the hero's journey demonstrates how the dark powers that once challenged the hero can be overcome. Regardless of the hero's personal fate, the deeper purpose of the journey reveals that light always triumphs over darkness. While the personal growth and rewards achieved along the way are significant, the true essence of the journey lies in the hero's ability to return to their community and share the wisdom gained.

When the hero comes back home, understanding the meaning of their experiences and effectively communicating the benefits of their journey to others, the cycle reaches its completion. This process of returning, sharing knowledge and contributing to the greater good transforms individual growth into a collective benefit. It highlights the importance of not only self-discovery but also of using that insight to positively impact the wider community.

Activity #11: Your hero's journey

Reflect on your personal journey, considering how challenges and growth have shaped, or could shape, your life.

Write in the table below what your journey looked like or could look like:

1. Recall a time in your life when you experienced a significant call to change, a turning point or a life-altering event.

2. Identify the internal or external challenges you faced during this journey, including beliefs, assumptions or behaviours you had to confront.

3. Consider how you overcame these challenges or how you might overcome them in the future, and what wisdom or growth resulted.

4. Fill in each column of the table with your reflections.

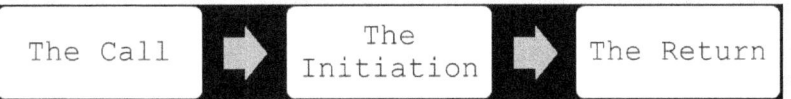

The incident that occurred in your life (The Call)	Confronted by outdated beliefs (The Initiation)	The dark power is overthrown (The Return)

Reflection:

- What patterns do you notice in the challenges you faced and the ways you responded?
- How did, or could, this journey contribute to your personal growth and the wellbeing of those around you?

Six archetypes of heroes

There are six archetypes of heroes that we can learn from in order to move forward on our own hero's journey.[55] The six hero archetypes reveal common patterns of behaviour and strengths we carry within us. Understanding them helps us navigate challenges, uncover our potential and make conscious choices on our personal journeys. While inspired by Jungian archetype theory, this specific categorisation of six hero types comes from Villate's interpretation and expansion of the concept.

They are:

1. **The Orphan** – embodied when people see themselves as victims and focus on their suffering. They need to learn to feel their feelings so they can move through them and let them go.
2. **The Wanderer** – seeks to discover through their journey their own identity so that their work and life reflect their purpose and feed their passion. Thus, their task is to find themselves.
3. **The Warrior** – focused on achieving their goals and defeating the competition. Their task is to prove their worth. However, the Warrior is a heroic archetype only when their courage and focus are employed for the greater good.
4. **The Altruist** – their task is to show generosity. They sacrifice for others, committing to something greater than themselves, seeking to make the world a better place.
5. **The Innocent** – guided by the gift of a deep faith in the unfolding of life, going with the flow. They trust that the various situations in life will lead them down a destined path, trusting in a higher power and

the universe. Through this surrender, they find happiness, which is their task.

6. **The Magician** – shares a basic worldview with the Innocent but claims a greater amount of power, which is their gift. Magicians take responsibility in an active and immediate way for the state of their lives or of the planet.

The following exercise will assist you to reflect on your life experiences, behaviours and responses to challenges and then identify which of the six hero archetypes best describe you.

Activity #12: Your archetypes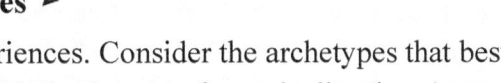

1. Reflect on your own experiences. Consider the archetypes that best describe your qualities and behaviours (refer to the list above).
2. Complete the table below. Your qualities may fit in more than one archetype. For example, you may have been the Orphan and the Wanderer. This is a useful way to understand yourself, your values and your path. Some examples are provided as prompts.

The Orphan	e.g. Felt abandoned after a friendship ended; learned to process emotions and move forward.
The Wanderer	e.g. Tried different career paths to discover what truly motivates me.
The Warrior	e.g. Trained for a marathon to prove to myself I could push through limits.

The Altruist	e.g. Volunteered at a community shelter, prioritising others' needs over my own comfort.
The Innocent	e.g. Accepted a sudden relocation and trusted it would lead to new opportunities.
The Magician	e.g. Used my expertise to improve a process at work, creating better outcomes for everyone

Reflection:

- What do these archetypes reveal about how you respond to challenges?
- How can this awareness help you make choices aligned with your values and goals?

Jung's stages of life

Carl Jung depicted archetypes of heroes that map four stages of our lives. These four archetypes represent the evolving stages of life, helping us understand our growth, purpose and the values that guide our choices:

1. **The Athlete**: In this early phase, we want to make a name for ourselves, create a good impression and be attractive. We are self-absorbed and pursue happiness, chase success, look for love and are full of ambition. In this state, we have not yet experienced a purpose higher than our ego.
2. **The Warrior:** At this stage, we want to conquer the world. For example, our aim is to be financially independent, to own our own home and assert our free will. We begin to realise that we are here to love, but our circle of love is still narrow.

3. **The Statement**: At this stage we begin to ask ourselves, 'Is there more to life than this? There must be!' The life that we are living feels too small for us now and we want to play a part in a bigger story. The most important question we can ask is 'What am I living for?'

Jung asked, 'What myth am I living?' A myth is a great story that you want to be part of, a story of love, a hero's journey to bring about change and make the world better, namely, a higher purpose that we give ourselves fully to. At this stage we look out for what truly inspires us and what we want to give our life to.

4. **The Spiritual**: Now we are living an inspired life. We are not just driven by the rational and small-minded person we once were. We now recognise what inspires us and do what we love. At this stage we are living for universal ideals. We no longer care about being normal. 'To be normal is the ideal aim of the unsuccessful,' said Carl Jung.

Activity #13: Your hero's journey, archetypes and life stages

1. Review the six hero archetypes and four stages of life above.
2. Write in the table below your own hero's journey and which archetypes and Jung's stages of life apply to you and why (examples provided).

Jung's stage	Your hero's journey example	Hero archetype(s)	Why it fits
The Athlete	*Started a new school in a different city and struggled to fit in.*	*Orphan / Wanderer*	*Felt out of place, had to navigate uncertainty, and discover inner strengths.*
The Warrior	*Studied intensively to earn a scholarship.*	*Warrior / Magician*	*Took responsibility, showed courage and focused on achieving a meaningful goal.*

The Statement	Volunteered in a community project	Altruist / Wanderer	Questioned previous life choices, sought purpose beyond self-interest and acted for a greater cause.
The Spiritual	Mentored others	Magician / Innocent	Integrated wisdom gained, lived according to values and contributed to others' growth.

Reflection:

- How do your archetypes and life stages intersect?
- What patterns of growth or challenges do you notice?
- How can this awareness guide your future decisions and actions?

Allowing our ego to die

To free ourselves of the chains of the narrow selves and narrow lives (our departure from the cave), it is necessary for the ego to die. This means surrendering our ego (our narrow self) and pursuing ideals greater than ourselves. Only when a single grain of wheat falls to the earth can it die and bear new fruit. Similarly, by letting go of the narrow self – which includes our self-image and the stories we tell ourselves about the world – we can be awaken to a greater awareness reality, who we truly are and why we are here.

Letting go of the narrow self also requires resisting our immediate impulses to achieve a goal or something we truly value. The destabilisation of the ego is sometimes experienced as a kind of death, with transformative energies released in the dying of the ego.(54)

Development is not a passive process; it requires an active interaction between the individual and their environment, as well as the triggering of significant events that propel them towards the next stage. In counselling and psychology, when the call to adventure is embraced, clients receive support to view the world from a new perspective and work towards a more fulfilling life.

Moreover, a new stage of personal growth involves releasing old frameworks for meaning-making and adopting new ways to perceive the world. This process represents the metaphorical death of the old self and the birth of a renewed way of seeing and being in the world.(56)

Activity #14: The values that define who you are

This activity helps you develop the ability to understand your values and identity. By reflecting on how your ego and choices influence your actions, you strengthen your capacity to align your behaviour with the person you want to become.

1. **Know thyself:** Write down what a better life means for you – what your dream life would look like.
2. **Your funeral:** Imagine you have just died. What would you like people to say about you at your funeral?

Compare your answers from Part 1 and Part 2. Are they the same? For example, if for Part 1, you wrote, *'Travel the world and make lots of money'*, and for Part 2 you wrote, *'Be a good friend, husband or mother'* then your answers are incompatible and inconsistent.

If your answers are the same, the chances are that you are currently doing what is important to you in your life.(57)

3. **Your identity:** Write down the values and behaviours that would make your life better.

Ask yourself, *'What are the values that define me – my identity? Why are these important to me?'*

4. **Your struggles:** Reflect on times when you did not live up to your own values or expectations. Consider the influence of your struggles on your reasoning, decisions and behaviour.

Reflection:

- What did you learn about yourself and your values from this exercise?
- How do your values shape your actions and interactions with others?
- What insights do your struggles provide about your growth and development?

'The mind and body are always in conversation. The more you listen, the better you understand yourself.'

—*Brenda Mapane*

4

Understanding Mind and Body Relations
Dr John Bellavance

Understanding the relationship between mind and body is essential for personal growth. Human development is often viewed from two perspectives. One focuses on external factors – physical needs and the scientific understanding needed to meet these needs. The other centres on the mind, aiming to elevate human consciousness through the pursuit of moral ideals and practices that transcend physical needs. These two perspectives shape the way we view human development. This distinction is crucial because values education is fundamentally about transforming our mind/consciousness, guiding us towards moral ideals and practices that shape who we are and how we act in the world. Hence, the mind plays a crucial role in how we act with our body.

In this chapter, we explore how a holistic view of life integrates mind and body, unites the inner and outer worlds, and reveals the dynamic balance between giving and receiving. Through this understanding, we learn how our inner thoughts and values influence our outward behaviour, and how unity between mind and body fosters personal responsibility, wellbeing and wholeness.

Mind–Body, Subject–Object, Giving–Receiving

> *'Realising that our minds control our bodies while our bodies reflect our minds amounts to understanding the most fundamental aspects of ourselves.'*
> —H E Davey

The mind/consciousness and the body have a beneficial reciprocal relationship where both exist in relation to each another through a continual process of giving and receiving. The term *mind/consciousness* refers to our inner awareness – the part of us that perceives, reflects and gives meaning to experience. It is the *subject* within us, the observer through which we interpret the world and ourselves. The body, in turn, expresses this inner life outwardly through action and interaction – the *object* side of our being. When mind and body are united, our inner awareness (subject) and outer expression (object) work together in harmony, creating a state of wholeness and integration.

While the mind/consciousness typically occupies the subject position, directing the body, the body may sometimes occupy the subject position depending on its physical processes.

An example of the beneficial reciprocal (giving–receiving) relationship between the mind and body is when we make a resolution to exercise. This process involves negative feedback – a self-regulating cycle in which the mind monitors and adjusts the body's responses to maintain balance and stay on track towards a goal. For example, exercising requires willpower, placing the mind in the subject position to guide the body. It also entails the mind pursuing a goal and resisting the body's impulse to be lazy and avoid exercise.

If laziness overpowers the mind's determination, the body assumes a subject role over the mind, reinforcing the lazy behaviour (see Figure 9). This situation exemplifies positive feedback, but in this case, it is unhelpful because it strengthens the undesired pattern. However, positive feedback from the body can also be beneficial. As we exercise and feel better, this positive feedback improves our desire to continue exercising, reinforcing the positive behaviour.

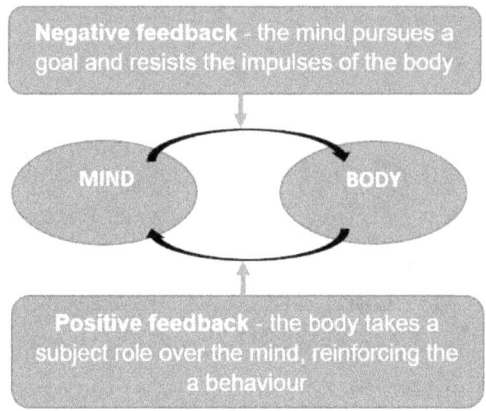

Figure 9 Mind and body positive and negative feedback

Giving and receiving in reciprocal relationships

The principle of giving and receiving between subjects and objects operates throughout much of the world and human life – not only within the relationship between mind and body but in every interaction where two or more parts exist in relation to one another. A parent and child, teacher and student, or even the sun and moon, all participate in ongoing exchanges of giving and receiving.

In essence, the nature of life is reciprocal, where all things exist in relation to one another through giving and receiving. The Latin root of *reciprocal* comes from the Latin – *reciprocus*, meaning 'back and forth' – which captures this dynamic perfectly.

These roles are not fixed; they continually shift depending on context. For example, a father may give love and advice to his son, placing him in the subject/giving position, but the son can also give love and advice, giving something back and temporarily taking the subject role himself. This giving and receiving of love and advice allows for personal growth and development to occur (see Figure 10).

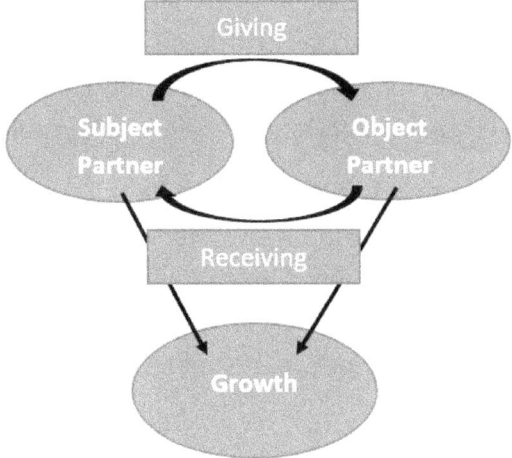

Figure 10 The reciprocal and interchanging nature of subject and object

Holism: An Integrative Explanation of Purpose

Recognising this constant reciprocity of giving and receiving allows us to see a larger pattern in life: when parts interact harmoniously, they create greater, integrated wholes. This is the essence of holism.

Holism is the idea that systems are the result of the properties and interaction of their component parts – such as mind and body within the human body – and that such systems are more than the sum of their parts. This program takes the perspective that both the development of consciousness/mind and attention to physical needs, supported by scientific understanding, are essential for human wellbeing. When mind and body work harmoniously, they form an integrative whole.[17]

Why is this important for your life and personal development?

Firstly, **the relationship between your mind and body largely determines how you behave in the world** – morally, ethically and physically. It influences how you manage your physical health, respond to challenges, and make choices that affect yourself and others.

When an individual's mind and body are united centring on love, values and purpose, they become an integrative, harmonious whole – a self-actualised individual – a person who has achieved their full potential and is living a life of purpose, meaning and fulfillment (see Figure 11). At a larger level, when a husband and wife (subjects–objects of love) are united in love, purpose and values, they form a larger integrative whole: a family (see Figure 12). This family expands into an even greater integrative whole: a nation and then the world.

Life tends to move towards more integrative wholes – combining two or more things to form effective units or systems – as matter becomes ordered into increasingly larger and more stable structures through the interaction of subject and object. Holism emphasises that the meaning of the whole emerges from the relationship between the parts, rather than from the parts alone.

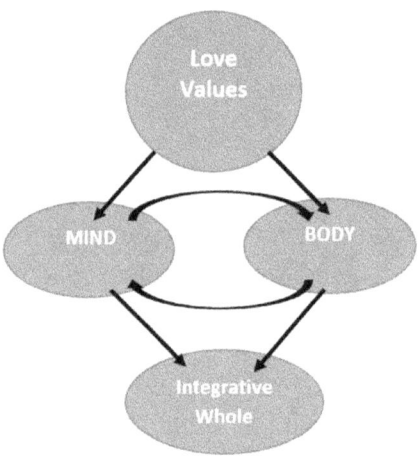

Figure 11 An individual as a self-actualised integrative whole

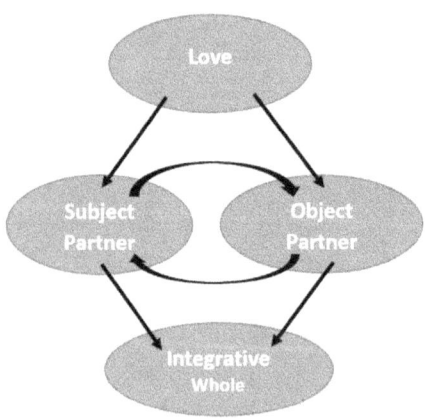

Figure 12 A loving family as an integrative whole

Secondly, **creativity arises from the process of giving and receiving between mind (subject) and body (object),** which enables the discovery of the self, others and the world around us. For example, through exchange with other people and our environment, we come to understand the world as we interact with it, while simultaneously nurturing it into existence, and it, in turn, nurtures us. The role and impact of love operate similarly. For example, a mother, in the subject position, loves and nurtures her child who occupies the object position as the recipient of her love. And the child returns love.

The third implication of holism is that **life has purpose.** Philosopher Thomas Nagel[2] suggests that the universe is not a random collection of disconnected entities drifting aimlessly through time and space. Instead, it consists of interconnected systems that interact in an orderly manner, driven by an underlying, unifying purpose.

It may seem that randomness governs life and that order is the exception. Order is the universal norm. The flow of the universe is always creative, though it has order. It is a process of collaboration and co-creation.[58]

ACTIVITY #15: Mind, body and giving and receiving

Write in your journal and share with others:

1. Provide an example of the benefits of giving and receive between mind and body in your life.

2. Describe one interaction this week where you felt connected and one where you felt disconnected. What influenced the difference?

3. Do you see order and purpose in your life? If so, what does this mean for you?

Debrief: Find one person to share about this.

Are We Our Mind or Our Body?

> *'Moral commitment enables civilised societies to become havens of decency for most of their members.'*
> **— William Damon and Anne Colby**

Human behaviour is influenced by many factors, including biology, environment and conscious choice. Understanding the influence of biological determinism – the belief that our genes, biology and physical makeup alone determine who we are – is important because it shapes how we think about personal development, responsibility and moral decision making.

Biological determinism suggests you're mostly a product of your biology and environment, with little real say over who you are or how you behave. While it's true that your biology plays a part (your brain and body shape some things) and your environment influences you too (like your family or community), this view overlooks something essential: your consciousness. We risk disregarding our personal responsibility, as well as the power of ideals and values in guiding and managing our lives.

Great leaders have shown that moral convictions rather than base emotions or social pressure can bring about great change in our world. If you ignore that part of yourself – the part that can dream, decide and believe in things – you basically let yourself off the hook for your own actions. You might think, *Oh well, it's just how I'm wired*, instead of taking responsibility. Or you might doubt your power to make a difference.

So, while biology and environment are important, don't forget the superheroes in your own story: your conscious mind – a heart of love and the ideals you choose to live by. They're what truly help you grow and become the person you want to be. Ordinary people can exercise control over important life decisions and pursue ideals that inspire us.[26]

Understanding the relationship between mind, consciousness and body is crucial to personal development. Yet, while consciousness is a defining characteristic of human life – it's what makes us 'us', from our thoughts to our feelings – scientists still don't have a single, solid answer for how it works. People often wonder…

- *Am I defined by my body and its impulses?*
- *Am I shaped by my thoughts, planning, mind and consciousness?*
- *Is human life merely a response to a set of physical impulses, or is consciousness the driving force?*
- *Is free will merely a myth?*

In this book, we take the position that our understanding of biological organisms and their evolutionary history must expand beyond the materialist view that biology alone determines destiny. Instead, we must incorporate an explanation of human life that recognises the crucial role of consciousness and reasoning and heart in shaping both ourselves and the world around us.[2]

Consciousness is a defining characteristic of human life. While it's what makes us 'us', from our thoughts to our feelings, scientists still don't have a single, solid answer for how it works. There are three main ideas or perspectives that researchers use to try and figure out the connection between our mind (our thoughts and awareness) and our brain (the physical organ)[59]:

> Consciousness is a defining characteristic of human life.

1. **Biological determinism**, which suggests that who you are is primarily determined by physiology.

2. The **science of consciousness**, where subjective human experiences and reasoning (the part of you that thinks, feels and makes choices) transforms your biological disposition (feeling hungry or scared). You might be super hungry (biological disposition), but you decide to wait until dinner because you want to be polite **(subjective human experience).**

3. **A holistic approach**, which suggests that consciousness and biological factors aren't separate things working on their own. Instead, they constantly influence each other.

Let's have a look now at these three perspectives:

Biological determinism

A deterministic view can lead to the perspective that that free will and consciousness are illusions.[10, 32] This view regards the brain as a kind of machine. Our bodies have inbuilt physiological responses – like hunger or fear when you hear a loud noise. These form our biological dispositions, which are innate, automatic patterns shaped by evolution – hardwired like the basic software that comes with your computer.[32]

- What is reductionism?

Reductionism is the idea that to understand something complex, we must break it down into its simplest components. Just as you could examine a smartphone by analysing its circuits and microchips, reductionism in science proposes that complex systems – such as living organisms – are best understood by examining their smallest physical parts. For example, to understand how a living cell works, reductionism suggests you start by looking at the molecules and atoms that compose it.

However, critics argue that this approach misses something essential. Even if we understand every part of a system, we may not fully understand how those parts interact to produce the system's overall behaviour. As the saying goes: *'The whole is greater than the sum of its parts.'*

Theoretical reductionism often proposes – though not without controversy – that biology will ultimately be explained by chemistry, and chemistry by physics.[60] How things are related and influence each other is viewed as a secondary matter.[10] However, it is argued that biological organisms are too complex to explain by looking at individual part numbers alone, as this can lead to oversimplification of the complexity of living things.[61]

- So, why does any of this matter?

In a reductionist framework, human consciousness, reasoning and emotions are understood as the product of electrochemical processes in the brain. They are just brain activities. Mental states and free will are material entities and are therefore completely determined by natural laws.[58] The brain's unconscious and automatic processes have led some to question whether conscious thought has *any* influence on behaviour at all.⁽⁶²⁾ From this perspective, physiology and neuroscience are viewed as the only disciplines capable of explaining human consciousness, reasoning and existence. Reducing mental events to physical ones is also a common answer to the mind–body problem in psychology.⁽⁶³⁾ Clearly, physiology plays a significant role in who we are. For example, evolutionary science and research into human behaviour have yielded a consensus that fairness, empathy and altruism are part of our biological makeup.⁽²⁶⁾ Additionally, our neural pathways produce automatic responses that protect us from danger and a host of other functions that we are not aware of.⁽³⁹⁾

All experiences in this life come to us through the brain and are therefore constrained and shaped by it. This becomes evident when a person suffers a stroke or brain injury causing some aspects of their normal experience to disappear from their world.⁽¹⁰⁾ However, the question of *which* specific electrical processes provide the most effective explanation for consciousness remains unsolved. Why should physical brain activity give rise to a rich inner life at all?

If any problem qualifies as the 'hard problem' of consciousness, it is this one.⁽⁶⁴⁾

It's not surprising that brain scans show certain areas 'lighting up' when you're in love. After all, every experience you have, from seeing a dog to solving a math problem, is accompanied by brain activity. But here's the thing: just knowing where those lights go on doesn't tell us much about what it *feels* like to fall in love.

Birch (cited in ³⁸) maintained that mechanistic science can explain what happens in the brain's cells when conscious thought is present. But it leaves unanswered the question about the *feeling* of consciousness. Science is highly successful at dealing with objective events in the brain but not so with the subjective side of human experience. The problem is not so much whether the brain works like a computer, but whether that helps us understand consciousness at all.⁽³²⁾

As Nagel (2012) argues, the failure of evolutionary materialism lies in its abandonment of the search for transcendent self-understanding.⁽²⁾

The science of human consciousness

In contrast to biological determinism, another approach emphasises the science of human consciousness. This other idea focuses on **human consciousness** (your mind and awareness), your **ability to reason** (think things through logically) and your **moral convictions** (what you believe is right or wrong). It basically says that to truly understand how people grow and develop, you must consider their inner experiences – their thoughts, feelings and beliefs – not just their genes or physical makeup.

But if you think that your conscious mind can influence your actions, it means you have the power to direct your own life. This is where personal development comes in.

Conscious thought and reasoning allow us to move beyond our biologically based dispositions. The key question is whether they play a crucial role in shaping our lives or are merely by-products of biology and chemistry.[62]

The noted psychiatrist, Viktor Frankl,[19] while in a Nazi concentration camp, pondered on whether human beings are unavoidably influenced by their body and their surroundings (nature), or have the capacity to shape their moral lives. He asked:

> '*Is there no spiritual freedom in regard to behaviour and reaction to any given surrounding? Is that theory true which would have us believe that man is no more than a product of many conditional and environmental factors – be they biological, psychological or sociological in nature? Does a man have no choice of action in the face of such circumstances?*
>
> '*The experiences of the camp life show that man does have a choice of action. There were enough examples, which prove that apathy could be overcome and irritability suppressed. Man can preserve a vestige of spiritual freedom, of independence of mind, even in such terrible conditions of psychic and physical stress.*' (Frankl, 1984, p. 66)

Our experience of both ourselves and the world is shaped by our perceptions of them. However, the immediate evidence of our senses should not be regarded as the ultimate authority on reality.[32] Conscious reasoning is required.

Imagine your senses – your eyes, ears, touch – are like a camera and microphone. They collect information, but they don't give you the full, perfect picture of what's happening. Your *perception* is how your brain processes and interprets that information. So, when we say, 'Our experience of ourselves and the world is shaped by our perceptions,' it means that the 'movie' you see is unique to you, filtered through your memories, emotions and past experiences.

Nagel[2] argues that the mind is not merely a by-product of physical laws but is central to our understanding of the world. Through reasoning, we can transcend our immediate sensory and instinctive perceptions to explore deeper realities, including nature and values. Even though what you see and feel seems real, it's not always the absolute truth. Optical illusions, a magician's trick or misinterpreting someone's words are examples of how our senses can fool us.

The key message is to not blindly trust what you see and hear. Be aware that your mind is actively shaping your reality. When we take a rational and objective approach to our pre-reflective tendencies – the automatic interpretations of sensory input – we engage in detached reasoning. This allows us to rely on structured systems of measurement, such as science and moral reasoning, to refine our perceptions and correct biologically ingrained tendencies.

> Your mind is actively shaping your reality.

This is the process of using our conscious brain to override instincts. It's about not just reacting but instead taking a moment to think and analyse a situation without letting our gut feelings or instant perceptions take over. For instance, reasoning enables us to regulate instinctive impulses like anger, hunger and sexual desire. Unlike cultural history or biological predispositions, systematic reasoning justifies our conclusions and actions through logical analysis.

Your *senses and instincts* give you an indirect connection to the world, like a blurry photo. They tell you something is there, but not the full story.

Reason is what gives you a direct path to the truth. It's like having the ability to take that blurry photo and sharpen it until you see every detail clearly. Reason is the tool that lets you step back and think critically about your automatic reactions, your gut feelings and what your senses are telling you. This allows you to interact with reality in a more objective way, not just reacting to it but truly understanding it.

In its evolution, humanity has now reached a point where we have moved beyond mere appearances and biological dispositions. Once we recognise the distinction between appearance and reality and acknowledge the existence of factual truths that go beyond perception and emotion, it becomes necessary to consider how we can discover these truths in the first place. It is not sufficient to assume that natural selection alone has given us the ability to discern right from wrong. Likewise, we can't merely rely on our natural biological instincts, impressions or emotions.[2]

Consciousness and reasoning transform biological dispositions

Let's look at some examples of how consciousness and reasoning can transform our biological dispositions.

1. **Neuroscientists have discovered that neurons in the brain play a crucial role in habit formation.**

    Engaging in new activities or ways of thinking trains the brain to create new neural pathways. As these behaviours, thoughts and emotions are repeated, the pathways strengthen, eventually making the behaviour feel natural and automatic. In this way, we are actively programming our brains.[65] In cognitive control research, brain scans show that regular mental training can change how the brain works and is built.[66]

2. **Positive mood states change brain patterns and improve cognitive performance in several ways**[67]**:**

    - *Enhanced brain connectivity* – Positive emotions increase activity in the prefrontal cortex (responsible for decision making and attention) and strengthen its connections with other brain regions, improving overall brain coordination.

- *Increased dopamine levels* – Positive moods boost dopamine, a neurotransmitter that enhances motivation, learning and memory. This helps the brain process information more efficiently.

- *Improved cognitive flexibility* – When you're in a good mood, you're more open to new ideas and able to switch between tasks more easily. This flexibility supports creativity and problem solving.

- *Reduced stress response* – Positive emotions help regulate the amygdala (the brain's threat detector), lowering stress and anxiety. This allows the brain to focus better and perform more effectively.

3. **Research in psychogenic pain shows that certain kinds of pain have no organic or structural cause but are a result of emotional and psychological problems**, including psychological trauma and the suppression of painful emotions.

   If a person can't accept and express these emotions, the memory of them is suppressed in their unconscious. As a result, every physical and emotional stimulus that can remind the unconscious memory of the trauma will reactivate the pain experience. The most important implication for treatment is that the patient *accepts* the psychological origin of the pain, suggesting the importance of conscious reasoning when dealing with this type of pain.[29]

4. **Conscious determinations cause behavioural outcomes.**

   Cognitive control is basically our ability to optimise goal-directed behaviours, that is, stay focused and make choices that help us reach our goals.[66] Mental practices such as planning, goal setting, reflection, reasoning, seeing from another's point of view, self-affirmation, communication and choosing not to act on impulse all show that our conscious mind plays a real role in shaping how we behave.[62]

   Exercise is a good example. Our bodies have a natural biological disposition to conserve energy. When you're running a long race and your muscles start to ache, your body's instinct is to stop and rest. It sends signals of pain and fatigue to your brain to get you to slow

5. **While your genes might give you a natural tendency for certain skills, a good education is what really helps you build on them and reach your full potential.**

   You can always get better at something with the right practice and teaching. There is a psychological perspective to learning, which requires many different cognitive functions such as working memory, cognitive control and attention. Therefore, one of the main goals of education is to form adaptable, versatile people who can make the most of their capabilities.

   > One of the main goals of education is to form adaptable, versatile people who can make the most of their capabilities.

   The brain is malleable and is affected by education, daily experiences and cognitive functions. It continues building and rebuilding the map of neural connections (new roads) throughout the whole of life. This process of neuronal plasticity is the cellular and neural basis of learning.[68] The great thing is your brain isn't set in stone. It's always being built and rebuilt. This amazing adaptability of the brain is called *neuronal plasticity*, and it's happening every single day. New experiences create new roads. Every time you learn a new fact in school, have a deep conversation or try to solve a tricky problem, you're building new connections in your brain.

6. **Moral reasoning is important with respect to moral development.**

Moral emotions are strongly shaped by prior deliberative moral reasoning.[23] This means that before we even feel a strong emotion about a situation, our brain has often already done some thinking. For example, you might feel a pang of guilt (an emotion) about not helping a friend, but that guilt is likely a result of your reasoning that being a good friend means helping people. Your conscious understanding of what's right and wrong makes you feel a certain way.

Moral development isn't just about feeling a certain way; it's about learning to use your reason to guide those feelings towards a more ethical outcome.

Considering all of this, human beings aren't just biological organisms; we're also conscious subjects with complex psychological structures and processes. Therefore, we conclude that rationality, consciousness and moral reasoning allow us to have a some level of free will.[2]

Activity #16: Are you your mind or your body?

1. How do you see the power of your mind and consciousness in transforming yourself and the world around you? For example, when you decide to help someone.
2. How do your values and reasoning help you move beyond your biologically based dispositions (natural tendencies)?
3. How does your body influence your behaviours? List how you can manage that.

Activity #17: Reasoning and instinctive impulses

1. List at least three instances when your reasoning corrected your impulses such as anger, desire for sex and hunger.
2. List when you recognised that you can't merely trust your instincts, impressions or emotions.
3. Have goal-directed behaviours changed your life? If so, how?

A holistic/systems approach

In this text, we're taking a holistic or systems approach to the mind–body relationship. This view argues that your mind and body aren't separate things that operate on their own. Instead, they're part of a single, integrated system that constantly influences itself.

Think of it as a *circular causation*. Who you are – your personality, your actions and your development – is a result of this continuous feedback loop:

- *Your mind affects your body* – Your consciousness and reasoning have the power to train and control your body's impulses. For example, your mental focus allows you to push through physical pain while exercising, or your willpower helps you resist an unhealthy craving.
- *Your body affects your mind* – The biochemical mechanisms in your body, like hormones and neurotransmitters, directly impact your mental states. Feeling anxious (a mental state) can be a direct result of stress hormones (a physical response), and a lack of sleep (a physical state) can make it harder to focus and think clearly (a mental process).

This approach suggests that to understand yourself, you must look at how both your mind and body work together in a single, dynamic system.

A systems approach and holism are an alternative to the reductionist approach that seeks to understand a system by examining its individual parts in isolation from each other. To understand what it means to be human, a holistic scientific approach looks at more than just our bodies. It considers both *biology* – which includes our genetics, brain chemistry and all the physical parts that make us up – and *psychology* – which involves our conscious reasoning, subjective experiences, thoughts and emotions.

For instance, while the brain is malleable and can be changed by education and everyday experiences, its formation and functioning are still based on a genetic substrate that influences it.[68] Also, physical conditions affect mental health, and mental conditions affect physical health. Science thus suggests that almost every human behaviour comes from a mixture of conscious and unconscious processing.[62]

Nagel[2] maintained that there is a need for a constitutive model such as holism that shows how the mental and physical are inseparable and depend on each other, and how the physical and the mental develop together – a theory of consciousness woven into the evolutionary story (see Figure 13). A model is required to explain how humans can detect and be motivated by reasoning and personal values, as well as by instinctive motivations.

LIVING WITH PURPOSE

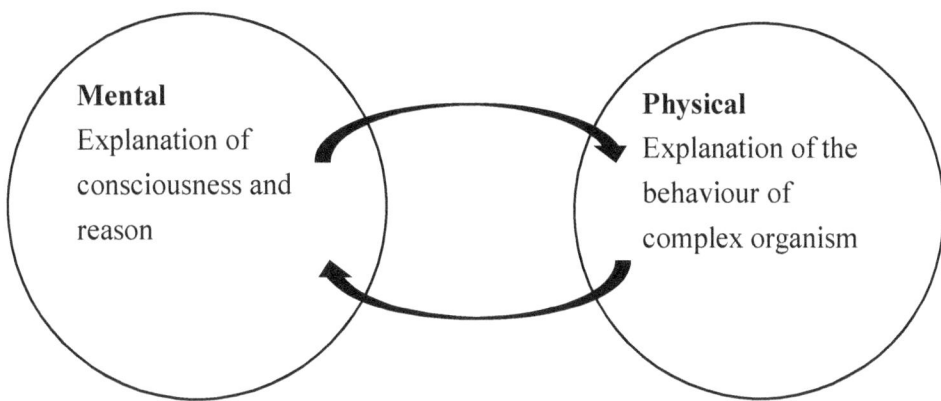

Figure 13 A theory of consciousness woven into the evolutionary story

Pereira[69] maintains that conscious experience is a fundamental aspect of reality, neither separable from, nor reducible to, the physical, chemical and biological. Accordingly, a change of the state of mind implies a change in the state of the brain and vice versa.[67]

Mind–Body Conflict and Inner Conflict

As the United Nations Educational, Scientific and Cultural Organization (UNESCO) Constitution states: 'Since wars begin in the mind, it is in the minds that the defences of peace must be constructed.'

If we are at war with ourselves – experiencing conflict between who we aspire to be (mind) and how we behave (body) – then peace cannot flourish. For genuine peace, our mind and body must be guided by the heart and love in harmony, forming an integrated whole rather than opposing forces.

The personal victories we achieve within ourselves lay the foundation for our relationships with those around us.[70] Both goodness and selfishness are driven by the thoughts, attitudes and actions of individuals. Our civilisation is shaped positively by people with high ideals who put them into action, and we can presume these individuals possess some degree of inner peace and unity between mind and body. Conversely, civilisation can be harmed by those whose selfish actions reflect a lack of this inner harmony.

While the mind and body typically work in harmony, there are times when they come into conflict. Understanding and resolving these conflicts is crucial for personal growth, inner peace and harmonious relationships, and to reduce internal and external conflict. Psychoanalysis, as the study of inner conflict, identifies various forms of internal struggles, including contradictions, self-deception and self-defeating behaviours.[71] Addressing inner conflict begins with self-awareness and making the necessary corrections.

The parable of the two wolves, a popular story often attributed to Native American wisdom, speaks of this inner conflict we all experience. It tells the following tale:

> *A grandfather tells his grandson, 'Inside me, there are two wolves. One is evil – he is anger, jealousy, greed, resentment, inferiority, lies and ego. The other is good – he is joy, peace, love, hope, humility, kindness, empathy and truth.'*
>
> *The grandson thinks for a moment and then asks, 'Which wolf wins, grandfather?'*
>
> *The old man replies, 'The one you feed.'*

This parable contrasts negative emotions like anger and jealousy with positive ones such as love and peace. The message is clear: **we have power over which side we nurture**. By focusing on positive thoughts and emotions, we cultivate peace and contentment, while feeding negativity only strengthens harmful patterns. It's a reminder of the power we have in shaping our own experiences and how we can influence our inner world with the choices we make.

Because of this inner tension between the inner self (mind) and outer self (body), our actions do not always align with our core values and wishes. This can leave us feeling anxious, restless or even angry. We are not at peace within ourselves.

On one hand, the mind/conscience strive to align with our cherished values, goals and ideals. On the other hand, the body's impulses pull us in the

> True peace comes when we bring mind and body into harmony.

opposite direction, driving us towards self-gratification and physical desires. This often leads to unethical and ineffective behaviours(see Figure 14).⁽³⁹⁾ True peace comes when we bring mind and body into harmony.

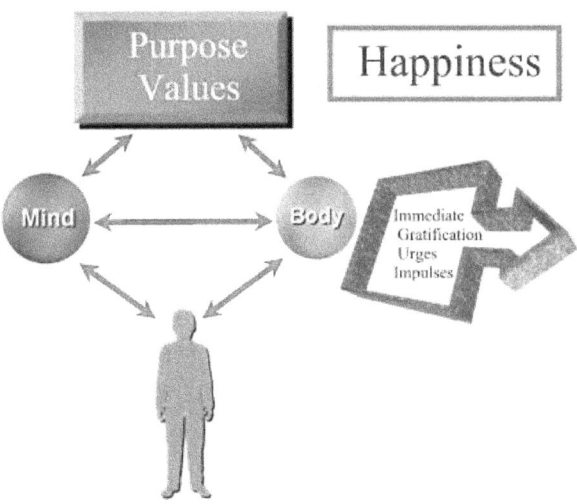

Figure 14 Managing self-gratification

Selfishness can have a strong influence on our lives and impact our relationships negatively. The body's desire for self-gratification can sometimes be overwhelming, leading to selfish behaviours that may unintentionally harm others and cause personal frustration, anger and guilt. These patterns can also cause us to view life from a self-serving perspective (*Oh well, it's the way I am*'), which can impact our relationships and behaviours. For example, constantly putting one's own needs first at the expense of others can create distance and conflict.

When impulse control is challenging, it can evolve into a disorder, where a person struggles to manage emotions or behaviours that conflict with societal values or others' rights. An inability to resist an urge can become a persistent, severe and harmful pattern of behaviour. Common types of impulse control disorders include persistent outbursts, violent or aggressive behaviour, substance abuse, frequent anger, irritability, resentment and disregard for social rules.⁽⁷²⁾

It takes discipline to live according to our values and goals. When we fail to do so, we experience regret and self-loathing, creating inner conflict. Personally, I've come to realise that when I'm anxious or angry, it's usually because I haven't lived up to my own values or managed my body well. I feel disappointed, sometimes even angry, with myself.

When such ingrained behavioural patterns takes over and conflict with our true self and values, the resultant anger and disappointment can lead us to feel inadequate – not good enough. This frustration may even manifest as aggression towards others, where we unknowingly take out our inner turmoil on those around us. We may try to fill our inner emptiness through self-gratification – sex, alcohol, drugs, food or other means – or by chasing after possessions, money, success, power or approval. Yet even when we achieve these things, the emptiness remains. This is when we are truly in trouble, as we can no longer deceive ourselves into believing these pursuits will bring lasting fulfilment.[44]

Feeling the need to be right all the time is another common form of inner conflict that comes from having a fragile ego. This can lead to external conflict with others. You may find yourself getting into arguments or becoming defensive because any disagreement feels like a direct attack on your identity. Power is often a weakness disguised as strength. Becoming aware of our defensiveness, and what we are actually defending, is an important step towards inner peace.[44]

Activity #18: Exploring inner conflict

This exercise may help you reflect on times when your actions didn't match your values, helping you increase self-awareness and align your mind, body and behaviour.

Reflect. Write. Share with a partner or small group you feel comfortable with:

1. Have you ever experienced regret and self-loathing for not living according to your values? What did that teach you?

2. Have you been disappointed or angry with yourself? How did you respond or cope?

3. When a lack of awareness or self-control left a gap inside you, how did you try to fill it?

'People with well-developed emotional skills are ...more likely to be content and effective in their lives, mastering the habits of mind that foster their own productivity.'
—Daniel Goleman

5

Managing Mind and Body Well
Dr John Bellavance

To actualise our values and purposes, we need to manage ourselves well by achieving unity between mind and body. This chapter explores several practical ways to do this: cultivating heart and love, practising self-control, setting goals and using mindfulness. While emotional intelligence (EI) and mindfulness are discussed more fully in other chapters, the focus here is on strategies to align thoughts, feelings and actions for intentional living. You will also practise applying these strategies to achieve your goals through S.M.A.R.T goal setting.

The quality of life is largely determined by how well we manage our mind and body. Both relationships and success in life's endeavours require this management. Achieving any goal demands unity and focus between mind and body. For example, truly listening to someone requires directing your mind, ears and eyes towards them to fully grasp both their words and body language. Attention, memory, learning and performance all depend on mindfulness and the harmony between mind and body. Whether playing tennis or the flute, success is influenced not just by skill but also by mental state; anxiety, for example, can significantly impact performance.

Mind and body are also most effective when guided by values and purpose. People experience wellbeing, happiness, self-esteem and success when their actions align with meaningful values and purpose (see Figure 15). Simply following bodily impulses is not enough. Effective self-management requires

LIVING WITH PURPOSE

regulating thoughts, emotions and physical impulses in line with the values and goals that matter most to us.[39]

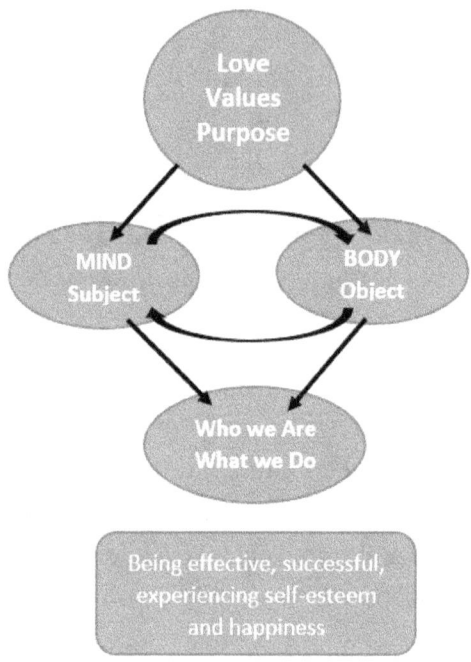

Figure 15 Managing mind and body and self-actualisation

Love's Role in Mind–Body Unity

> *'When we focus on ourselves, our world contracts as our problems and preoccupations loom large. But when we focus on others, our world expands.'*
> *—Daniel Goleman*

The first and most important method for bringing our mind and body into unity is by cultivating a state of loving kindness – becoming a person of love. This is because love is the precondition for unity within oneself and with others. Unity is established on the basis of love, and peace on the basis of unity.[17]

Love and emotions such as empathy, gratitude and remorse are deeply connected to our relationships with others, fostering the growth of our hearts and our capacity to care.[23] No experience unites the mind and body more powerfully than love (see Figure 16). When we perceive another's emotional pain through empathy, we too feel a part of that pain.

In many ways, our values, judgements and motivations are rooted in love. Research suggests that acts of loving kindness have an immediate impact, and the more people practise kindness and compassion, the stronger these tendencies become, both in the brain and in behaviours.[73]

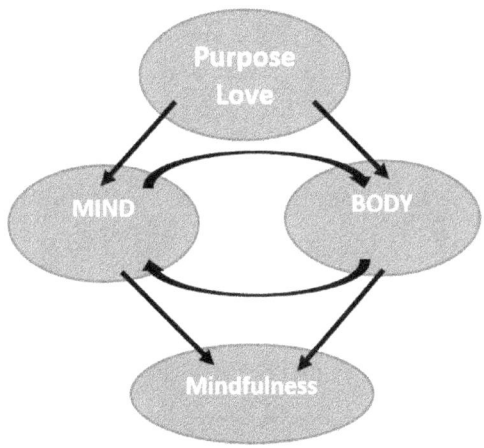

Figure 16 Love and mind/body unity

Depression can often turn our attention inward, narrowing our focus to our own pain – sometimes so deeply that it becomes difficult to connect with others or see beyond it. Yet, when we're able, even small acts of care or kindness towards others can gently shift our attention outward.

Personally, one of the greatest means to focus my mind and body and manage emotional issues has been to consider the needs and feelings of others. Shifting the emotional focus from myself to others has created opportunities to cultivate a heart of love and allowed me to understand others better.

Loving another brings the mind and body into focus. Adopting a mindset that prioritises the wellbeing of others helps diminish self-preoccupation and a self-serving attitude. Since the body is driven by biological needs, these impulses can sometimes interfere with our ability to truly love others.

Practising love involves learning to manage these impulses thoughtfully and to cultivate empathy, recognising that 'it's not all about me'.

People often avoid relationships, but this robs us of the opportunity for the growth of our hearts and our self-actualisation. In my own experience, love brings harmony between my mind and body and puts so many things into perspective.

Love takes discipline

Choosing love isn't always easy. Loving another requires discipline, especially when you're physically exhausted; just ask any parent! One day, my son eagerly asked me to play pool with him on our newly purchased table. After a long day at work, I told him I was too tired and promised to play the next day. When he asked again the following day, I postponed it to the weekend. He accepted my answer, but in that moment, I felt a deep conflict – the battle between my mind and body, between my physical need to rest and my desire to show love by spending time with him, even at the cost of my fatigue. As the saying goes, 'The spirit is willing, but the flesh is weak.' I knew, if I continued to put him off, his trust in me would diminish – and I would lose trust in myself. I played a game with him, and we were both happy.

Activity #19: Loving another

This exercise explores how love unites your mind and body, helping you understand how caring for others supports inner peace and self-mastery.

Prompts:

- How does loving another bring your mind and body into unity?
- How does it create a sense of peace within you?

Use a Y-Chart to describe:

- What it looks like for you (actions, body language, posture, presence)
- What it sounds like for you (tone of voice, word choice, way you communicate))

- What is feels likes for you (internal state: calmness, confidence, warmth, vulnerability)

Reflect in your journal: You could 'think, pair and share' with someone else.

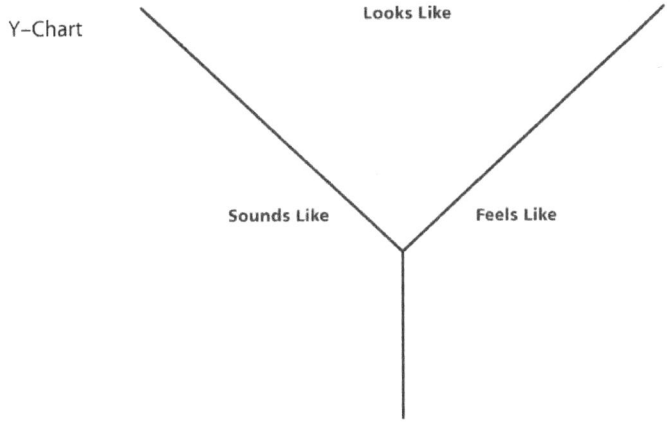

Self-Control and Mind–Body Unity

The second approach to uniting the mind and body is through practising self-control – the ability to suppress inappropriate emotions, desires, impulses and actions in favour of those that support important values and goals and maintain good habits.[6, 74] Psychology, philosophy, social and emotional learning (SEL), and many spiritual texts consider self-control key to managing ourselves and our relationships with others.

Self-control is vital for being a person of integrity. Some ethicists define moral integrity as maintaining high moral expectations, feeling a deep sense of personal responsibility and accountability,[75] and consistently living according to one's moral values.[76, 77] Holding moral values alone doesn't make us moral. It is through acting rightly – in alignment with our values – that we demonstrate true integrity.[78, 79]

We all desire the freedom to do as we please, yet responsibility is important. True freedom comes when you can choose between right and wrong and

> Freedom without responsibility... leads to a loss of freedom.

take ownership of your decisions. Consider the internet and online anonymity. The freedom to express yourself without revealing your identity can promote openness and protect privacy, but when used irresponsibly – for example, to cyberbully, commit fraud or coordinate illegal activities – it creates a toxic and dangerous environment. Freedom without responsibility, however, leads to a loss of freedom.

Managing yourself well and embracing responsibility allows you to fully realise your goals and purpose. For instance, a child's development depends on both the freedom to explore, and the structure provided by the rules and responsibilities set by an adult.

Activity #20: Responsibility

This exercise helps you understand how self-discipline supports your values and actions.

1. Reflect on how you balance freedom with responsibility, including freedom of speech.
2. Use a Y-Chart to describe what it looks like (actions, body language, expression, posture, choices), sounds like (tone, word choice, communication style) and feels like (internal state: confidence, calmness, discomfort) for you.
3. You can also *'think, pair and share'* another person.

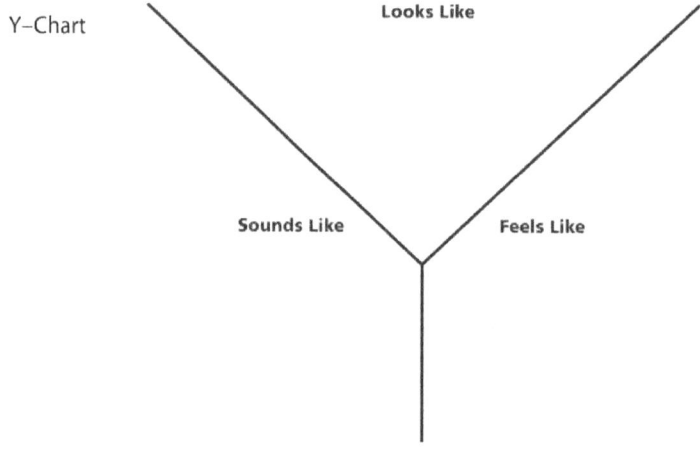

From freedom to self-mastery

Why do some people turn to drugs or other destructive behaviours or addictions? The answer may seem straightforward. A more complex question, however, is why do others successfully manage themselves when it comes to alcohol consumption or overeating?[40] You might say self-mastery is one key. Let's explore this further.

Bodily impulses to seek pleasure and avoid displeasure are important for happiness and survival. However, impulses to pursue here-and-now rewards can be at odds with our cherished values and goals. In a world that glorifies the pursuit of pleasure and self-gratification, why would we seek to control our impulses? Many may say, 'I just want the freedom to enjoy myself!' This view is based on a misunderstanding of how we need to be purpose-driven to be happy and free.

Poorly managed desires and impulses can lead us astray and can hurt others. A lack of impulse control can contribute to issues such as substance abuse, gambling and sexual disorders.[72] For instance, a person may turn to alcohol to cope with stress or social anxiety. Without the self-discipline to adopt healthier coping mechanisms – such as exercise, meditation or talking to a friend – they rely on alcohol's immediate relief. After a difficult day, the short-term relief of a drink overshadows their long-term goal of health and sobriety. Over time, this repeated behaviour can lead to a dependency as the brain begins to associate alcohol with relief from negative emotions.

People with good self-control have a healthy self-esteem, a strong will and resilience.[80] Self-control is important for controlling what we say and supports academic, occupational and social success. Studies also show that adolescents with higher self-control experience less stress.[81] (see Figure 17)

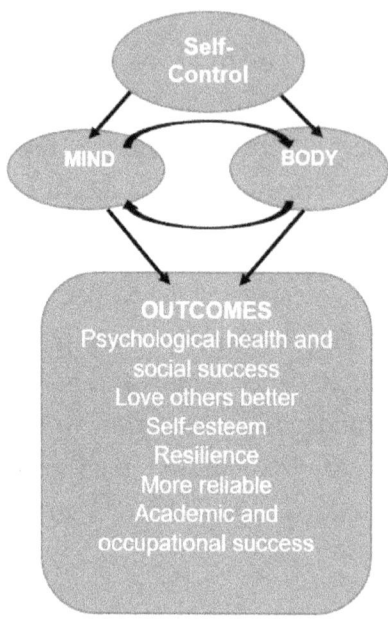

Figure 17 Outcomes of self-control

Compassionate note on self-control and trauma

For many people, especially those who have experienced trauma, chronic stress or difficult life circumstances, practising self-control can feel genuinely hard. Trauma can impact the brain's ability to regulate impulses and emotions, making it challenging to manage behaviours, even when there is a strong desire to change.

If you find self-discipline difficult, it doesn't mean you lack strength or willpower. It may simply mean that your past experiences have shaped how you respond to challenges.

Remember, growth takes time, and kindness towards yourself is an important part of the process. Support from friends, family or professionals can also make a meaningful difference on your journey towards greater balance and wellbeing.

Activity #21: Exploring impulse control

This exercise explores the impact of self-control on your goals, wellbeing and relationships. Consider how managing impulses unites your mind and body.

Write. Reflect. Share with another person or small group:

Figure 18 is an example of a concept map that could be used to complete this task.

Where it says sub-topic, write how your mind influences your body and behaviours, and how your body influences your mind, values and goals, for good or ill.

Debrief:

- Why is controlling yourself important?
- What strategies do you use to manage impulses?
- Do you control your impulses well? How does it this affect your life?
- Recall a time when you were not in control of yourself. How did you feel, and what did you do after?

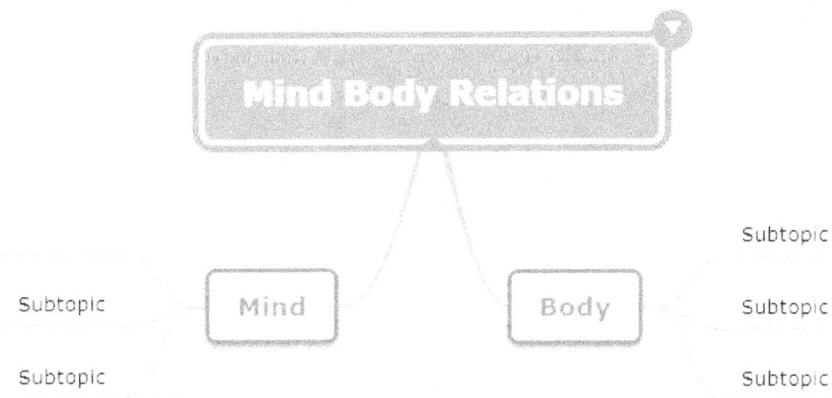

Figure 18 Self-control concept map

Setting Goals and Mind–Body Unity

The third way to unite your mind and body is by setting goals and actively working towards them. Being goal-oriented suggests that you can self-regulate and manage your impulses.

Setting goals is a practical exercise in self-control and delaying gratification. It fosters personal growth and helps you reach your full potential. Achieving your goals brings significant rewards – both personal and external accomplishments. You experience a range of positive emotions when you succeed in the goals that matter to you. Ultimately, true happiness comes from witnessing your own progress.

Delaying gratification

Delaying gratification is a fundamental life skill because it's essential for achieving long-term success and wellbeing in various areas of life. It's the ability to resist an immediate, smaller reward in favour of a larger, more valuable reward in the future. Saving is a good example. Instead of spending your entire pay on immediate pleasures like a new gadget or eating out, you choose to save a portion of it for future goals. Individuals who practise delayed gratification tend to be less impulsive and more effective in life.[39]

The well-known Stanford experiment illustrates this principle.[82] In this study, a child was given a choice between one small, immediate reward, such as a single biscuit, or two biscuits if they waited for 10 minutes. A single biscuit was placed in front of them while the researcher left the room. For a six-year-old, 10 minutes can feel like an eternity.

A follow-up study conducted years later, after the children had finished high school, found that those who were able to wait for the preferred reward (two biscuits) tended to be more confident, persistent and trustworthy, and they showed better educational and social outcomes. In contrast, those who took the immediate reward were more anxious and more easily upset.[39]

This research reinforces the idea that when we delay something we want in the moment for a greater benefit later, life tends to work out better.

It is important to recognise the emotions, desires and actions in our daily lives that hinder us from achieving our values and goals. Self-awareness and self-reflection – examining our values, reasoning, and the impact of our actions on ourselves and others – are essential for developing self-control. Equally important is identifying the emotions, desires and actions that support our goals.

Practise, practise, practise. Set boundaries for yourself. Self-control involves goal-directed behaviour, even when faced with distractions and competing impulses. Deny one desire to achieve a goal and make it a habit. Then reward yourself. Behavioural psychology has shown that reinforcing actions with rewards strengthens habits, whether for better or worse.[40]

Procrastination

Sometimes self-control is not just about what we do but what we avoid. One of the biggest obstacles many people face in reaching their goals is procrastination: the voluntary delay of an intended course of action, despite knowing that the delay will likely lead to worse outcomes.

It is estimated that at least half of university students regularly procrastinate, postponing studying for exams or writing papers. Procrastination is linked to depression, anxiety and stress, as well as loneliness and reduced life satisfaction.[83]

Activity #22: What hinders you in achieving your goals?

Write. Reflect. Share with another person or small group:

This activity helps you identify the obstacles to your goals and explore ways to overcome them, strengthening your mind–body connection.

1. Use a Y-Chart to describe the three aspects of what hinders you – what it looks like (e.g. procrastination, distracted body language, avoiding tasks), sounds like (e.g. negative self-talk, hesitation, distracted or rushed speech) and feels like (e.g. anxiety, frustration, lack of confidence, restlessness).

2. Think about your habits, impulses and emotions that interfere with achieving your goals.

3. You could also *'think, pair and share'* with another person or small group about this.

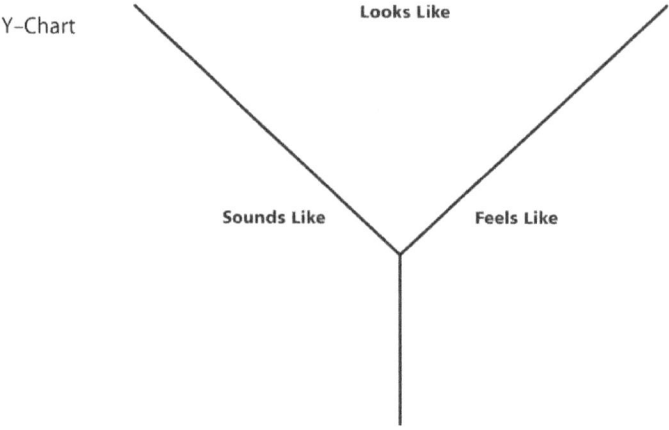

Developing a growth mindset

Your belief about your own abilities will significantly impact how those abilities develop. Setting goals is closely linked to a **growth mindset** – the belief that your basic abilities, like intelligence and talent, can be developed through dedication and hard work. You can think of your abilities like a muscle: the more you challenge them, the stronger they become.

The opposite is a **fixed mindset**, where abilities are seen as fixed traits that can't be changed.

When you cultivate a growth mindset, you begin to see challenges as opportunities for learning and growth, not as obstacles you can't overcome. [84] You recognise that improvement comes from effort, not from some innate talent you were born with. This belief makes you more resilient and willing to try new things, even if you fail at first.

For example, a growth mindset sounds like:

> *'This math problem is really hard, but if I keep trying and ask for help, I can figure it out.'*

Here, you see the challenge as a chance to improve your problem-solving skills. You focus on the process of learning, not just the outcome.

The opposite is a fixed mindset:

'I missed that shot. I'm a terrible basketball player.'

Here you see a single failure as proof of your permanent lack of skill.

Starting something new and setting meaningful goals will always come with risks and challenges. Uncertainty. *What if I fail?* Failure can be uncomfortable and impact your self-esteem and resilience – and even how others perceive you. However, without taking risks and embracing new opportunities, how can you grow and reach your full potential?

Life is inherently full of risks. Having a child is a risk; trying a new outdoor activity is a risk. But without these experiences, life would be far less fulfilling. Embrace the challenge, step outside your comfort zone and cultivate a growth mindset.

Activity #24: Growth mindset

This exercise helps you see how your beliefs shape growth and goal setting, and how reflecting on challenges and barriers can build resilience and a growth mindset.

Reflect. Write in your journal:

1. Do you have a growth mindset? What does that mean for you?
2. What are the barriers you face when setting goals and starting new initiatives?
3. List the risks you take in your life. Are these rewarding?
4. Do you find it hard to set goals. If so, why is that?
5. Explore whether goal setting feels worthwhile and why.

Goals, habits and emotions

The goals and tasks we set for ourselves can eventually become habits. BJ Fogg[85], author of *Tiny Habits*, argues that the key to building new habits lies in behaviour design: we need to 'hack' and 'code' our brains.

Fogg suggests linking a desired behaviour to an existing routine to make new habits or goals ridiculously easy at first. For example, to stay fit, he did two push-ups every time he went to the toilet. By linking a desired behaviour (push-ups) to an existing routine (going to the toilet), the action becomes automatic over time. The more we repeat a behaviour in response to a specific trigger, the less we need to think about it, until it becomes a habit wired into our brain.

Positive emotions also play a crucial role in rewiring the brain. When we have achieved our goals from consistently practising a new habit, we receive a reward – emotional satisfaction. This reinforces the habit even more by tapping into the brain's reward circuitry, which helps encode the sequence of behaviours we've just performed. So, it's not just repetition over time that solidifies habits, but rather the emotions we associate with them. When we feel good about completing a habit, our brain strengthens the neural pathways that make it easier to repeat the behaviour in the future.

For example, a student decides to learn to play the guitar and practices for 20 minutes every day (*the habit*). At first, it's frustrating, with squeaky chords and awkward finger positions (*the repetition*). But one day, they play a song perfectly and feel a surge of pride and joy. That emotional reward reinforces their motivation, linking their effort with success and helping the habit stick.

Goal setting can be learned, even as young as five or six years old.[86] Well-defined goals allow us to choose, design and implement the important targets necessary to achieve our desired results. They establish direction for ongoing activities, identify expected results and improve teamwork through a common sense of purpose.[87]

Goals can be both internal and external. External goals might include writing a book, learning a new skill, managing our diet or exercising more. Internal goals focus on personal growth – being true to yourself, practising mindfulness (see next chapter), avoiding actions or words that lead to self-regret, and refraining from unnecessary criticism of others (something we are all too skilled at).

Abilities: Setting S.M.A.R.T. goals

Setting goals is not just about deciding what you want; it's about planning how to achieve it. A structured framework can make your goals realistic, actionable and measurable. One of the most widely used frameworks is **S.M.A.R.T.**, which ensures that goals are:

Specific – clearly defined

Measurable – progress can be tracked

Action-oriented – includes steps to take

Realistic – achievable given your resources

Time-bound – has a clear deadline

By applying this method, you strengthen the connection between your mind and body, focusing your thoughts and actions towards meaningful outcomes.

Why S.M.A.R.T. goals matter

Setting and achieving goals requires unity between the mind and body. It involves focusing mental energy on a task while managing challenges and physical impulses that may arise along the way. Qualities such as optimism, commitment, effort, perseverance and resilience make goal achievement possible, especially in the face of difficulties.

Setting goals enables us to:

- identify a problem and define the desired accomplishment or solution
- recognise barriers to solving the problem
- overcome challenges
- self-evaluate our performance (see Figure 19).

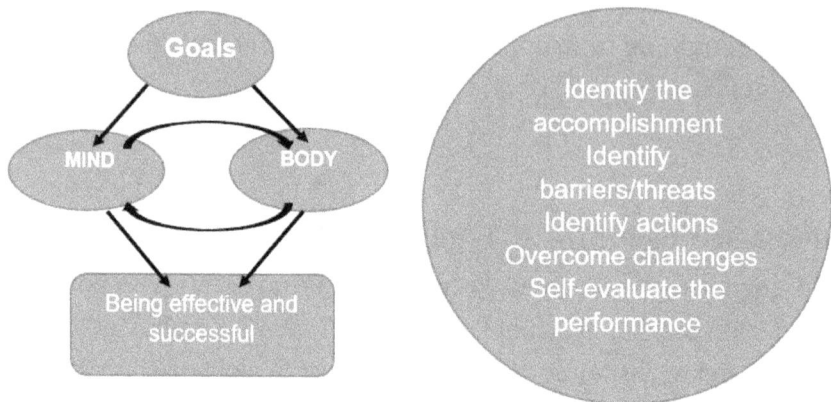

Figure 19 Managing mind/body and setting goals

However, even the most structured plan can fail if we don't address the inner mindset that drives behaviour.

The psychology behind goal setting

One of the main barriers to achieving our goals lies in the psychological obstacles within our own minds. As the ancient saying goes, 'Know thyself'.

Ask yourself:

- Why can't I achieve this goal?
- Why haven't I achieved it yet?

We must genuinely believe that our goal is attainable. Any doubts can become mental blocks that limit forward action. Common internal obstacles include:

- a defeatist or deficit mindset
- procrastination
- engaging in unproductive activities

These can be overcome through:

- **Adopting a growth mindset** – believe that abilities can improve through effort and persistence.
- **Setting small, achievable goals** – break large tasks into manageable steps.

- **Practising self-compassion** – learn from setbacks rather than criticising yourself.
- **Eliminating distractions** – focus attention and energy on what truly matters.
- **Visualising success** – picture the satisfaction of achievement to stay motivated.
- **Developing routines** – build consistency to reduce procrastination.
- **Staying accountable** – share your goals with someone who can encourage you.

Your mindset plays a pivotal role in determining your success. As Henry Ford said, 'If you think you can do a thing or think you can't do a thing, you're right.'

Steps for setting S.M.A.R.T. goals

The following list outlines the abilities and activities involved in setting S.M.A.R.T goals.[87] Each step presents a challenge that requires effective management of both the mind and body to achieve success.

1. **Define your goal / desired accomplishment:** Identify personal or professional goals that align with your values and purpose.

    Critical questions: What are my needs, roles and responsibilities? What am I trying to build or improve?

    Example: 'I will establish a daily writing routine to complete my book manuscript.'

2. **Visualise success** – Imagine your goal as already achieved. For example:
    - Listen to a speaker's praise and description of your accomplishments.
    - Stand on the podium to accept an award.
    - Write out the deposit slip for a bonus earned.
    - Experience a sigh of relief at turning in a completed project.

3. **Determine specific and measurable outcomes** – Can you measure if your goals have been met? If so, define them clearly. Ask yourself: *How will I know when I've succeeded?*

Examples:

- The business will have a location with equipment like….
- I will stand up for myself each day by doing …

4. **Plan your actions:** Break your goal into short-term and long-term steps, mapping out the actions needed to achieve them. Create a timeline of activities and deadlines, then identify the resources – people, time, finances and tools – required for success. You can prepare a simple project plan using a **Gantt Chart** to visualise each step and track your progress. Many short instructional videos and free templates are available online

5. **Identify barriers and strategies to overcome them:** Be honest about potential obstacles – both external and internal. Many obstacles are psychological, rooted in self-doubt, fear of failure or a defeatist mindset. Recognising these early helps you manage them effectively.

Common psychological obstacles include a defeatist or deficit mindset; procrastination; and engaging in unproductive activities. To overcome obstacles, use strategies like:

- Adopt a growth mindset
- Break goals into small, achievable steps
- Practise self-compassion
- Remove distractions
- Visualise success
- Build routines and habits
- Stay accountable to someone else

6. **Stay focused on achieving goals despite distractions and problems** – Persist despite setbacks. Achieving goals is mostly effort and consistency. Accomplishing a goal is 95% perspiration and 5% inspiration.

7. **Evaluate and adjust** – Actively monitor performance against goals and milestones (key events that mark progress towards a project's completion), adjusting plans and expectations as required. Keep a logbook that evaluates your performance with respect to achieving a goal(s).

8. **Reward yourself** – Reinforce good habits by rewarding yourself for your achievements. This could be a small thing such as giving yourself a treat, or a big thing like booking a holiday.

Activity #26: Set a goal and make it a habit

Your task is to delay gratification to achieve one goal and make it a habit. This activity helps you practice applying S.M.A.R.T goals while strengthening your mind–body connection. Use your journal.

1. **Define your goal**

    Think of one personal or one career goal.

    Complete the sentence: "I will achieve … by …"

2. **Identify obstacles**

    List bodily urges, distractions and mindsets that might prevent success (e.g. procrastination, fatigue, negative self-talk).

3. **Plan your steps**

    Break the goal into small, actionable steps.

    Decide on deadlines and resources needed.

4. **Overcome obstacles**

    Choose at least two strategies from the list above (growth mindset, routines, accountability etc.) to manage barriers.

5. **Track and reward**

    Keep a log of your progress.

    Celebrate milestones, even small ones, to reinforce positive habits.

'Remember then: there is only one time that is important – Now! It is the most important time because it is the only time when we have any power.'
—*Leo Tolstoy*

Mindfulness and Mind-Body Unity
Dr John Bellavance and Dr Rafia Naz

In the previous chapter, we discussed three methods for bringing the mind and body into harmony and unity: cultivating love, self-control and setting goals. The fourth method is practising mindfulness.

Mindfulness is a state of non-judgemental awareness characterised by decreased attachment (less clinging) to thoughts and emotions.[88] Children naturally live in the present moment – finding joy in simply being alive and enjoying the company of their family and friends. But as adults, do we live with the same awareness?

Eckhart Tolle[44] encourages us to embrace the 'power of the now' by fully living in the present moment – the only moment we truly have – as explored in his book *The Power of Now*.

Now, the present moment, is where our attention belongs. Many of us, however, spend too much time in our minds, dwelling on the past or worrying about the future. If you struggle to be in the present moment, what can you do? Start by simply observing your mind's tendency to escape the 'now', noticing when it drifts into memories or future anxieties.

Mindfulness, Attention and Flow
Dr John Bellavance

We cannot truly love or connect with others if we aren't fully present with them. Have you ever listened to someone and later realised that you didn't fully absorb their words? This illustrates the importance of focus, attention and presence, especially when learning.

It's not the amount of time we spend on a task that matters, but the quality of our attention that shapes our experience. In a society filled with sound bites and streaming media, where our minds are trained for continuous partial attention, the ability to concentrate deeply has become more crucial than ever.[24] The internet is an interruption system that fragments our attention. Research shows that frequent interruptions scatter our thoughts, weaken memory, and increase stress and anxiety.[89] Developing the ability to focus and immerse yourself fully in a task is therefore essential for learning, creativity and overall wellbeing. Psychology suggests that a wandering mind is often an unhappy mind, while living in the present moment can make even ordinary activities more interesting and joyful.[84]

When listening to someone, don't think about what you'll say next; just listen and be present. I often remind myself, 'John, if you're making coffee, focus on that – don't let your mind wander to the past or the future.'

Being fully present is challenging. Those who practise meditation know how the mind tends to wander, jumping from thought to thought like a monkey hopping from branch to branch. Focused meditation helps quiet the habitual chatter of the mind, allowing us to feel grounded in the present and at peace.

To be focused on the now and what is really going on – to be mindful – requires being fully present in the moment, with a constant reflective attitude of attention and non-criticism. It is about maintaining self-awareness – noticing your thoughts, feelings and surroundings without judgement.

Paying attention and noticing don't just happen automatically.[90] We need to regularly create the space and time to experience beauty and to connect with others. This is another aspect of mind–body unity. Many of us spend too much time in our minds, dwelling on the past or worrying about the future.

Flow: immersion and mind–body unity

When we engage in captivating activities, time often seems to 'fly'. We enter a state of absorption and timelessness, like a child experiencing wonder. This state is called 'flow', where the mind is fully immersed in a task and the body remains relaxed. Mindfulness and flow are closely connected, with mindfulness often serving as a gateway to flow. While both involve deep focus on the present, they differ:

- **Mindfulness** is non-judgemental awareness of the present.
- **Flow** is complete absorption in an activity.

By cultivating mindfulness – training your attention and reducing mental clutter – you strengthen your ability to stay present and focused, making it more likely to enter flow states. Learning in flow is joyful and nourishing. Conversely, anxiety and agitation hinder flow. Strained concentration, driven by worry, creates heightened cortical activity – a 'strained brain' (Goleman 2004) – weakening mind–body connections and reducing productivity.

Personally, I find peace in the moment when learning to write new computer code or engaging in writing. My mind focuses entirely on a single task, and time seems to pass by unnoticed. Most of us have experienced this kind of immersion when engaged in something we enjoy. Athletes call it 'being in the zone,' where excellence feels effortless. It's a relaxed yet highly focused state, exemplifying true mind–body unity.

Flow illustrates the unity of mind and body through focused awareness. In the next section, Dr Rafia Naz examines the scientific and therapeutic foundations of mindfulness and meditation in promoting wellbeing.

Mindfulness, Meditation and Wellbeing

Dr Rafia Naz

The World Health Organization defines health as 'a state of complete physical, mental and social wellbeing'.[91] Perceived psychological, social and emotional states of wellbeing are assessed in relation to an individual's personal frame of reference.[92]

Mindfulness meditation has gained significant attention in recent years, with decades of research exploring its connection to health. This practice, shaped by self-regulation, has been shown to enhance overall wellbeing.[93, 94]

It is associated with adaptive outcomes because it helps people develop key skills to better manage stress, cope with change, and respond to challenges in healthy and effective ways. Mindfulness is not just a stress reduction technique; it trains the mind to be more flexible and resilient, fostering psychological health.[95, 96]

Interrelation of mindfulness and meditation

Bear maintains that mindfulness and meditation are interrelated. Mindfulness, a way of paying thoughtful attention, originated from Buddhist meditation practices.[95, 97] It has been used as a tool for achieving psychological wellbeing.[98]

Since then, mindfulness-based practices have rapidly expanded with a substantial body of research over the past two decades confirming their effectiveness in treating psychological disorders,[99, 100] and having affirmative effects on many psychological symptoms of distress.[101, 102] It also aids in reducing psychological and physical problems.[103-106]

One central practice is mindfulness meditation, the purpose of which is to learn to let go of attachment to sensations and feelings, both pleasant and unpleasant.[107]

Mindfulness, Brainwaves and Practising Mindfulness

Dr John Bellavance

Meditation is the intentional self-regulation of attention, aimed at managing the flow of information and monitoring our experience in the present moment. One way it works is by regulating brainwaves – electrical impulses generated by the brain that enable communication between neurons and influence our behaviours, emotions and thoughts.

Because of the effect on brain activity, meditation can serve as a powerful mind–body therapy. It has been used as a complementary approach to manage pain, reduce anxiety and alleviate self-criticism. Research supports its effectiveness; for example, studies have demonstrated that mindfulness meditation can help individuals manage chronic pain.[29]

One of the most notable benefits of mindfulness is its ability to alter our physiological state. For example, when we close our eyes and focus on our breath, we send signals throughout our body–brain system that help reduce blood pressure, lower heart rate and decrease cortisol levels – cortisol being the primary stress hormone.[24]

Mindfulness meditation can be practised during simple daily activities by fully engaging in what we're doing at that time. One common technique involves focusing on the body's breathing and sensations, which helps regulate alpha brain waves, enhancing the ability to relax and focus.[108]

Practising mindful meditation can:

- reduce anxiety
- lower stress levels
- improve coping mechanisms
- enhance attention
- strengthen emotional regulation
- boosts performance and educational outcomes.

Additionally, mindfulness fosters better relationships through improved EI, empathy and communication skills, while promoting neuroplasticity. Neuroplasticity is the brain's remarkable ability to reorganise and form new neural connections throughout life in response to learning, experiences and even injury.[73, 84, 109]

Foundations of mindfulness

The three foundations of mindfulness, rooted in ancient Buddhist teachings, are: focus, mindful awareness and dhamma. Together, these foundations help cultivate a deeper state of mindfulness, promoting mental clarity, emotional stability and a sense of inner peace.

Focus – involves directing and sustaining attention on a particular object, sensation or thought in the present moment. It helps cultivate concentration and reduces distractions.

Mindful awareness – refers to being fully aware of your thoughts, emotions and sensations as they arise, without judgement or attachment. It's not clinging to them but simply observing them as they pass by. It encourages a non-reactive awareness of the present as we pay attention to what is going on inside us and around us.

By observing ourselves, we can better manage habitual patterns of feeling and thinking such as living in the past and future and worrying. Tolle[44] referred to mindful awareness as the basic principle of being present as 'the watcher' of what is happening inside you.

Practising mindful awareness (becoming conscious) is the first step to inner freedom by focusing on the ethical and unethical qualities of the mind. *Is my thinking based on truth or some dysfunctional thinking?* This involves self-evaluating what is arising in the mind – such as jealousy, hatred or resentment – and noticing when the mind is free from attachment. For example, when greed or wanting is absent, we observe that the mind is not attached.

Dhamma – encompasses understanding the nature, and wisdom, of reality, the interconnectedness of life and the practice of ethical conduct. This Buddhist teaching encourages a mindful approach to life, rooted in moral principles and an understanding of suffering and liberation. This practice goes beyond self-reflection into the realm of self-transformation. We are encouraged to let go of our hindrances and attachments, freeing ourselves from our mental prisons.

The ego is vulnerable and insecure, perceiving itself as constantly under threat. It always seeks something to attach to, to strengthen its illusory sense of self. Ego, in this sense, is negative because it is the false mind-made self. Mindfulness helps us recognise that these mind-made fictions are not who we truly are.[44]

As we become aware of what supports our understanding, we are invited to cultivate, develop and strengthen these qualities. As mindfulness grows, mental capacity shifts from external objects to the process of self-awareness and personal growth.[110] In this respect, Dhamma also involves key practices of mind and body unity such as mindfulness, joy, tranquillity, concentration, loving kindness, and skilful understanding and thinking.

Mindfulness also helps us shift our perception of events and release the hindrances that hold us back in life, laying the groundwork for cultivating non-attachment.

Activity #28: Mindfulness

Use a Y-Chart to describe the three aspects of mindfulness for you – what it looks like (internal state: e.g. slow, deliberate movements; relaxed posture, focused attention), sounds like (e.g. soft, steady voice, calm and gentle words, mindful pauses) and feels like (internal state: calmness, presence, gentle awareness, peacefulness).

You could also *'think, pair and share'* with another person about this.

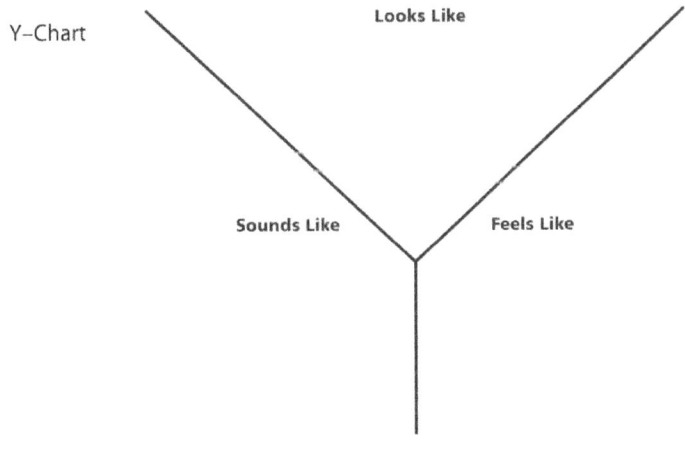

Non-attachment improves mindfulness

Non-attachment is the psychological freedom from being controlled by our thoughts, feelings and desires. It's not indifference or lack of care; rather, it's the ability to observe internal experiences without being swept away by them.

By cultivating non-attachment, a person becomes better at mindfulness. They can acknowledge sadness or desire without letting it define them or dictate their actions. Non-attachment allows us to accept things as they are and be open to new possibilities. It involves letting go of past mistakes, old behaviours and emotional baggage, whether they stem from our own actions or the actions of others. It also means releasing attachment to unhealthy aspects of our lives, creating space for growth and positive change.

Personal reflection: I had to let go of my need for approval and the irrational worries that held me back, to be authentic and free myself from the mental prisons I had created. As I released these attachments, I found greater acceptance of both myself and others, allowing me to see people more positively and open new possibilities. This freedom gave me the ability to be more present, to truly listen to others, rather than focusing on what I might say or do next to gain approval or impress them.

How can we truly listen and understand others if we are caught up in our own unresolved issues or worries? To be fully present requires being self-aware and mindful of our inner dialogue – able to pay attention to what we're focusing on and to notice our thoughts as they arise.

The absence of misapprehensions is the natural state of the mind – a peaceful mind. A misapprehension is a wrong idea or a mistaken understanding of something. It's a failure to comprehend a situation, fact or motive correctly, leading you to hold a belief that isn't true. Perception plays a key role in how you experience stress, as your level of stress often depends on how you perceive events. Is it your thoughts, feelings or events themselves that cause stress, or is it your attitude towards them?[84] The Greek philosopher Epictetus wrote:

'It's not the things that happen to us that are upsetting, but the view we take of those things.'

Activity #27: Non-attachment and mindful presence

This activity helps you develop the ability to observe your thoughts and emotions without becoming entangled in them. Through self-reflection and mindfulness practice, you'll explore how non-attachment enhances your focus, peace of mind and emotional freedom.

Reflect. Write. Share with a partner or small group:

1. Take a moment to observe whether your thoughts often drift or whether you feel present in what you're doing. Is your mind wandering or focused? Write in your journal about any patterns you notice.

2. Reflect on how frequently you replay past events or worry about the future. Write specific examples if you can.

3. Explore practices or techniques that help you stay present – mindfulness, breathing exercises or simply pausing to notice your surroundings. Write the steps you could take to be more present.

4. Recall a time when you were completely absorbed in an activity, when time seemed to disappear. What were you doing? How did it feel?

5. Are events inherently stressful or are they stressful depending on how you perceive them?
   - Can you recall a past event that felt different once your perspective changed?
   - What happens when you are more present in the moment, rather than preoccupied with the past (what I did wrong, or others did to me) or future (what will happen to me)?

6. Have you ever felt so focused on something you were doing that you forgot the time? What activity were you engaged in? How did it feel? What do you think contributed to that deep state of focus?

Debrief:

Take your time to journal these reflections and share your thoughts with someone you trust. Discuss how non-attachment and mindfulness can improve your focus, emotional regulation and ability to listen deeply to others. You might discover new insights about how your mind works and how to better manage your focus and presence in daily life.

A Teacher's Reflection on Mindfulness, Meditation and Wellbeing During COVID

Dr Rafia Naz

During the COVID pandemic, many teachers encountered significant challenges[111, 112] including the sudden shift to online remote teaching. Stressors varied from a lack of support and overwhelming workload demands to emotional exhaustion, time pressures, challenges with managing online work, workplace stress, strained relationships with colleagues, and difficulties with training and adapting to new working methods. These stressors often extended to pressures with family and balancing family life, digital literacy challenges for both students and teachers, and issues with internet connectivity. Moreover, these factors negatively affected overall wellbeing and work-life balance.[113-115]

Mindfulness played a crucial role in supporting me as a teacher during those challenging times. It helped me maintain better focus and stay relaxed as I devoted my mind, body and soul to the present moment. By embracing the challenges with greater acceptance, I was able to not only anticipate the difficulties but also navigate through them with more adaptability. This clarity allowed me to find solutions with increased precision and effectiveness.

I come from a cultural and religious background where meditation plays a significant role in my life. This practice helped me become more aware of issues, improve my observation skills and maintain self-control. However, during the COVID pandemic, it often felt nearly impossible to stay grounded. With mounting workload pressure, two children under three years old, and the challenge of teaching remotely, it truly felt like being caught in a snowstorm.

I remember working from home as a constant juggling act – tackling household chores, attending online meetings with staff, students and management, all while racing against time to keep up with online teaching and discussions. Mindfulness meditation, however, helped me tap into the positive aspects of life. It allowed me to cultivate a healthier state of mind, which had a profound effect on my ability to regulate my emotions, attitude and overall reactions.

By focusing on self-control through mindfulness, I became more disciplined than I had been before and my ability to resist temptation developed into a stronger, more patient and tolerant version of myself.

As I deepened my mindfulness practice and meditation, I experienced both psychological and physical benefits, leading to greater satisfaction and positive experiences. I no longer felt overwhelmed or fraught with stress. Instead, my mind became more tranquil and at ease, creating a ripple effect that extended to my physical wellbeing and overall behaviour.

Several studies have established that augmented levels of mindfulness can facilitate improved self-regulation, enhance a person's ability to control attention and regulate emotions,[97] suppress impulsive behaviour and thereby increase a person's level of self-control.[103, 116]

Mindfulness meditation strengthened my self-control and reaffirmed my ability to self-regulate. It enhanced my communication skills and enabled me to respond more effectively to unexpected challenges during the pandemic. Ultimately, it played a crucial role in helping me navigate and stabilise my emotions amidst the chaos.

Overall, I found that mindfulness, meditation and wellbeing are well interconnected and transformed my overall outlook and response. I felt a sense of self-compassion and gratitude through mindfulness meditation. My level of self-awareness, EI, emotional resilience and cognitive clarity were heightened.

LIVING WITH PURPOSE

Activity #29: Reflections on mindful awareness
Write in the table below or in your journal:

1. What are the challenges for you to practise mindfulness in your daily life?

2. What does mindful meditation mean to you? What are your thoughts on this? Could mindfulness help you have greater acceptance of challenges in your life?

3. Outcomes – How have you applied mindful meditation in your daily real-life activities? In the table below list the challenges, thoughts, and benefits and positive outcomes of mindful meditation.

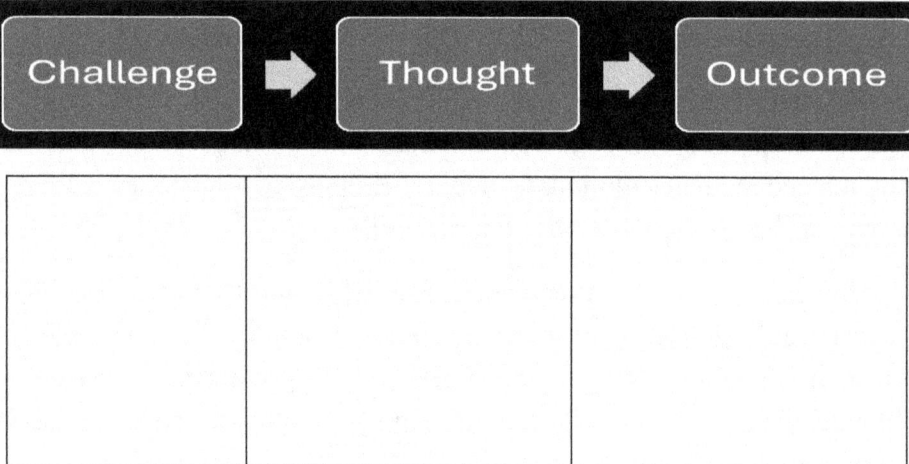

Challenge	Thought	Outcome

'...great leadership depends primarily on vision – not just any type of vision, but one that we can appreciate intellectually, emotionally and spiritually.'
—Danah Zohar

7

Emotional and Spiritual Intelligence and Mind–Body Unity
Dr John Bellavance and Dr Rafia Naz

The fifth method for bringing our mind and body into unity is understanding and applying emotional intelligence (EI) and spiritual intelligence (SI) in our lives. Zohar[117] proposed a new paradigm of intelligence (see Figure 20).

...balancing your emotions with reason is key to making thoughtful and meaningful decisions.

EI is demonstrated through empathy, self-awareness, self-control, and the ability to recognise and appropriately respond to one's own emotions and those of others. It contributes to social capital, reflected in trust and empathy within a community, which can be assessed by indicators, such as crime rates, divorce rates, literacy levels and the prevalence of litigation.

SI serves as the foundation for both IQ (Intelligence Quota) and EI. IQ is the ability to think logically and solve problems in a goal-oriented way. SI is the ability to connect with your deepest values, motivations and sense of purpose. SI shapes who you are, what you stand for, believe in, aspire to and take responsibility for. It also encompasses the capacity to access higher meanings, values and unconscious aspects of the self, embedding them into daily life to cultivate a richer, more creative and fulfilling existence.

Capital	Intelligence	Function
	IQ	
Material Capital	Rational Intelligence	What I think
	EQ	
Social Capital	Emotional Intelligence	What I feel
	SQ	
Spiritual Capital	Spiritual Intelligence	What I am

Figure 20 Three types of intelligence

Four Features of Emotional Intelligence

Dr John Bellavance

There are four features of EI: emotional self-awareness, balancing emotions and reasoning, understanding emotions in others and managing our emotions.

Emotional self-awareness

Emotional self-awareness – understanding the connection between your thoughts, emotions and behaviours – is essential as emotions influence every decision you make. Emotional self-awareness enables you to recognise how your feelings impact your actions, helping you make wiser choices. By harnessing emotional learning, you can navigate challenges effectively, prevent negative outcomes and align your actions with your true self.

Emotions carry profound wisdom about our relationships and surroundings, and learning to channel them productively is key to self-actualisation and lasting happiness. Too little awareness of our emotions can lead to flawed reasoning.[39] For example, when in a negative or sad mood, people tend to focus on details and look for errors. Conversely, those in a positive state of mind are often more optimistic, creative and open to new possibilities.

Balancing emotions and reasoning

Your emotions shape your thinking, just as your thoughts influence how you feel. Achieving a healthy balance between the two requires recognising how emotions impact your decisions and learning to use them to guide your thoughts and actions. This is the second feature of EI.

Your emotional responses also stem from how you interpret your experiences through reasoning. Reason and emotion continuously and reciprocally influence each other (see Figure 21). Striking the right balance between them is essential for making sound decisions and leading a fulfilling life.

This balance fosters both wisdom and wellbeing. EI teaches us that navigating relationships and daily challenges requires integrating rational thinking, emotional awareness and the right mindset. Whether you are making moral choices, selecting a lifelong partner, pursuing a career or raising children, balancing your emotions with reason is key to making thoughtful and meaningful decisions.[39]

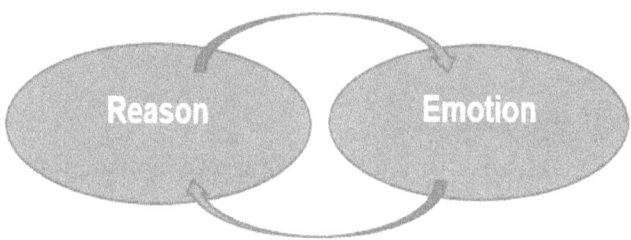

Figure 21 Reciprocity between reason and emotion

The interplay between reasoning and emotion mirrors the relationship between subject and object, much like the connection between mind and body, where both continuously influence each other. Depending on the situation, either reason or emotion may take precedence. Understanding emotional cues – the signals your body and mind give you in response to experiences, such as tension, heart rate changes or gut feelings – and correctly interpreting their underlying meanings allows you to manage your responses more effectively. For instance, feeling guilty for acting against your values may manifest as anger. Being aware of this connection helps you regulate your emotions, ensuring they don't negatively affect you or those around you.

Activity #39: Exploring emotional balance

Reflect on your own experiences and answer the following questions in your journal:

1. In what situations do reasoning tend to guide your decisions more?
2. In which circumstances are emotions more dominant?
3. How do your emotions influence your thoughts and behaviour?
4. What are your common emotional cues?
5. In what ways do these emotions influence your behaviours?

Understanding emotions in others – social awareness

Social awareness is the ability to understand the emotions of others, the third feature of EI. This involves empathising with others: recognising their feelings, reading situations accurately, identifying the underlying issues and responding with empathy. The capacity to perceive emotional cues in others and interpret their meaning is a vital cornerstone for building strong working and personal relationships.

By recognising and monitoring the emotions of others, you can adjust your thinking and behaviour in ways that foster better relationships. This skill requires mindfulness and being fully present in the moment (see Chapter 6). Research shows that children who are more successful at understanding emotional cues in others tend to develop stronger social skills, demonstrate prosocial behaviour and build positive relationships with others.[118]

Activity #40: Practising empathy

Reflect on a recent interaction and journal your answers:

1. What underlying issues or emotions might someone have been experiencing?

2. What emotional cues (tone, expression, body language) did you notice?

3. How could recognising these cues have changed your response?

4. How can you be more present and mindful in future interactions to understand others' emotions better?

Managing your emotions

Practising self-control and effectively managing your emotions is the fourth feature of EI. Emotional self-control isn't about suppressing your feelings but about *acknowledging* negative emotions and addressing them in a healthy way. You don't need to avoid unpleasant feelings, rather, learning to regulate emotions helps balance negative emotions with positive ones. Self-care and emotional soothing are essential for maintaining emotional wellbeing.[39]

> ...learning to regulate emotions helps balance negative emotions with positive ones.

It's crucial to be mindful of how we manage emotions. In times of anger, frustration, stress, anxiety or self-doubt, we may turn to unhealthy coping mechanisms like alcohol, comfort food or unintentionally taking our emotions out on others.

Emotional self-control involves using emotions constructively, particularly in relationships. For instance, when someone hurts or undermines you, the instinct may be to retaliate. However, after taking a moment to cool down, you can reconsider your response is aligned with your values and consider the other person's perspective before drawing conclusions.

Regaining control often means noticing and stepping back from the self-righteous inner monologue that insists you are right and questioning irrational thoughts. Interrupting and detaching quickly from the inner dialogue that fuels anger can be helpful. While it's important to stand up for yourself, it can be done without intending to retaliate. Self-awareness and self-evaluation, based on values, play a crucial role in managing emotions effectively.

Another important aspect of emotional self-control is being able to regulate how long our emotions last and how strongly we feel them – their duration and intensity. The brain's chemistry plays a significant role in emotions like fear, anger and anxiety, which can impair our ability to think clearly and rationally. These emotions trigger the emotional brain, causing it to focus solely on the immediate threat and neglect other important factors. While this response is beneficial in life-threatening situations, it is less helpful in everyday stressful or frustrating scenarios. For example, chronic worry often results from this low-grade emotional hijacking.[39]

The positive aspect of worry is that it can help us address potential threats and engage in problem solving. However, anxiety and worry often involve low-grade stories that spiral in our minds, consuming our energy and attention. These worries can persist for a long time if left unchecked, but they can also be stopped by employing constructive reflection and mindfulness techniques.

> *A cooling-off period, such as engaging in a calming activity or exercise, is invaluable in these moments. It allows us to step back, gain perspective and prevent worry from taking control.*

Research shows that expressing anger by venting increases emotional arousal, making it hard to calm down, especially if the anger is directed at the person who caused it. My boss once told me that everything looks darker when you are tired. He suggested a good night's sleep would make things look brighter in the morning. He was right. In fact, neuroscientists have found that sleep deprivation amplifies anxiety in the regions of the brain associated with emotional processing.[119] Being aware of, and understanding, such processes can help us manage our emotions better, for example, to respond more calmly in stressful situations.

Abilities: Emotional regulation and authenticity

Below are some behaviours that you can practise to better control your emotions[120]:

- ❖ *Shift your focus to the purpose and needs of others*

    Paying attention to the needs or perspectives of others can sometimes reduce the intensity of personal emotional reactions.

- ❖ *Exercise self-control*

    Be true to your values and control your impulses. This strategy is the most important for emotional self-control. Don't act in ways that will cause you to go against your values, causing you to become frustrated with yourself.

- ❖ *Select your battles*

    Avoid circumstances that trigger unwanted emotions. For example, you must accept that you can't change others. Trying to change others triggers unwanted emotions. You can be true to yourself and others, but you can't change others.

- ❖ *Reappraise and change your thoughts*

    Let's say that you feel inferior to the people around you; they appear better than you. Shifting your focus away from comparisons to your own attributes and abilities will allow you to feel more confident. Emotions are often linked to beliefs. By changing your thoughts, you may be able to change the way you believe the situation is affecting you. **Write down your negative thoughts, then you can reappraise them.**

Another approach is to **discuss the issue with a trusted person** to help you change the way you appraise situations. This is known as Cognitive Behavioural Therapy (CBT – discussed in Chapter 2). The focus is on modifying dysfunctional thoughts, emotions and behaviours by interrogating and uprooting negative or irrational beliefs. For example, it is irrational to believe that school or work should always be fun.

You can ask a spouse or a trusted friend to act as your personal therapist in moments like this. They can help by asking you hard questions that challenge your thinking. You might feel annoyed at first, but with time, you may come to appreciate the wisdom behind these questions. They can help you identify irrational beliefs, ruminations or catastrophising thoughts.

Asking yourself critical questions can also help. For instance: *Is my thinking rational? Am I confusing a thought with a fact?*

For example, if you think, '*She didn't smile at me. I must have done something to offend her*' or '*She doesn't like me anymore,*' you might realise that her behaviour had nothing to do with you. She could be dealing with challenges in her own life. It's important to avoid rushing to conclusions about others. You never know what they're going through.

Another useful question to ask is, 'What effect is this thinking having on me?' Reflecting on how your thoughts influence your emotions can help you manage them better.

❖ *Change your responses*

Take control of your responses by recognising when your emotions start to take over. If you're feeling anxious or angry, your body might be sending signals like a racing heartbeat or tense muscles. In these moments, pause and take deep breaths to help calm yourself. Closing your eyes for a moment can also be a great way to centre yourself.

Just like teachers ask children to take a 'time out' when they're frustrated, adults can benefit from a similar pause. When your emotional mind is racing, it's essential to give yourself space to cool down before reacting. Another productive way to release angry feelings is through **physical activity**, like going for a walk or exercising. This not only helps release built-up tension but also redirects your focus in a healthier way.

Activity #41: How do you manage your moods?

Ask yourself: How do I manage negative emotions or regulate my moods?

Journal your answer.

Honesty is the best policy

As we have seen, emotions can lubricate rather than impair rationality. Try to be honest with yourself and others about how you feel. Then you can more freely get in touch with and express your true feelings appropriately and make better decisions. You can also listen to your negative emotions and understand what they are trying to tell you. Silencing or ignoring them won't make problems go away.

Organisations that encourage people to be open and honest about their emotions perform better at collaboration and establishing stronger ties with colleagues. Razzetti suggests being yourself and allowing people to be themselves.[121]

Activity #42: How do you honestly feel?

Write in your journal and share with another person or small group:

Ask yourself if being open and honest with others would establish better relations, even if it is not easy. *Am I confusing a thought with a fact?*

Finish the sentence....

- When I see a friend suffer, I feel...
- When I am sensitive to others, I usually...
- I felt that someone I love did not understand me because...
- This made me feel ... and I responded...

Debrief:

How did you feel others understood you, and why is that important to you?

Spiritual Intelligence
Dr John Bellavance

Danah Zohar[117] identified 12 key aspects of Spiritual Intelligence (SI) that contribute to a deeper sense of meaning, purpose and personal growth (see Figure 22):

1. **Self-awareness** – Understanding oneself deeply, including strengths, weaknesses and motivations
2. **Being vision- and values-led** – aligning actions with personal beliefs and values
3. **Positive use of adversity** – transforming challenges into opportunities for growth
4. **A holistic view of life and connections** – recognising the interconnectedness of all things
5. **Compassion and empathy** – feeling *with* someone rather than just *for* them
6. **Celebration of diversity** – appreciating differences and learning from them
7. **Standing up for convictions** – maintaining integrity even in the face of opposition
8. **Asking deeper fundamental questions** – seeking meaning beyond surface-level concerns
9. **Ability to reframe worldviews** – seeing situations from a broader perspective
10. **Spontaneity** – letting go of fear and inhibitions to fully embrace the present moment
11. **A sense of vocation** – feeling called to contribute to the world in a meaningful way
12. **Humility** – recognising one's place in the larger scheme of life.

While many of these concepts have already been discussed, taking a closer look at them can help deepen our understanding of how SI influences our choices, self-awareness and journey to self-actualisation.

Figure 22 12 Spiritual intelligences (Blackbyrn 2022)

SI is the ability to recognise life as having meaning, purpose and values, linking people's actions and intellectual abilities to deeper questions of human existence. The focus is on shifting from the ego – our smaller, less mature self – to the soul, fostering greater mental clarity.

It the mental ability to become conscious of the meaning of life. Research suggests that individuals with a higher level of spirituality experience greater inspiration in their work, enhance their decision-making skills, and improve their ability to set and achieve goals by cultivating self-awareness and personal meaning.[122]

Activity #43: Describe your spiritual intelligence (SI)

What does SI mean for you? Complete the sentences below:

1. Being vision- and values-led means…
2. A holistic view of life and connections means…
3. Celebration of diversity means…
4. Asking deeper fundamental questions means…
5. A sense of vocation means…
6. Humility means…

Emotional Intelligence for Enhanced Leader Relations
Dr Rafia Naz

The purpose of this section is to explore the relationship between Emotional Intelligence (EI) and leadership. EI is essential for effective leadership. It is the ability to accurately perceive, assess and express emotions; understand emotional knowledge; and regulate emotions effectively to support both emotional and intellectual growth. Leaders with high EI are better equipped to navigate social complexities, communicate effectively and make informed decisions.[123, 124]

> *While EI is a skill set, Emotional Quotient (EQ) is the measure or score of that ability, often assessed through tests or evaluation.*

Salovey and Mayer[125] identified five core domains of EI: self-awareness, emotional regulation, self-motivation, empathy and relationship management. Goleman[39] later refined EI into four key dimensions: self-awareness and emotional regulation, self-motivation, empathy for others and social skills. These abilities are not optional for leaders. They are fundamental to achieving influence, trust and organisational success.

EI and leadership

Leadership can be defined as the process of influencing others to align their efforts towards achieving goals.[126, 127] Scholars suggest that leaders who can perceive and understand both their own emotions and those of their followers tend to be more effective in their leadership roles.[128, 129] Leaders with heightened emotional understanding possess the ability to understand followers' emotions and to interact with followers in order to achieve their desired goals.[128, 129]

Leaders with a higher level of emotional understanding possess the ability to anticipate others' responses in various situations, enabling them to strategize effectively and adapt their approach accordingly[123] they can also use their own emotions to inspire positive feeling in followers, while leveraging emotional awareness to enhance critical thinking, demonstrate empathy and utilise interpersonal relationships to their advantage.[129]

Effective leadership necessitates the ability to distinguish authentic from inauthentic emotions, and to recognise the difference between expressed emotions and true emotions. This awareness fosters trust, understanding and better communication within teams.[129] It requisites higher levels of problem-solving skills and understanding of human resources and social systems. [130-133]

Leaders with higher EQ also display self-control, and combined with their problem-solving skills, this leads to greater trust and respect.[128] Leaders who can manage their emotions can adapt their behaviour to meet their followers' emotional needs, which helps in gaining their respect. This emotional adaptability allows leaders to build stronger connections, foster trust, and create a supportive environment where followers feel understood and valued.[129]

Gill[134] highlights that managers require planning, organising and controlling skills, while leaders need EI. Patterson[135] further argues that EI becomes twice as important as IQ and technical skills as individuals advance in their careers. As leaders progress within an organisation, EI becomes increasingly critical for success, shaping their ability to lead and manage effectively.

It is essential for leaders to first develop an understanding of themselves, including their emotions and how to manage them, before attempting to understand and guide others.

EI enables leaders to:

- solve complex problems
- make more informed decisions
- effectively manage their time
- adapt their behaviour to various situations and navigate crises better.[136]

Given the challenges of the 21st century, the evolving work environments and the impact of the global pandemic, fostering EI in future leaders is crucial for developing effective leadership.[137] This has implications for performance management and training and human resource management.

Leading through self-reflection

As a leader, you need to reflect on yourself effectively, which means you must mirror your behaviours and understand the impact of your actions on others. This *Mirror Leadership* should be an ongoing, evolving practice where you continuously assess and adjust your approach to better align with your followers' needs and the changing environment.

You can't expect your followers to change if you aren't willing to change yourself. It is crucial to recognise your own blind spots and demonstrate adaptability, self-confidence, innovation and initiative. By acting as a catalyst for change, as a leader you are to model EI and create an environment that fosters greater employee engagement, commitment and satisfaction.

While EI has been shown to have a positive impact on leadership, further research is needed to explore the relationship between EI and various leadership styles, particularly within the university context. Additionally, it is important to examine how EI practices may differ across different settings and individuals.

Organisations can become mental prisons if leaders fail to set the right tone. Without EI, leaders may struggle to navigate the complexities of the workplace, leading to far-reaching consequences such as decreased employee engagement and higher turnover rates. Some leaders may excel in their roles and be highly productive, but without EI, they are unlikely to thrive in the face of the challenges and uncertainties that arise in today's environment.

Activity 43: Use a Y-Chart to describe emotional intelligence

For each question below, using the Y-Chart, describe what it looks like for you (attentive eye contact, open posture, thoughtful facial expressions, difficult), sounds like (empathetic tone, clear and respectful words, active listening) and feels like (confidence, calmness, self-awareness, emotional balance, emotional discomfort).

Reflection prompts:

- What does Emotional Intelligence (EI) mean for you personally or professionally?
- Have you applied or used EI as a leader in any capacity, either at school, university or work? Yes/No?
- If yes, how has EI impacted your leadership role? How?
- If No, do you believe you would benefit by developing your EI skills?

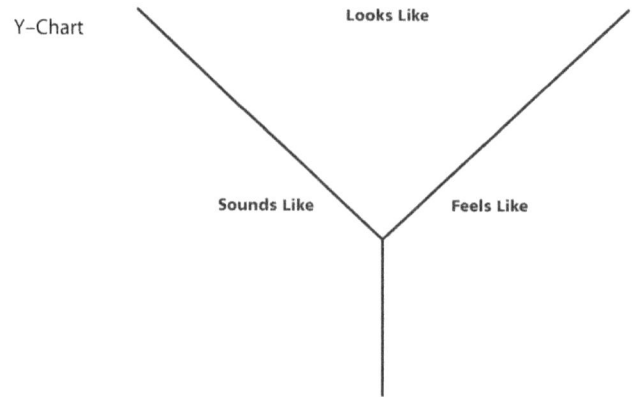

Emotional Intelligence for Enhanced Relations and Conflict Management
Dr Rafia Naz

This section explores the relationship between EI and conflict management, highlighting the strong positive connection between the two. It further provides practical implications for leaders on how to effectively manage conflicts using EI, enhancing their leadership capabilities and fostering a more harmonious work environment.

Conflict is a pervasive phenomenon that influences various organisational processes and outcomes. Its presence is recognised across diverse fields, including psychology, communication, organisational behaviour, information systems and marketing, highlighting the importance of effectively managing conflict within organisations.[138]

Scholars identify various conflict management styles in the workplace, with the integrating style being considered particularly significant. This style focuses on collaboration, open communication and finding mutually beneficial solutions, which helps manage interactions during conflict scenarios. By fostering cooperation, the integrating style not only leads to more effective conflict resolution but also produces better outcomes and greater productivity in the workplace.[139]

Research also demonstrates that EI plays an important role in resolving conflicts.[140, 141] Greater emotional awareness and the ability to act accordingly facilitate conflict resolution and contribute to better team performance.[140-142]

With higher EI, leaders demonstrate greater empathy, which encourages individuals to consider others' interests when resolving conflicts. This empathy not only helps in understanding others' needs but can also foster altruism,[143, 144] as individuals become more aware of and responsive to the needs of those around them.[145] Additionally, empathetic leaders are more skilled in anticipating how others will behave and respond, enhancing their ability to navigate and resolve conflicts effectively.[143, 144]

With these characteristics, emotionally intelligent leaders tend to adopt integrating and compromising conflict management styles, which emphasise collaboration and finding mutually acceptable solutions. These approaches enhance both efficacy and suitability in resolving conflicts.

By balancing the needs of all parties, such leaders foster more harmonious relationships and create long-term positive impacts within the organisation. [139, 146, 147] Given that integrating and compromising styles have positive effects on conflict resolution, these styles are preferably the styles selected by EI leaders as part of their approach.[139]

EI in leadership selection, training and organisational dynamics

Scholars have suggested that EI plays a crucial role in both selecting effective leaders and in leadership training.[128] Mayer and Goleman further emphasise that leaders must be attuned to the emotional climate of their organisations, highlighting the necessity of EI abilities in effectively managing and responding to organisational moods and dynamics.

The ability to perceive others' feelings and empathise with their emotions can help to establish a stronger interpersonal bond, which in turn is beneficial for leadership and constructive conflict management. Kellett Leaders' use of emotions can also enhance cognitive processes and decision making.[129, 148]

Considering the skills that EI provides enables us to develop effective conflict management strategies for organisations. This further highlights the importance of EI training in equipping leaders to better navigate workplace conflicts. Furthermore, EI can serve as a tool for distinguishing between authentic and inauthentic emotional expressions in the workplace, as well as for integrating different leadership and conflict management styles across diverse national and cultural contexts.

In conclusion, this research advocates for more investigations on the topic in different contexts, nationalities and cultures. It also stresses the significance of assessment/appraisals, trainings and evaluation of the importance of EI for individual, team and organisational effectiveness. A multi-tiered approach in investigating leaders, peers and all echelons of staff is essential.

Activity #44: Applying emotional intelligence

Write in your journal and share with others:

1. Have you applied or used EI for conflict management in any capacity either at school, university or at work? If so, explain with an example?
2. If yes, has EI impacted you in any positive way in conflict resolution?

3. If no, do you know of anyone (could be someone you don't know personally) whom you believe has a high level of EI and has used this for conflict management and resolution? What qualities and strategies did they use?

'We propose cultivating virtuousness and self-actualisation at work as a project of the self, a project of growing, becoming and evolving towards the ideal self.'
—*M Fernando & RMM Chowdhury (2015)*

8

Cultural Impacts on Self-Actualisation and Self-Development
Dr Tuong Thi Phan

Managing ourselves (self-actualisation and personal development) forms the first pillar of the *Six Pillars Framework for Wellbeing, Positive Relationships, and a Sustainable and Peaceful Future*. This chapter explores how culture influences a person's ability to achieve their potential.

By working towards enhancing positive self-actualisation and managing self, this chapter aligns with and contributes to the attainment of four UN Sustainable Development Goals: Goal 3 – Good Health and Wellbeing; Goal 4 – Quality Education; Goal 16 – Peace, Justice and Strong Institutions; and Goal 17 – Partnerships for the Goals (revitalised global partnerships).

Self-management is essential for human development in any social settings. [149] A key aspect of self-management is self-actualisation, which represents fulfilling one's potential. Research across various disciplines – including healthcare, behavioural and cognitive modifications, sports, education, organisations and leadership – highlights the significant role of assertiveness in supporting self-actualisation and personal growth.

Assertiveness is the ability to express your thoughts, feelings and needs directly, honestly and respecting the rights and beliefs of others. Rather than being passive (avoiding conflict) or aggressive (being hostile or dominating), assertiveness strikes a healthy balance that is essential for fulfilling your potential.

Eastern-Asian perspectives on virtues and self-actualisation

To foster values education in our global village, it is vital to consider non-Western views. Self-actualisation and its foundation, assertiveness, are often considered Western approaches to self-management. Studies have documented that individuals from non-Western cultures, particularly in East and Southeast Asia, may not be as familiar with the paradigm and practice of self-actualisation, as their cultural values often emphasise collective wellbeing over individual self-expression.[151]

In these countries, the group's welfare is often seen as more important than the individual's desires. This is rooted in a collectivistic mindset, where a person sees themselves as an integral part of a larger whole – be it their family, community or company. This contrasts with the more individualistic cultures often found in the West, which emphasise personal autonomy and self-expression.

According to Eastern-Asian doctrines, self-cultivation – the process of developing one's mind, character and abilities through one's own efforts – is the marker of self-growth and social order. Confucianism, during the 6th–5th century BC, emphasised that personal and governmental morality is the benchmark for good government. Fostering correctness of social relationship, justice, kindness, sincerity and social rules will lead to virtue (behaviour showing high moral standards).

In Confucianism, moral responsibility is linked to bloodline, namely the family – specifically, the filial piety children show to their parents. People are to first take responsibility for their family and then extend that to fulfil their responsibility to others.[151] Confucianism emphasises self-cultivation through a commitment to lifelong learning, personal improvement and ethical living. This process involves observing rituals, following moral principles, seeking guidance from teachers and respecting authority. Righteousness is central to human conduct: one must first strive for self-correction while also encouraging others to do the same. Moreover, Confucian thought upholds the virtue of prioritising love and care for others above oneself.(151)

Taoism, which emerged in ancient China around the 6th–4th century BCE and is associated with thinkers such as Laozi, offers a complementary yet distinct perspective to Confucianism. Taoist principles encourage simplicity, humility, and living in harmony with others and nature. Good behaviour is the virtue of self-improvement and the improvement of the world. Taoism promotes altruistic, helpful and kind conduct while prohibits competitive behaviour of any form – overt, covert or inadvertent.(152) In Western countries, such as Canada, many people of Chinese descent continue to uphold Confucian and Taoist values, which influence their approach to self-actualisation and workplace dynamics. As a result, despite growing up in Canada and being familiar with Western concepts of assertiveness and self-promotion, many of these talented individuals choose not to adopt an assertive approach in professional settings.

While Confucian and Taoist values and practices have positively influenced health, educational development, family happiness and socialisation, their emphasis on humility and low assertiveness can negatively impact professional advancement. As a result, individuals may be less likely to advocate for themselves in the workplace.(150)

Activity #45: Exploring your assertiveness

Use a Y-Chart to reflect on your assertiveness in everyday life.

1. In the centre, write the word 'assertiveness'.
2. What does it *look* like for you? (actions, body language, expression, posture, choices)
3. What does it *sound* like for you? (voice tone, words, the way you communicate)
4. What does it *feel* like for you? (internal experience: confidence, calmness, hesitation, discomfort, strength)

Reflection:

- What does assertiveness mean for you?

- Do you express your thoughts, feelings and needs directly and honestly while respecting the rights and beliefs of others? If yes, give an example. If no, consider moments where you wanted to speak up but didn't – and why.

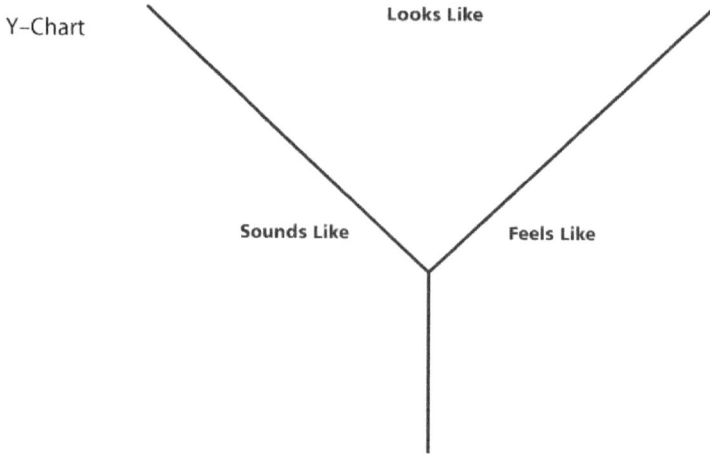

Challenges of Low Assertiveness in Southeast Asian Communities

How can individuals of Eastern-Asian origin achieve self-management and self-actualisation while living in Western society?

As discussed, leadership styles and culturally low assertiveness among various Southeast Asian communities have negatively impacted professional promotion.[153] However, the root cause of this low assertiveness is not a lack of understanding of self-actualisation itself. Fieldwork conducted by the current writer within Eastern-Asian ethnic communities in Sydney and Melbourne indicated a lack of recognition and *acceptance* of assertiveness, even among individuals familiar with concepts of self-actualisation in education and workplace environments. This reluctance to embrace assertiveness commonly led to unfavourable outcomes, including delayed professional advancement, limited personal autonomy in decision making, and increased personal or family dissatisfaction.

The first generation of this refugee-immigrant community worked tirelessly to provide for their children, ensuring they were healthy and successful in their studies. In return, children were expected to honour family traditions and adhere to their parents' wishes, following their guidance on which schools to attend, academic fields to pursue and professional careers to enter. Many children from Vietnamese, Chinese, Korean and Indian refugee backgrounds have indeed excelled academically, frequently entering careers in medicine, dentistry, pharmacy and law and engineering.

However, qualitative interviews with several families of these backgrounds highlight the conflicting family dynamics experienced by many. In several cases, adult children refused to follow the professional paths their families had envisioned for them, leading to tension and discord. Some even took time off study without setting a return date. Many of these graduates explained that they had chosen their fields of study to honour their parents' desires and expectations. Once they fulfilled their duty to their families, they felt free to pursue their own paths.

On the other hand, parents viewed their children's pursuit of personal choices as a reflection of their own failure in fulfilling their parenting obligations, adherence to traditional expectations and socio-moral norms. As a result, many parents fell seriously ill and were hospitalised, deeply affected by their perceived failure.

These cultural dynamics are explored in contemporary literature as well. *Three Holidays and a Wedding* by Marissa Uzma Jalaluddin illustrates the deep influence of Confucianism and Taoism on Canadian-American families of Pakistani-Indian background. The book delves into the prolonged and often undesirable effects these cultural philosophies have on the intertwined aspects of self-management, academic and career choices of their children, spanning from youth through to adulthood.[154]

A tragic, stark example of the consequences of unresolved cultural and intergenerational conflict was presented in the 2024 Netflix murder documentary *What Jennifer Did*.[155] Jennifer was a Canadian teen from a Vietnamese refugee family. Although brilliant in piano, in contrast to her parents' expectations, she had low scores in core subjects required for entry into medicine or pharmacy studies. Jennifer experienced tremendous pressure from her parents to the point where she didn't report her actual high school study results and provided forged reports.

After high school, Jennifer continued lying to her parents, pretending to attend university, and even producing a fabricated bachelor's degree certificate. Meanwhile, she formed a toxic relationship with a Vietnamese-Canadian male classmate and together they conspired to murder Jennifer's parents. Fortunately, her father survived and was the key witness of Jennifer's involvement.

The Importance of Acculturation

The examples shared above highlight the significance of acculturation: adapting to the new culture and norms of the communities and social groups one is joining and integrating with. Even when there is no desire for cultural change, embracing the new culture becomes essential for recognising and understanding why and how people behave differently.

What is needed in these social situations is for both generations, parents and children, to acknowledge the differences in their beliefs and ways of living. If both parties understand that the children have adapted to the culture of their host country while the parents have not, it will lead to a more harmonious experience in their personal, familial and social interactions.

This information highlights the importance of self-expression for true self-actualisation and self-management. However, sharing one's thoughts and feelings, even with loved ones, is not always easy, straightforward or simple. It requires courage, assertiveness, and the relevant skills and techniques to communicate effectively.

However, the information gathered though the writer's study indicates that previous knowledge of self-actualisation and assertiveness alone does not necessarily translate into effective self-expression. Rather, these capacities must be actively developed through intentional guidance and practice.

Cultural Aspects of Self-Management

Cultural differences between Western and Eastern societies are often described in terms of contrasting orientations. Western cultures are often characterised as 'egocentric' or 'individualistic', whereas Eastern culture is described as 'sociocentric,' or 'collectivist'. These distinctions highlight the contrasting approaches to self and society, with the West focusing on individual autonomy and personal control and the East prioritising social harmony and group-oriented values.[156]

However, such broad cultural contrasts are insufficient for effectively monitoring and enhancing community integration and social belonging for several key reasons:

- Culture is not fixed; it is fluid, continuously shifting and adapting over time.
- Cultural transformation can be subtle and gradual, making it difficult to observe, track and analyse.
- Cultural changes may manifest in behaviour, thinking, or both, requiring assessment of personality traits, situational factors, cognitive processes and motivations to evaluate shifts in cultural perception.
- Individuals interpret and engage with cultural values differently due to personal perspectives, cognitive and motivational differences, and situational influences, resulting in significant variability within cultural groups.

Research in cultural cognitive behaviour indicates that individuals can integrate multiple cultural frameworks, even when these cultures have conflicting theoretical foundations or moral perspectives.[157] Changes in cultural perspectives and behaviours are created by learning experiences; however, this can only be guided by one system at a time. In other words, typically one guiding cultural orientation will be dominant at any given moment.

Assertiveness and Self-Actualisation

As stated in the first pillar, self-actualisation is the driving force behind self-management. It reflects the desire and commitment to reach one's highest potential and make a meaningful impact on the world. The core motivation for self-actualisation is the pursuit of self-fulfilment.

In the pursuit of self-actualisation, individuals are motivated to:

- express themselves
- seek challenges and opportunities for growth
- achieve personally meaningful goals while gaining recognition for their accomplishments.

Self-actualisation is characterised by an outward orientation and requires assertiveness. According to the *Oxford English Dictionary*, assertiveness is defined as 'having or showing a confident and forceful personality'. For example, *'The job may call for assertive behaviour.'*

Conceptually, the term 'personality' may suggest that assertiveness is an innate trait, but this may not be the case. However, assertive skills can be learned and developed over time. Assertive behaviour exists on a spectrum, where individuals express self-confidence in varying degrees depending on their interactions with others. For instance, a person may be communicative and suggestive in one situation but appear confrontational or aggressive in another.

In the context of self-management, self-actualisation relates to assertiveness as effective communication, enabling individuals to express their thoughts, feelings and desires, particularly in pursuing their goals and ensuring they aren't dismissed.

> *Verbal and behavioural violence, aggression and rudeness do not fall within the scope of assertiveness.*

Assertiveness is a crucial skill for self-advocacy, enabling individuals to move away from passivity towards self-confidence while respecting others' viewpoints and feelings, rather than disregarding them in a domineering manner.(158)

Activity #46: Mapping your assertive self

Effective self-expression is essential for true self-actualisation and self-management. It requires courage, assertiveness, and the relevant skills and techniques to communicate effectively.

Use a Y-Chart to describe your assertiveness in life. What does sharing your thoughts and feelings about what you want to do with your life with loves ones look like, sound like and feel like? Examples:

- **Look** like steady eye contact, open posture, confident gestures, shaky hands and voice
- **Sound** like clear, honest tone, direct but respectful words, calm communication, stuttering
- **Feel** like internal state: confidence, calmness, occasional nervousness or discomfort.

Reflection:

Are you assertive in your life? If so, why? If not, why not?

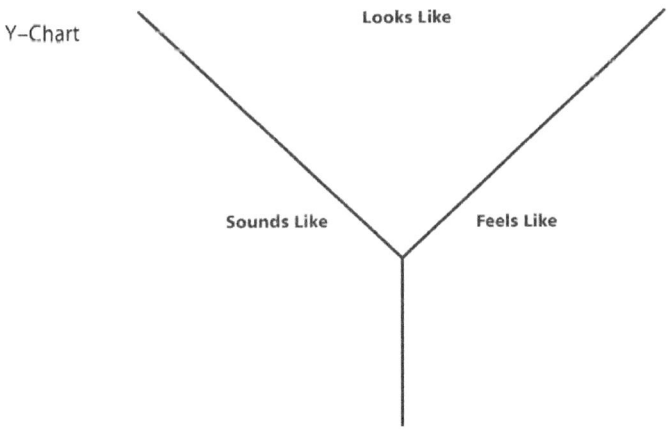

Self-Cultivation and Self-Actualisation

Self-cultivation and self-actualisation are linked concepts and processes. Self-cultivation is derived from Confucianism,[151] prescribing self-directed learning methods for acquiring self-growth and self-management. This moral disciplinary process guides the learner towards the practice of self-actualisation – gaining deep recognition of the inner self or true nature – with the goal of self-improvement.

Confucius established key moral principles, including obedience to elders and superiors, showing respect to rulers, parents and even social inferiors, and adhering to ritual and ethical living. He emphasised the cultivation of wisdom, trustworthiness and the pursuit of righteousness in all situations.

From an Eastern perspective, the journey of self-realisation is inward-focused, emphasising reflection and awakening. Self-improvement encompasses both independence and interdependence, with a strong emphasis on the latter. Interdependence is paramount, extending beyond close family members to include the broader network of extended relationships.[158] The desire to know oneself goes parallel with making changes for the better of oneself but not changing others. The highest achievement of self-cultivation is self-content, gaining internal peace.

Taoism emphasises the principles of 'Zhong' and 'Shu'. 'Zhong' refers to 'other-regard' or loyalty, particularly towards rulers, but its application extends to all relationships, including those with younger individuals, those of lower socio-economic status, elders in society and filial piety towards parents. 'Shu' represents self-reflection and embodies the golden rule: *'What you do not desire for yourself, do not do to others.'* This principle ties self-reflection to outward virtue – a moral quality or habit that reflects a person's commitment to doing what is good and right, such as telling the truth. In the doctrine of Kongzi (Confucius), there is no strict separation between self and others, inner and outer, or individual and whole. Self-cultivation is not merely a personal endeavour but also a collective, social and cosmic pursuit.

Practising cultivation means living in harmony with oneself, family, the local community and the world. It doesn't imply weakness, submission, neglecting one's rights, avoiding interactions or disregarding others.

Acknowledging the philosophical uniqueness of cultural practices, particularly the principle of 'Rectify oneself but not rectify others' within Zhong and Shu, raises questions about the appropriateness of assessing self-management among individuals of Southeast Asian origin based on 'low or high assertiveness'. It is evident that assertiveness is not a core concept in the doctrine of self-cultivation and self-realisation. While self-actualisation aligns with individualism, self-cultivation is inherently social. This distinction highlights cultural origin's influence on how individuals from different nations approach self-actualisation and self-management.[159]

Acculturation and Transculturation

Before examining acculturation in more depth, it is important to define culture. Culture is a pattern of shared meanings and ideas that shapes how people think and act. It is a product of a specific environment and experiences. We create culture through our behaviours, and in turn, culture influences our future behaviour.[156]

Transculturation involves the creation of a new cultural identity that draws from multiple cultural sources. Acculturation and transculturation have both increasingly been recognised as essential processes that facilitate social assimilation, enabling subgroups of the population to learn about and adapt to the cultures of their host countries.

As mentioned earlier in the chapter, acculturation is the process within which contact between people of two or more different cultures occurs. Through acculturation, members of these groups acquire the new culture(s) and practise cultural exchanges, fostering social assimilation. For example, refugees and immigrants from Vietnam, China or Sudan experience acculturation when they settle in Australia or the USA. These newcomers would be expected to learn about their host country's culture so that they can integrate into the host country's community. Acculturation occurs through such encounters, learning and exchanging cultural perspectives.[162]

At the same time, through these interactions, people in host countries also gain exposure to the cultures of newcomers. However, there is often little expectation or social obligation for host communities to acknowledge or understand the cultures of refugees and immigrants. This is largely because the host community belongs to the majority group, which holds economic power and dominance over land ownership. Worldwide, the culture of the host country is perceived as the dominant culture.[160, 163]

The unwillingness to understand the culture of newly arrived individuals can lead to a reciprocal reluctance among newcomers to engage with the host culture. As a result, community assimilation may be hindered, creating social, financial and political challenges for both newcomers and the host government.

Transculturation

The prefix 'tran-' signifies going beyond or moving across from one side to another. Trans-culture refers to the transformation or transition from one culture to another. The term 'transculturation' was introduced by Cuban anthropologist Fernando Ortiz in 1940 to describe the merging and convergence of cultures.[164] According to Ortiz, transculturation occurs in three phases[160]:

1. **Acculturation** – the process of acquiring a new culture
2. **Deculturation** – the loss or uprooting from one's original ethnic culture
3. **Neoculturation** – the emergence of a new cultural identity resulting from the interplay of acquired and former cultures.

It's important to note that acculturation does not always occur when individuals from different cultures come into contact, and when it does, the phases involved don't occur in a fixed order.

Transcultural studies examine how cultural perspectives and linguistic identities are formed and consolidated through contact between group. The central aim is to promote transculturalism, which calls for cooperation, interaction and exchange across communities. Transculturalism theory and practice extends its goal to encourage connections between cultural and ethnic boundaries to globalisation.[160]

Advocating globalisation, transcultural development emphasises the egalitarian recognition of universal human nature, where individuals enrich their cultural identities by appreciating and valuing their own ethnic culture while also learning from and recognising the merits of other cultures.[160]

Transformative learning is a process by which we transform our taken-for-granted frames of reference and make them more inclusive, discriminating, open, emotionally capable of change, and reflective in order to guide (personal and social) action(s).[165] This information on culturation is valuable for enhancing self-management. While maintaining the perspective of your own culture, you can also be open to other cultures, acknowledging various ways of managing self.

Wellbeing and Acculturation

Wellbeing is the fundamental aspect of living and is closely tied to the cultural environment we inhabit. Culture, though intangible, is essential to our existence. It is absorbed into our subconscious and manifests in our behaviour, gestures, conversation and thinking. It silently guides us to become who we are. Moving to a new environment and living among people who practise a culture unfamiliar to us can be highly challenging, for both our physical and mental health, particularly as we adjust to a new way of living and responding to it.[159]

This is a collective ordeal, experienced by all family members and individuals within the same ethnic community. It is important to share thoughts, feelings and concerns about such experiences with friends, family and community members. Seeking counselling from professional services can also be highly beneficial.

Social welfare is closely linked to how well you integrate into a new culture. When entering and becoming part of a new environment, whether it's a new community or organisation, you are expected to adapt and merge into the social and cultural dynamics of the situation. To do this successfully often involves developing new skills or adjusting existing ones to meet the new requirements. These include linguistic skills, vocational skills – such as knowledge and qualifications – awareness of the political situation, legal requirements, and understanding social customs and protocols. These new sets of skills and practices can equip you for your survival and wellbeing in the new environment.

The speed of settlement varies. For some, it can be quick and smooth, while for others, it may be slow, rough or even stagnant. Generally, this variation is influenced by your ability and capability to develop new skills. However, the willingness to adapt to the new culture is key to adjusting to sociocultural changes. Inconvenience and disadvantages can arise during settlement if you are reluctant to understand the new culture or join the new society.

> ...the willingness to adapt to the new culture is key to adjusting to socio-cultural changes.

Morality and acculturation

Morality is closely linked to how well we integrate into culture. The desire not to explore or merge into a new culture is not inherently immoral. Conversely, the effort to understand and become familiar with a new culture is not an act of disloyalty to one's own ethnic culture.

The overall benefits that acculturation and transculturation can bring to newcomers and their communities have been highlighted earlier. From a moral perspective, trying to understand and engage with the culture of a new country or organisation reflects respect for the host organisation and its government, fostering positive relationships with local residents.

Respecting others' lifestyles and living harmoniously with them are core virtues in Southeast Asian culturation. Respectful social exchanges between hosts and newcomers are viewed by all parties as gestures of goodwill and signals of peace. This shared sense of peace serves as a powerful motivation for self-satisfaction, contentment and the integrity of the community.

State of affairs

As mentioned in the social welfare section, successful settlement into a new community requires developing a new set of skills, including linguistic proficiency, vocational abilities, and an understanding of socio-legal and customary practices. The settlement process varies for individuals. Some may lack the ability or capability to acquire these skills, even if they are financially desperate and seeking social affiliation, while others may be reluctant to integrate socially. At the same time, other family members may be more comfortable adapting to the new society's lifestyle, culture and customs.

This uneven pattern of social integration within families can lead to serious conflicts, sometimes unresolvable, resulting in regrettable outcomes, as seen in the true story of Jennifer and her family. Field studies conducted in Sydney and Melbourne have similarly reported health deterioration and unhappiness linked to these dynamics. Children were reluctant to share their perspectives and experiences with their parents, possibly due to a lack of assertiveness skills and fear of parental rejection. For individuals of Southeast Asian origin, nothing is more valuable than connection with the family blood line.

Such cultural and familial tensions deeply impact individuals' ability to develop their identities, express their needs and pursue their potential. When communication and understanding break down, self-actualisation becomes difficult to achieve, further highlighting the critical role of cultural awareness and adaptive self-management in these contexts.

At a broader community level, we have witnessed how cultural ignorance or misunderstanding can spark disputes between neighbouring villages, communities, regions and even countries. Social segregation is a common outcome of cultural incongruity and is regularly reported. An unwillingness to acknowledge the nature and value of other cultures can be as damaging as bigotry, often leading to unresolvable sectarian conflicts.[166] The widespread aftermath of these conflicts typically includes community riots and wars, far beyond mere bickering.

Whether or not you want to practise a new culture, any effort made to acculturation is worthwhile, not only for personal benefit (self-development) but also for family interaction and community integration. Community harmony and peace are the most honourable rewards to humankind.

> Community harmony and peace are the most honourable rewards to humankind.

Activity #47: Understanding culture and connection

Journal exercise:

1. How have your family values and culture helped you in life, or not?
2. Have you experienced cultural misunderstanding? If so, what happened?
3. What challenges have any of your family members, or someone you know, experienced when introduced to a new culture?

PILLAR 2:

Managing Our Relationships and Self-Actualisation

A key element of mental health, wellbeing, happiness and self-actualisation is the ability to experience and sustain loving relationships. Our happiness and health are deeply connected to both receiving and giving love. Pillar Two explores how we grow socially and emotionally through our connections with others.

Related UN Sustainable Development Goals (SDGs)

Goal 1: End poverty in all its forms everywhere.

- **Indicator 1.2.2:** Proportion of men, women and children of all ages living in poverty in all its dimensions according to national definitions.
- **Target 1.2:** By 2030, reduce by at least half the proportion of men, women and children of all ages living in poverty in all its dimensions according to national definitions.

Goal 3: Ensure healthy lives and promote wellbeing for all at all ages

- **Target 3.4:** By 2030, reduce premature mortality from non-communicable diseases (NCDs) by one-third through prevention and treatment, while promoting mental health and wellbeing.

- **Target 3.5:** Strengthen prevention and treatment of substance abuse, including narcotic drug abuse and harmful use of alcohol.
- **Target 3.7:** By 2030, ensure universal access to sexual and reproductive health care services, including for family planning, information and education, and the integration of reproductive health into national strategies and programmes.

Goal 4: Ensure inclusive and equitable quality education and promote lifelong learning opportunities for all.

Our relationships, especially with family members, play a vital role in our education, mental health and wellbeing. Learning to relate well to others is essential for personal and social development.

- **Target 4.7:** By 2030, ensure that all learners acquire the knowledge and skills needed to promote gender equality, a culture of peace and non-violence, global citizenship, and an appreciation of cultural diversity and its contribution to sustainable development.

Goal 5: Achieve gender equality and empower all women and girls.

Gender equality and empowerment begin within the family. The education and behaviours modelled at home are fundamental in reducing violence and exploitation.

- **Target 5.1:** End all forms of discrimination against all women and girls everywhere.
- **Target 5.2:** Eliminate all forms of violence against women and girls in both public and private spheres, including trafficking and other forms of sexual exploitation.
- **Target 5.4:** Recognise and value unpaid care and domestic work through the provision of public services, infrastructure and social protection policies, and the promotion of shared responsibility within the household and the family as nationally appropriate.
- **Target 5.5:** Ensure women's full and effective participation and equal opportunities for leadership at all levels of decision making in political, economic and public life.

- **Target 5.a:** Undertake reforms to give women equal rights to economic resources, as well as access to ownership and control over land and other forms of property, financial services, inheritance and natural resources, in accordance with national laws.

Goal 16: Promote peaceful and inclusive societies for sustainable development, provide access to justice for all, and build effective, accountable and inclusive institutions at all levels.

The values and practices established within families and extended families shape the way individuals contribute to society and the institutions they influence.

Goal 17: Partnerships for the Goals

'The simple math of love is the more you love, the happier you feel, the more you love the healthier you are, the more you love the more successful you are at everything. In sum, your life works when you love, and it doesn't when you don't.'
—Robert Holden

9
Love Is the Central Value of Life
Dr John Bellavance

A truly fulfilling life is not built on power, knowledge or wealth alone. The happiness they provide eventually diminishes, leading us to seek deeper fulfilment in our relationships. While some may view love as merely a sentimental concept, this chapter explores its tangible impact on our personal growth – shaping our hearts, character, moral development, psychology, physical wellbeing and interactions with others. In this context, both altruistic and selfish or dysfunctional expressions of love have profound consequences, not only for our own wellbeing but for everyone around us.

Love forms the foundation of a healthy, functional human being and serves as the primary driver of social competence. To truly practise love, we need values and structure, such as those provided by family and community. In an era where superficial or distorted expressions of love often masquerade as the real thing – when the outward display of affection often conceals the absence of true love and countless individuals have never known genuine love – it is crucial to develop a clear understanding of what love truly is. Yet, in our modern world, the study and genuine practice of love is often treated as an afterthought.

The challenge is that relationships can be a source of significant struggles. For example, difficulties within the family or partnerships are major causes of depression.[167] Considering this, fostering abilities to strengthen relationships and families is critical for happiness and wellbeing.

Difficulties in relationships generally fall into two categories: social/relational and physical/financial[168, 169]:

- **Social and relational challenges** stem from issues related to love, values and self-management:
  - Love-related struggles include poor communication, lack of support, withholding affection and infidelity.
  - Value-based conflicts arise from disagreements on core beliefs and goals, trust issues, differing parenting styles, toxic influences from a partner's social circle and dishonesty.
  - Self-management difficulties involve unhealthy behaviours, poor habits, ineffective stress management and misdirected anger.
- **Physical and financial challenges** include infertility, emotional and physical abuse, substance abuse, and financial struggles such as theft and unemployment.

Activity #48: Your challenges

Write in the table below.

What social/relational and physical/financial challenges have you encountered in your relationships? What were your thoughts about this, how did you deal with it and what was the outcome?

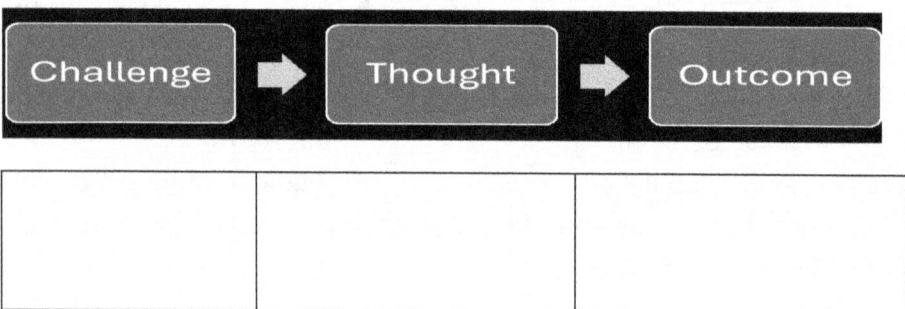

Challenge	Thought	Outcome

Reflection:

- What values and mindsets enabled you to cope with these issues?
- How did you communicate with your loved one to resolve issues?

Love Gives Life Meaning

Understanding the challenges of love reveals its deeper significance. Beyond the ups and downs of our relationships, love is the thread that holds life together. It is the central value that gives meaning to our lives and lies at the heart of what matters most. On its foundation, the values of truth, beauty and goodness take root, leading to genuine happiness. Our wellbeing is deeply tied to our relationships, and you could say that hell is the absence of those we love.

In *Man's Search for Meaning*,[28] Viktor Frankl recounts his experiences in a Nazi concentration camp, where, during a moment of 'deep clarity', he came to a profound realisation: 'Love is the highest ideal to which we can aspire.'

Standing in the freezing cold with a work crew, he found solace in a silent, imagined conversation with his beloved wife, who was imprisoned in another camp. In that moment, he understood that love gives life its ultimate meaning:

> *'For the first time in my life, I saw the truth as it is set into song by so many poets, and proclaimed as the final wisdom by so many thinkers. The truth – that love is the ultimate and the highest goal to which man can aspire. Then I grasped the meaning of the greatest secret that human poetry and human thought and belief must impart: the salvation of man is through love and in love.'* (Frankl, p. 37)

We have all questioned the source of our individual value. Many tie their sense of worth to their jobs, yet if asked, they often admit, *'There is more to life than work.'* With the rise of artificial intelligence and robotics, many fear the loss of employment and wonder where these so-called 'irrelevant' workers will find meaning.

For insight, we can turn to people in less economically developed countries, who often find meaning not in work but in relationships. Observing this reveals a deep truth: love is the true purpose of life. Like Frankl, we have all experienced moments of pure, deep joy simply by thinking of a loved one. How extraordinary that love alone can awaken such joy!

Joy is an Outcome of Love

If love is the foundation of meaning, then joy is its natural expression. Joy to some extent arises from possessions or achievements, but the greatest joy comes from loving and being loved – from the living exchange that sustains human connection.

Giving and receiving love is essential to happiness and wellbeing. Healthy human relationships rely on a balanced exchange of both, and when this balance is disrupted, relationships can begin to break down. For instance, if one partner takes too much, gives too little or fails to communicate effectively, they are not properly applying the principle of giving and receiving. Maintaining this balance is key to nurturing strong and lasting connections.

A long-term Harvard study has shown that close relationships are what keep people happy and healthy throughout their lives. These ties protect people from life's discontents, delay mental and physical decline, and are better predictors of long and happy lives than wealth, social class, IQ or even genetics. Additionally, individuals' satisfaction with their relationships at age 50 were a stronger predictor of physical health than their cholesterol levels. Those who reported the highest level of relationship satisfaction at age 50 were also the healthiest at age 80 (Mineo 2017).

Once you understand that love is the central value of life, then you need to know how to realise the ideal of love in your relationships. Unification Thought (UT) maintains that love, ideals and joy can't be achieved alone and are primarily found in relationship with others (your subject or object partners of love) – your spouse, children, parents, relatives and friends. Love is the emotional force that the subject and object partner give to each other[17, 20] (see Figure 23)

> ...ideals and joy can't be achieved alone and are primarily found in relationship with others...

Joy is an outcome of giving and receiving love. It remains dormant until we exchange love. Human beings have an unrestrainable impulse to seek joy through love – connection. Without our connections to others, we feel isolated and lack support and meaning. This was confirmed by research by the Centers for Disease Control and Prevention, which shows that 19.6% of individuals who live alone and never or rarely receive social and emotional support experience depression, compared to 11.6% of those who live with others. These findings were consistent across all demographics.[170]

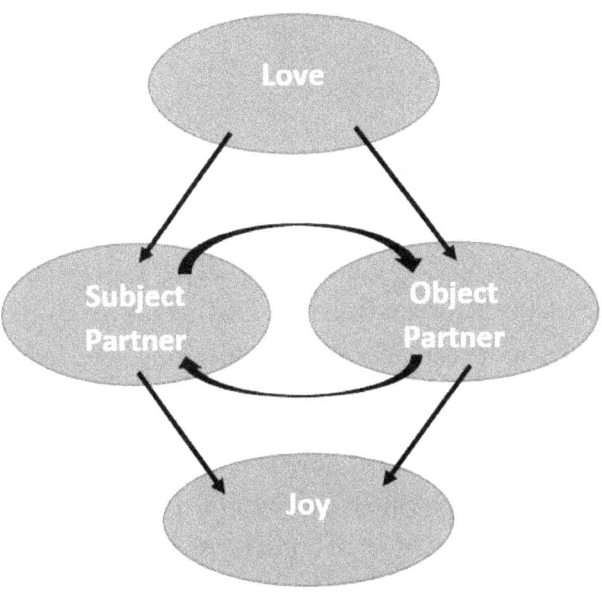

Figure 23 Joy is an outcome of relationships

Activity #49: How your people help you

1. Write your name in the middle of the spiderweb.
2. Write down in the surrounding web sections the names of your spouse/partner, children, parents, relatives and friends.
3. Now, write down how these people help you mentally and physically.

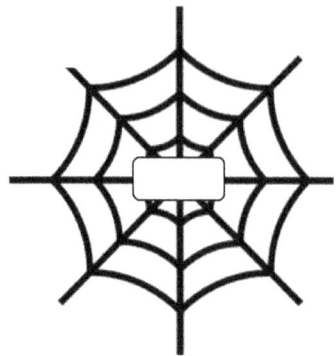

Systems and Connections

The principles that govern love and joy are mirrored in the natural world. Just as our happiness depends on connection, all living systems thrive through connection, interdependence and relationships, as shown by systems theory and neuroscience. This understanding is vital to fostering good human relationships.

The systems theory model helps us understand the complexity of the world by viewing it as a network of relationships among interconnected wholes – where the whole is greater than the sum of its parts. This kind of systems thinking represents a higher level of consciousness that fosters self-awareness and helps us grasp a deeper understanding of reality – particularly our relationships with others and the natural world. Everything from economies to human beings, consists of multiple interconnected facets that can't be fully understood or changed in isolation.[32]

Our natural environment, for example, consists of many interconnected systems – such as the solar system, electrical, biological and ecological systems – and human-made systems like economic and political structures. Similarly, human life is maintained through the relationship among our cells and organs, limbs and circulatory systems and so on.

Systems theory demonstrates that life on Earth is a complex web of natural and social systems, where actions, inputs and outputs in each system reciprocally feed back into one another in a circular manner.[171, 172] Disrupting one system therefore creates ripple effects in others: deforestation negatively impacts animal life, while trade wars disrupt global exchange and lead to economic difficulties. The components of any system influence one another, creating a feedback loop – a process where an output (effect) feeds back as input into its own cause.[173]

The system in Figure 24 illustrates the feedback loop between humans and our natural environment. Human inputs – our purposes, values, directions and behaviours – affect the environment's quality, either positively or negatively. These, in turn, feed back to us through nature's outputs. For instance, if we pollute the environment, it adversely impacts our health. This demonstrates how reciprocal actions between one system (subject) and another (object) generate outcomes that can either create or diminish value.

A family also functions as a system, where the behaviour of one member affects everyone else. For example, if a teenager, Maya, starts to struggle with her grades (**input**), it can create a ripple effect. Her parents, concerned about her future, might increase their oversight and pressure (**output**). Maya, feeling a loss of autonomy, may withdraw from family activities or become defiant (**feedback**), prompting her parents to become even more controlling (**new output**). This negative feedback loop escalates tension within the family system.

To understand a young persons' behavioural problems, it is therefore important to consider the family system in which they live, as this environment significantly influences behaviour.

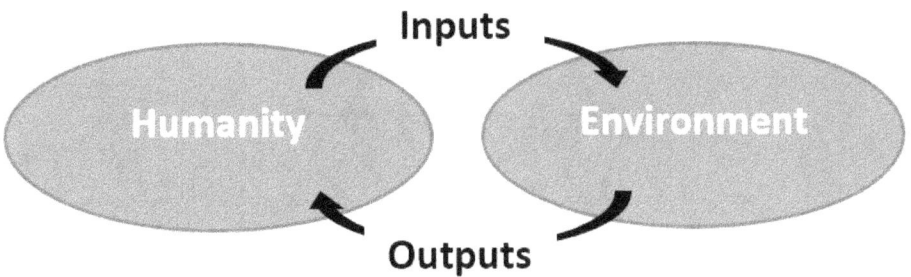

Figure 24 Feedback loop between humans and their natural environment

Giving and Receiving

All beings exist in a reciprocal relationship of giving and receiving between subject and object, and the purpose of this is to establish a relationship with a counterpart. For interaction to occur, one initiates the relationship (the subject) and the other responds (the object). Giving and receiving love between subject and object partners is the central objective of our lives. Children growing up in homes that are full of vivid discussions learn how to share ideas and receive ideas. Babies enjoy exchanging sounds with other babies, and later, they have fun turning those sounds into real words with other people. This giving and receiving is vital for their brain development.

Activity #50: Are you a systems thinker?

1. Write your name in the middle of the spiderweb.
2. In the surrounding web sections, list:
   - The countries where your food, clothing and transport (e.g. your car or public transport parts) come from.
   - The animal and plant life you rely on in your daily living (e.g. rice, wheat, cotton, bees, cows, water ecosystems).

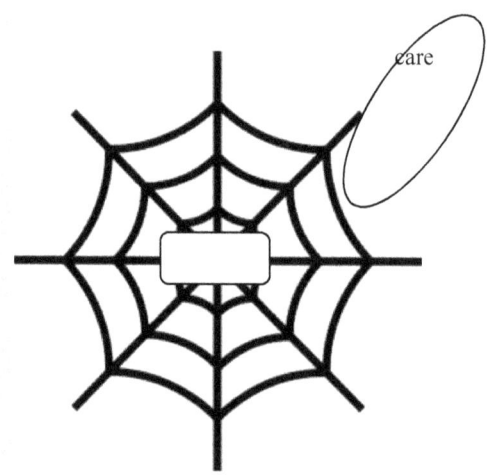

Reflection:

Human understanding is always shaped by context. We make meaning within relationships, environments and systems – not in isolation. Consider a time when someone's behaviour made more sense once you understood the context they were in.

- Write down an example of a context-bound situation (this could be from your own life, your community, workplace or a story you know).
- What does this activity show you about how connected, or dependent, you are on broader systems?

Giving and receiving love

It is crucial to assess the quality of your interactions with others – what you give and receive in your relationships. Often, we become so focused on ourselves that we forget that the greatest joy and meaning can be found in our connections with one another. Joy arises from the act of giving to another and receiving positive responses in return. What you put into a relationship (the input) is what you will get back (the output) from the other person.

In Figure 25, the system represents the relationship between two people.

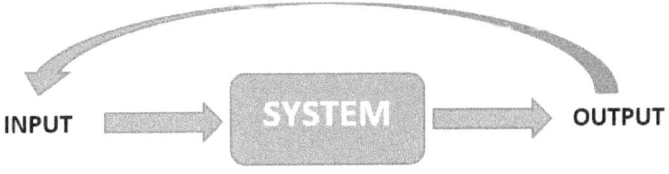

Figure 25 Giving and receiving feedback loop

As mentioned in the previous section, life systems exist based on circularity, where an effect (an output) feeds back (an input) into its very cause[173]. This circularity plays a significant role in human

> For love to work, both parties need to exist for the other...

relationships. You may have heard the saying, 'What goes around, comes around,' or the concepts of karma and cause and effect. What people say and do in their relationships has consequences that feed back onto themselves. For example, if I am more caring, I am likely to receive more care in return. Similarly, poor communication and a lack of mutual giving and receiving can cause relationship issues. On the other hand, good communication fosters positive relationships.

The importance of giving and receiving can be seen in children. A child who doesn't learn to share struggles to create friendships. A child who only receives without giving can't progress. They must learn to give back.

Research also suggests that living a lonely, self-centred life almost guarantees unhappiness and poor health. Loneliness is as harmful as smoking or alcoholism. It can literally kill.[174]

Certain values and behaviours underpin harmonious and mutually beneficial relationships. The most important is the giving and receiving of love, which causes the value of the exchange to increase for both parties. As a result, partners are naturally inclined to give more to each other, further enriching the relationship. For love to work, both parties need to exist for the other – be attuned to the other. The problem is that we can be self-centred, which short-circuits the principle of giving and receiving.

Activity #51: The balance of giving and receiving

Write in your journal and share with another:

1. What does giving and receiving mean for you in your relationships?
2. What are the qualities that allow for good giving and receiving?
3. Describe when your giving and receiving was not so good in your life and what the effects were.

'An individual has not started living until he can rise above the narrow confines of his individualistic concerns to the broader concerns of all humanity.'
—*Martin Luther King*

10

Values and Practices that Underpin Good Relationships

Dr John Bellavance

This chapter discusses the values and abilities that underpin good relationships, particularly the importance of living for the sake of others, shared values and communication. You may think that this knowledge requires changing how you are currently operating – and you might be right. You are the architect of your life!

> ...loving yourself ... means appreciating your uniqueness and the qualities that make you a responsible and loving person.

Living for the Sake of Others

> *'This is the true joy in life, being used for a purpose recognised by yourself as a mighty one. Being a force of nature instead of a feverish, selfish little clod of ailments and grievances complaining that the world will not devote itself to making you happy. I am of the opinion that my life belongs to the whole community, and as long as I live, it is my privilege to do for it whatever I can. I want to be thoroughly used up when I die, for the harder I work, the more I live.'* — **George Bernard Shaw**

A core value and practice that underpins healthy relationships is living for the sake of others (altruism) – orienting one's life towards the wellbeing of others, while recognising that mutual care and interdependence sustain all. Selfishness – the excessive focus on one's own needs, desires and interests at the expense of others – undermines our mental wellbeing and our relationships.

Research by Fuller examining youth suicide rates in 21 developed nations found that male suicide rates were highest in the most individualistic countries. The study suggests that the greater the personal freedom and control young people feel over their lives, the higher the suicide rate.[175] This challenges the assumption that greater personal freedom inherently enhances wellbeing. This finding is counter intuitive, as personal freedom is often assumed to be the road to happiness.

Young people struggle to develop a healthy sense of self-worth not only when they lack love, but also when their focus is solely on themselves. In highly individualistic societies, the emphasis on personal freedom and control can inadvertently weaken communal bonds and social networks. Hence, it is vital to foster socially oriented concerns. Research shows that as children move through adolescence, their understanding of right and wrong shifts from mostly self-oriented concerns about personal consequences to more socially oriented concerns regarding the impact of their behaviours on others.[6]

The essence of goodness

> *'Every man must decide whether he will walk in the light of creative altruism or the darkness of destructive selfishness. Life's most persistent and urgent question is, "What are you doing for others?"'*
> —*Martin Luther King*

- Why should I live for the sake of others?

The essence of morality is service, namely subordinating oneself for the sake of a higher purpose or showing love for another.[35] The essence of goodness is living altruistically, with consideration for others at the foremost of our minds – acting from empathy and service rather than self-interest, which is argued by many philosophers as the ultimate *societal necessity* – cooperation.

Being conscious of others inspires us to be part of something bigger than ourselves.

Let me share a personal experience. For 40 years, I've believed that living for others is essential – not just for my loved ones and the people around me, but for my own wellbeing too. Yet, there came a time when I found myself in a dark and cynical place, questioning everything. I asked myself, *'Why should I care about others? What's in it for me?'*

At the time, I was part of the Nelson Mandela Committee in Australia and was invited to attend the annual Nelson Mandela Lecture. I didn't want to go. *What's the point of all this service-for-others talk?* I thought. But out of a sense of duty to our president, who is a friend, I reluctantly went.

The speaker that evening shared the story of a man who deeply understood the power of living for others. I wasn't convinced. I was stuck in a disillusioned space, unable to see the meaning in it all.

A week later, I meditated on this topic, which helped me snap out of that dark mindset. I began to remember the value that comes from caring for others. The mindset of living for others had provided me with the joy and meaning that relationships bring to my life. I changed my mindset to one of gratitude.

At that point, I truly understood the core purpose and meaning of life: love. Service to loved ones provides meaning. We need our subject of love, and we need our object of love. We are relational beings who find joy in relationship with others. Joy and love require an object and a subject of love.

In essence, goodness is relational. It draws individuals beyond self-interest into a web of mutual care and responsibility. This recognition forms the basis for a broader understanding of interdependence – what Scharmer and Kaufer call 'ecosystem awareness'.

Ecosystem awareness

Otto Scharmer and Katrin Kaufer,[16] in their book *Leading from the Emerging Future*, propose a crucial shift in consciousness – moving from an 'ego-system awareness', which centres on individual wellbeing, to an 'ecosystem awareness', which emphasises the wellbeing of the whole, including oneself.

This transition involves expanding our focus from personal concerns to a broader perspective that considers the health and sustainability of our entire ecosystem. Operating with ego-system awareness often drives actions based on self-preservation and personal gain, sometimes at the expense of others. In contrast, ecosystem awareness encourages actions informed by the collective wellbeing, fostering interconnectedness and shared responsibility.

Take, for example, social responsibility and shared spaces like social media. An 18-year-old with a purely individualistic mindset might use social media to promote themselves and their personal brand, without much thought for the content's impact. With ecosystem awareness, however, they would recognise their role in a larger social system. They might use their platform to share information about social justice issues and promote mental health awareness, fostering a sense of shared responsibility and collective action.

All the ends we seek can be attained selfishly without thinking of others, justified by 'the ends justify the means'.[70] It is so easy for humans to operate under unprincipled, immoral values with respect to the means we use to achieve our ends – pleasure (an end) without conscience (a means), knowledge (an end) without character (a means), commerce without morality, science without humanity and politics without principles, and so on. That's why Gandhi (cited in [70]) placed altruism as the central value of morality.

What comes first?

- So, what comes first, giving or receiving?

I say giving. This simple principle has brought happiness into my life. The love between my wife and I has always been strengthened when I remember that life is not about me alone. Considering her needs has always helped shift the focus away from myself, which fostered our loving relationship. She, in turn, has loved me in the same way.

Research supports this importance of *balance* in giving and receiving within relationships. Healthy partnerships thrive on a reciprocal exchange where both individuals take on the roles of giver and receiver in roughly equal measures. This balance sustains and deepens commitment, contributing to overall relationship satisfaction.[176]

The simple principle is that genuine, sustainable love is realised by giving first, while conditional or self-serving love operates out of self-interest first. The self-serving individualism we often encounter in society is due in part to not understanding how love is generated and maintained. I realised that while we humans are intelligent learners, we are often still developing when it comes to learning to love. We may find ourselves waiting to be loved first, rather than discovering the joy that comes when we are willing to offer love openly and mutually.

Activity #52: Does giving work for you?

1. Write your name in the middle of the spiderweb. In the surrounding sections, write how people in your life respond when you give to them (e.g. with appreciation or discomfort).

2. Reflect on how *you* feel when giving(e.g. energised, valued, taken for granted).

3. Think about a time when giving didn't feel good or safe. What made it difficult? What could have supported you better in that situation?

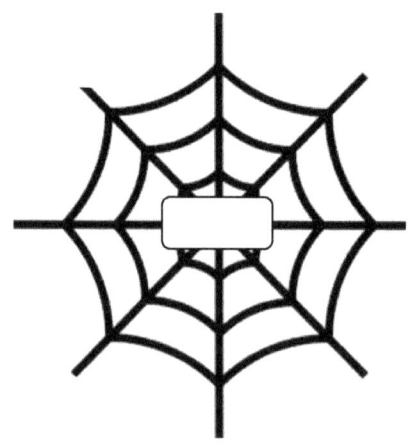

Embracing a mindset that prioritises giving can transform your relationships, fostering deeper connections and mutual fulfillment. By shifting your focus from expecting love to actively offering it, you not only enrich the lives of others but also experience profound personal growth and happiness.

Genuine and healthy love is based on the qualities of living in the best interests of the other, serving, and being sacrificial, unchanging, unconditional, forgiving and ethical.[52] It means giving and forgetting that you have given and living in the best interests of the other – the basic mission statement of parents.

As we love others in a genuine way, our self-esteem also develops. Our popular culture and society often send the message, 'Think of ourselves first. Look out for number one.' But loving yourself doesn't mean being selfish and ignoring others' needs. It means appreciating your uniqueness and the qualities that make you a responsible and loving person.

Living for the sake of others is good for your mental health and personal growth, giving those who serve others a great advantage over those who are primarily self-seeking. Genuine love is also beneficial for your physical health. One study found that women in midlife who were in highly satisfying marriages had a lower risk of cardiovascular disease compared with those in less satisfying marriages. Additionally, there is a link between negative interactions with family and friends and poorer health, while caring behaviours trigger the release of stress-reducing hormones.[177]

Studies have also shown that altruistic behaviours can alleviate physical pain. For instance, acts of kindness have been associated with reduced intensity and awareness of physical discomfort, highlighting the interconnectedness of mental and physical health.[178]

Self-centred love, driven by personal interests, often fluctuates and lacks stability. In contrast, genuine love, rooted in selflessness and a genuine concern for the wellbeing of others, tends to be steadfast and unchanging. I have been married for many years, and the love of my wife and I for each other is unchanged. We still want to take care of each other, and this desire increases with time. The driving force is the love that we experience through our relationship and the mindset of wanting to live for the sake of each other. The best thing about life is knowing that you are loved and cherished.

When giving first isn't safe

Giving and receiving should take place in relationships that feel safe and respectful. Sometimes giving first is not appropriate – for example, in relationships where boundaries are ignored, power is unequal, or giving feels one-sided or unsafe. Healthy giving includes caring for yourself as well as others.

Altruism and balancing personal and social interests

- How can we reconcile personal needs and the needs of others? Don't we have to love ourselves?

My answer is that embracing self-love and caring for others are not mutually exclusive but deeply connected. Your capacity to genuinely care for others is directly linked to how you treat yourself. The two work together in a reciprocal cycle: when you nurture yourself with self-awareness and self-acceptance, you have more emotional and mental energy to give to others. And when you show compassion towards others, it reinforces your own sense of self-worth and connection.

> ... when you show compassion towards others, it reinforces your own sense of self-worth and connection.

This dynamic between self and others is not just personal; it is shaped by how we learn and grow within society. To understand this better, we need to look at the working and evolution of both the human mind and human society.

Our basic biological instincts drive us to advance our own interests. However, from a young age we learn through socialisation to regulate and control these impulses. Throughout life, we continue to balance personal and social interests. Every parent knows that children must be taught to act with consideration for others. It takes effort to develop the will to align their behaviour with others' needs rather than just their own.[9]

This is where the socialisation of morality plays an important role. Within the family, love naturally harmonises the needs of the individual family members and the whole family.

Activity #53: Giving and receiving in relationships

Write in your journal and share with another:

1. What comes first for you, giving or receiving? Do you mostly give first or expect to receive first? Why is this?

2. What are the qualities and behaviours that make good relationships? What can you do to improve your relationships?

3. In the table below, write down the challenges you have faced trying to live for another person, your thoughts and the outcomes (what happened).

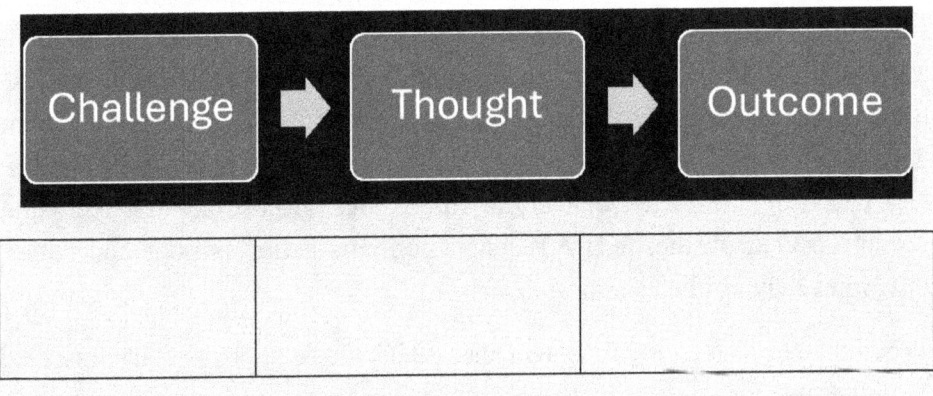

The Importance of Shared Values

To understand the importance of shared values in a relationship, we must first consider what we expect from the relationship – what we value in the other person, and what we ourselves bring to the relationship. When we relate to others, both parties have some expectations or hopes for that relationship. Good relationships are based on values and qualities that both parties value and share. These foster cooperation, trust and care.

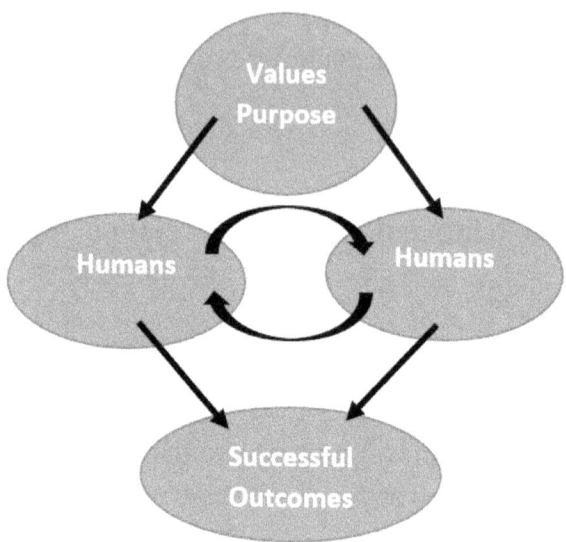

Figure 26 Outcomes based on shared values

An operating theatre nurse once explained to me that when all members of a surgical team have the best interests of the patient at heart (shared values and purpose), the surgical team work harmoniously and successfully to achieve the best outcome for the patient (see Figure 26). Open communication and good teamwork in the theatre are possible because of the shared values and purpose. She added that if the values and purpose are not the same, the atmosphere in the theatre is tense, communication is poor and patient outcomes may not be as good.

When shared values break down, the quality of relationships declines and the potential for conflict increases.[179] Moreover, people are more likely to engage with rules and systems when there is a foundation of common values. For example, imagine you're starting a club to raise money for a charity, but half the people in the club just want to hang out and have fun. They're not going to follow your rules about fundraising events. They don't share that core value of giving back, so the system (the rules, the meetings, the events) won't work for them.

Shared values create discipline and order without demanding it.[70] In organisational settings, shared values act as steady markers guiding actions and empowering individuals, leading to improved performance and reduced conflicts.[180]

Activity #54: Discovering shared values in relationships

Write in your journal and share with another:

1. Pair and share with another about your ideas about relationships. Did you find some shared values? You will find that you have a lot more in common with others through discovering shared values.

2. In the table below, write down what you expect from a relationship and what you bring to your relationships. Are there any shared values?

What you expect	What you bring

Communication

Effective communication nurtures relationships, fosters closeness and strengthens trust. Trust takes time to build, is not always easy to establish and can be quickly broken. Communication depends not only on conveying accurate information but also on *how* we communicate. Genuine communication begins with engaged dialogue, motivated by a sincere desire to understand others' perspectives and experiences. The aim is mutual understanding and benefit.

Achieving this involves considering others' perspectives, continuing dialogue until understanding is reached and developing actions that support the wellbeing of all involved.[181] Imagine you're in a group project with people who have different ideas. Instead of just pushing your idea, you listen to your teammates. You try to see the pros and cons from their point of view. This is adopting the perspectives of others. Continued communication means you don't give up after the first disagreement. You keep talking, maybe over text or in a group chat, until you find a common ground.

Communication occurs on multiple levels[181]:

1. The first is **polite conversation,** where interactions remain surface-level and nothing new is explored.
2. The second is **debating**, where you actively seek new information and engage in argument.
3. The third is **reflective dialogue**, which involves stepping into another's perspective to truly understand their position.
4. The fourth and most profound level is **generative dialogue**, where participants share a sense of common purpose and the potential for transformation, experiencing themselves as part of a greater whole.

Activity #55: Communicating for mutual understanding

Write in your journal and share with another:

1. Do your communications lead to mutual understanding and benefits?
2. Are you willing to adopt others' perspectives and continue to communicate until understanding is reached? Is so, why and how?
3. What does debating mean to you?
4. What does reflective dialogue mean to you?
5. What does generative dialogue mean to you?

Abilities: Speaking

When you communicate with others, it is important to express your feelings, thoughts, beliefs and attitudes clearly and appropriately. This skill can be developed and refined by engaging with public institutions and local communities on matters of shared concern. Through such interactions, you learn to communicate your views effectively, using language and approaches suited to the context. Additionally, by expressing your genuine beliefs – whether in writing or speech – you gain valuable insights your own perspectives, motivations and insecurities.

Through communicating honestly and authentically about who you are, you learn about yourself and your relationships. Others may challenge your views and help you perceive something you can't see on your own, thereby increasing your capacity to communicate well and develop relationships.

The language we use is equally important. Are our words demeaning, antagonistic or provocative? Using language that humanises others – conveying respect and affirmation – can strengthen relationships and communication. This means looking beyond labels, stereotypes and group identities to recognise the person beneath them. Words like 'illegal', 'thug' or 'addict' reduce people to a single, often negative characteristic. By contrast, humanising language promotes justice and peace, embedding these values into daily language and interactions.[182] For example:

Instead of *'illegal'*, say *'undocumented immigrant'*.

Instead of *'thug'*, say *'individual struggling with difficult circumstances'*.

Instead of *'addict'*, say *'person experiencing substance abuse challenges'*.

Finally, when engaging in debate, it is best not to view it as a conflict nor to assert your opinions as absolute truths; instead, listen with the openness of someone who might be wrong. It is essential to interpret others' perspectives respectfully, acknowledge areas of agreement, and recognise what you have learned from them.[109]

Activity #56: Expressing your views

Write an article about an issue in the news or one that affects your local community. Through this, you can learn to express your views appropriately and with the right language.

Abilities: Reflective listening

We must be attentive listeners and keen observers. Listening is just as active and important as speaking. A key test of effective communication is to ask yourself: **Am I truly listening?**[35] People like good listeners because they show interest in what others are saying and ask good questions. Listening involves developing sensitivity to verbal and non-verbal messages.

Reflective listening is a communication tool that helps us strengthen our listening skills by focusing on attentiveness, paraphrasing and thoughtful reflection while withholding judgement and advice. It involves mirroring or rephrasing what someone says to show you're actively listening and to help them feel heard and understood. After listening, we summarise the speaker's thoughts and feelings, repeating them back to ensure our understanding is accurate.

This process demonstrates genuine listening and understanding and fosters deeper connection. Additionally, we are responding with compassion, attachment and acceptance, creating a supportive and respectful dialogue.

Example of active listening:

Friend says: 'I'm so overwhelmed with all my assignments, and I have a huge exam next week. I just don't have enough time for everything.'

You could say: 'It sounds like you're feeling really stressed and worried about managing all your work.'

Why it works: This response shows you've heard their core feeling (stressed) and the main cause (too much work), which helps them feel heard and understood. It's a simple reflection that encourages them to continue talking.

Activity #57: Practise reflective listening

Practise reflective listening with a friend or loved one and ask them if they felt listened to. Get them to fill out the assessment sheet below about your listening skills.

There is no doubt that it is around the family and the home that all the greatest virtues, the most dominating virtues of humans, are created, strengthened and maintained.'
—Winston Churchill

11

Families As Schools of Values and Love
Dr John Bellavance

The UN maintains that families as the central hub of intergenerational interactions that nurture and support individuals. This is a foundational sustainable development goal that underpins mental, physical and economic wellbeing. Article 16 of the *Universal Declaration of Human Rights* states, 'The family is the natural and fundamental group unit of society and is entitled to protection by society and the state.'

Families are regarded as the basic social unit through which individuals form relationships and develop identity. The nuclear family is the most widely recognised type, consisting of two parents and their children, living together in the same household. The parents can be married or unmarried, and the children can be biological or adopted. However, beyond the traditional model, there are many variations, including the single-parent family, the blended family, the childless family and the extended family, which includes relatives beyond the nuclear family, such as grandparents, aunts, uncles and cousins, often living in the same household or in proximity. For instance, a teacher friend of mine was raised by her grandparents with much love and care.

Families as Foundations for Moral and Emotional Development

According to the Australian Institute of Family Studies, the rate of marriage has declined in Australia, and couples are marrying later in life. Nevertheless, most adults today are married or will marry at some stage in their lives. Cohabiting relationships have also become increasingly common, especially among young people.[183] Beyond these social structures, families serve as vital arenas for moral and emotional development, forming the foundation upon which individuals grow.

Ideally, family life is to provide the emotional and social learning essential for our personal growth and wellbeing. The relationships within a strong, well-functioning, nurturing, loving family form the foundation for the emotional content necessary for happiness, helping us develop our capacity to love and build positive connections with others in society. Healthy, happy, supportive family relationships enable us to grow into confident, balanced and socially functional individuals.

How we think and feel about ourselves, as well as how we respond to and give to others, is first learned within the family. Familial love is more than a comforting bond; it is also a strategic biological and moral mechanism that helps related individuals benefit from cooperation.[184]

Parents and teachers recognise the importance of raising children to act ethically and make sound judgements. Every child deserves the opportunity to develop strong moral habits and critical reasoning skills. Without these abilities, children may struggle to trust their own judgement or become vulnerable to negative influences they can't properly assess or resist.[52] Young people need consistent positive moral guidance to help them find their identity and feel safe and cared for at home and at school – and the family is key in this. Genuine love does not encourage young people to do what they want and let them believe anything they want. It sets boundaries and guides children towards values that promote their wellbeing and the wellbeing of others.

Families that display empathy, responsibility and the ability to form social relationships enable individual family member to internalise these values. Young people from supportive and nurturing families are more likely to develop moral aspirations that prioritise the welfare of others. Conversely, families that lack empathy can hinder the development of moral values and behaviours in their children.[27]

Family members in a loving family care for one another and cultivate relationships based on shared values, interdependence, mutual responsibility and collective prosperity. Kim[185] suggests that co-ownership is crucial for fostering mutual prosperity within families and society. The family can serve as a model for co-ownership and mutual prosperity, harmonising the needs of both the individual and the whole family through love. In many families, this interdependence is reflected practically, such as when the family home is passed down to children when parents pass away.

Wood[186] highlights that the spirit of mutual support within families should be celebrated, as it provides a vital social safety net that governments alone can't offer.

Ultimately, the family does more than shape moral understanding; it nurtures the very capacity to love. It is within this intimate setting that we first learn empathy, trust and care – lessons that form the foundation of all future relationships. In this sense, the family truly becomes a school of love.

The Family as a School of Love

'The family is the school of love; it is the most important school in life.'
—**S M Moon**

Families form the foundations of society, serving as the building blocks upon which communities are built. They are intended to serve as schools of love, values and personal development – sources of life, love, ideals and peace. Peace is not only a global aspiration but also a vital condition within families, societies and nations. Its foundation lies in the inner peace within each individual and each family. When peace and love thrive within families, they radiate outward, shaping society and ultimately contributing to global peace.[17]

Children are naturally self-focused, but through interactions with their parents, siblings and extended family, they gradually learn to consider the needs of others. They come to learn that the wellbeing of the family is just as important as their own. When sibling love is nurtured and developed, it creates a foundation for deeper connections, making it easier to extend that love later in life to a spouse or partner, or others beyond the family.(52)

The values and ideals instilled within the family have a profound and lasting impact, often shaping our lives and being passed down through generations. My life and values were shaped by the love and hope my parents had for me, even if at times I resisted this. When parents express their expectations and hopes for their child, these aspirations become integral to the child's self-image and identity, helping them develop their own expectations and hopes for their future.(187) Conversely, when misguided values are passed on, children may internalise them with damaging consequences to themselves and to their relationships.

> My life and values were shaped by the love and hope my parents had for me.

Activity #58: Your formative emotional experiences

Write your name in the middle of the spiderweb and write down in the surrounding web sections the emotional experiences you have had in your family that have formed your personality.

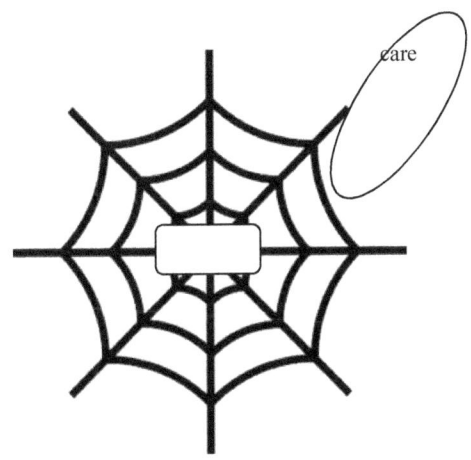

Social Challenges to Family Life

In the modern world, family life has undergone major social and economic changes. These shifts have created challenges that strongly indicate the need to foster strong, stable families. Demographers studying developed nations have expressed concern about the erosion of the family as an institution, with dire consequences for society.

For instance, the time and energy invested in children within their homes form a vital component of a nation's social capital. Such investment creates a strong foundation for children's future relationships and their ability to contribute positively to society. When parents spend time helping with homework, reading to their children or talking about school, they do more than support their academic success. They model care, perseverance, hard work and the value of education.

Even simple habits such as regular family meals create valuable *bonding social capital*. Shared meals provide a consistent opportunity for open communication, where family members can share their day, discuss challenges and reinforce family values. It is undeniable that this form of investment is declining as parents spend less time assisting their children to achieve academic and life outcomes. Reduced family time, longer working hours and high levels of family break-ups all reduce this form of social capital.[175]

Shifting attitudes towards marriage and family

The relationship between husband and wife serves as the foundation of family life, highlighting the importance of establishing this relationship on stable and healthy terms. Over the past 50 years, however, some academics, the media and the entertainment industry have promoted perspectives and agendas that undermine the foundational role of marriage in family life and the family as a core facilitator of values and communal life. This agenda has gradually been institutionalised through education, law and politics, reshaping societal views and structures over time.[9]

Media has increasingly highlighted personal happiness and fulfillment as a primary goal, even if it conflicts with family roles. Marriage is often portrayed with scepticism. Television shows and movies frequently depict divorce, infidelity and the challenges of long-term relationships, normalising these experiences and sometimes presenting marriage and family as a difficult or optional path rather than a societal cornerstone. Likewise, academic perspectives increasingly challenge the notion that marriage is a prerequisite for a fulfilling life.

Divorce

Separation and divorce have had the most profound impact on family life.[188] In Australia, there is a general acceptance for an unhappy marriage to end, even if there are children involved.[183] Divorce is a complex and often painful process, and there is no single reason that applies to every couple. This could be because of a lack of commitment, infidelity, abuse and other issues.

Divorce introduces a significant disruption to a child's sense of security and routine. It comes with significant negative health, financial, emotional and social costs. In contrast, marriage offers important benefits related to wellbeing, longevity and wealth, contributing to a healthier and more stable life for individuals and families.[174]

The impact on children

Children raised by single parents are at greater risk of living in poverty and experiencing health, academic and behavioural problems than children growing up with both parents.[189] Research consistently indicates a correlation between family structure and high school dropout rates. Children from one-parent families are about twice as likely to drop out of high school compared to those from two-parent families. They have fewer years of schooling and are less likely to attain a bachelor's degree compared to those from two-parent families.[190] These children are also more likely to have a child during their teenage years and to be idle, both out of school and out of the labour force, as young adults.

Furthermore, children from divorced families often have less access to the time and attention of two adults, leading to reduced parental supervision and emotional support.[191, 192] Research also suggests that having divorced parents is the highest risk factor for divorce in one's own marriage, which may be because children of divorced parents receive poor socialisation and role modelling for healthy marriages. Additionally, children of divorced parents often have more behavioural problems that negatively affect their intimate relationships in adulthood.[188]

For children, divorce is associated with difficulty relating to peers and family members, lower scholastic achievement, lower self-esteem, and more strained peer and parent–child relationships than those of their same-age peers from intact families.[193]

However, it should be noted that many single parents and extended families do a very good job at parenting despite additional challenges. Parental involvement is a powerful predictor of a child's educational success and single parents can successfully raise children who achieve academic success.

The impact on mental health
Mental health issues associated with divorce for women and men include disruption of a primary affectional bond, insecurity, depression, hostility, self-acceptance issues, and a decline in personal growth and positive relations with others.[188, 194] Additionally, problem drinking is more prevalent among unmarried men, and the end of marriage often leads to increased cigarette and alcohol consumption in men, likely linked to the stress and emotional challenges associated with divorce.[191]

Economic Challenges to Family Life
Some economists advocate for fostering and supporting strong families as a key to societal wellbeing. A 2011 report from the Organisation for Economic Co-operation and Development (OECD), which analyses policies aimed at improving economic and social wellbeing worldwide, warned that governments over the coming decades will face difficulties in sustaining social security expenditure for seniors, single-adult households and single-parent families. As the number of such households rises, governments may struggle to provide the necessary care, leaving more individuals without

adequate support. The OECD report argued that single adults, single-parent families and the elderly will become 'new poor' in the future.[195]

Without family support, individuals living alone rely heavily on government assistance. Conversely, fostering and supporting families and extended families allows them to naturally provide the physical and mental care family members need.

Rapid population ageing, as seen in China and other nations, further challenges social security systems and expenditure and economic growth. Changes in population age and birth rates have long-term economic impacts, highlighting the importance of strong family structures.[196]

Activity #59: Your family challenges

1. Reflect on challenges your family has faced. How did your family cope with these challenges?
2. Use a Y-Chart to describe the three aspects of the topic: what family challenges look like (actions, body language, expression, posture, choices), sound like (tone of voice, words, the way you communicate) and feel like (your internal experience: confidence, calmness, hesitation, discomfort, strength).
3. You may also *'think, pair and share'* with another person.

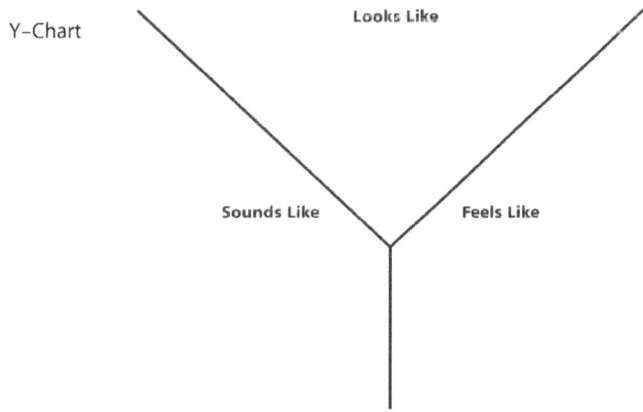

The Source of Morality is the Family

The greatest influence on our values and morality, for most of us, is our family values and love. The foundation of morality is love – considering the good of others, even at one's own expense. For Gandhi, love was a powerful tool for social transformation.[197] It's clear that a standard of values is shaped by the ethics of love cultivated within the family. As Nelson Mandela wisely said…

> 'No one is born hating another person because of the colour of his skin, or his background, or his religion. People must learn to hate, and if they can learn to hate, they can be taught to love, for love comes more naturally to the human heart than its opposite.' — Nelson Mandela

The love shared between a husband and wife establishes the standard of values guiding their behaviour towards one another and serves as a model for their children. It provides a powerful foundation for fostering respect, understanding and compassion within the family. When a couple marries, they make a commitment guided by the standard of love they have established between them. For parents, their standard of values – and their primary moral compass – is their love for their children, which shapes their decisions and actions. For children, their standard of values is their love for their parents. These intergenerational bonds of love help establish the core values that guide our lives.

Activity #60: Explore the values of love in your relationships

Write in your journal and share with another:

1. What are the values associated with love in your relationships – with your partner, children, siblings and your parents?
2. Are you willing to change for your partner, parents or siblings? If so, how?

The Family is an Integrative Whole

An integrative explanation of existence, rooted in holism in science, suggests that life has a purpose that progresses towards increasingly complex, interconnected wholes. (See Chapter 4) Life is a process of integration, where different elements combine to form more effective, unified systems. [58]

As previously explained, the purpose of life for an individual is to achieve a state of inner unity by harmonising mind and body and aligning thoughts and actions with love and personal values, forming a unified whole. By doing so, we move towards becoming a fully integrated, authentic individual. The process is called 'individuation' by Karl Jung. Psychological challenges are seen as opportunities for growth on this path.

Similarly, relationships within families – between husband and wife, children and the extended family – can also reflect this unity, forming a larger unified whole grounded in love. [20]

The four sphere of love in the family

Within the family unit, we can potentially experience four distinct spheres, or expressions, of love:

- Conjugal love
- Parental love for children
- Children's love for their parents
- Sibling love

The emotions and experiences within these spheres play a crucial role in shaping our values and who we become. Love is central to these bonds, influencing how we connect, develop and interact with each other (see Figure 27).

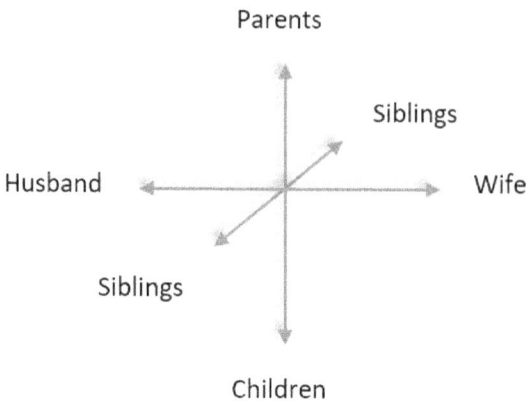

Figure 28 Four expressions of love

In our lifetime, we can develop our hearts in these four spheres of love so that we can experience the richness and depth of love that these relationships offer. If we have not loved our parents, our siblings, our spouse and our children enough, we can still do this, if time and circumstances permit. When my mother was alive, I always felt that I must love her more. I am sure she felt the same way about me.

We can also love others outside our immediate family, embracing others as part of our extended family. Family, love and connection are never far away if we look – and are open – to seeing them!

Activity #61: Your experience of four spheres of love

Write in the boxes below.

How did emotional experiences associated with the four spheres of love shape who you are, for good and for ill?

Debrief: What did you learn from this? What would you change?

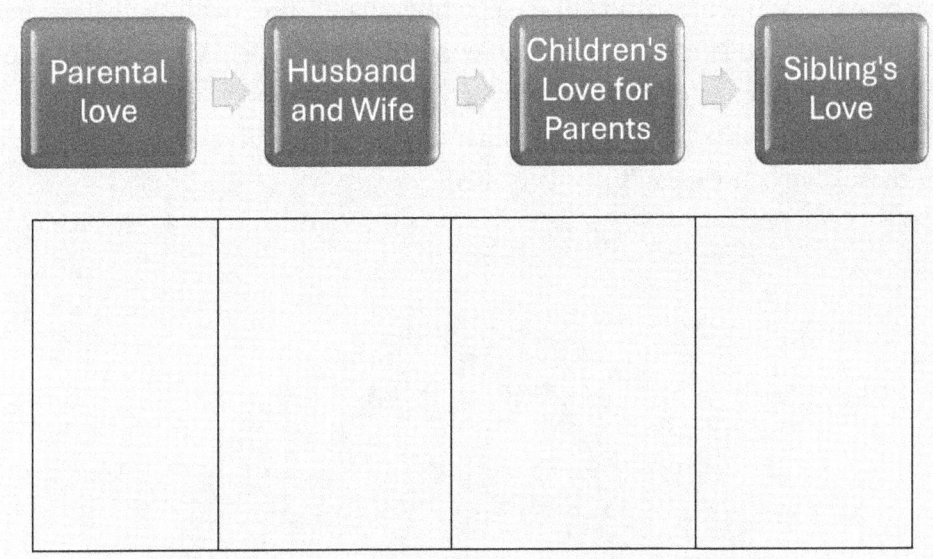

Extended Family and Spheres of Support

In the family, each sphere or relationship opens a new and richer experience of love and support. Each sphere builds upon the previous one, expanding like concentric circles that nurture growth at every stage of life. Beyond the nuclear family, grandparents, aunties and uncles, friends, schools, spiritual communities, clubs and so on form additional layers of connection and support.

Dr Ungar[198], a noted scholar on resilience, maintains that relationships and support structures that exist in the extended family, friendships, community and society are the spheres of love that allow children and adults to develop and experience wellbeing (see Figure 28). These are important developmental assets.

People who enjoy social support from family, friends and their community are generally happier, have fewer health problems and live longer. Conversely, a lack of social ties is associated with depression, cognitive decline in later life and increased risk of premature death.[174, 177] Positive peer relationships can also buffer against the negative behavioural impacts of parental discord.[199]

Moreover, individuals who enjoy spending quality time with their partner's family and friends are less likely to commit infidelity.[200] Grandchildren of divorced families often benefit from increased involvement with grandparents through emotional support and having less strain in their lives. The importance of these connections can't be overstated.

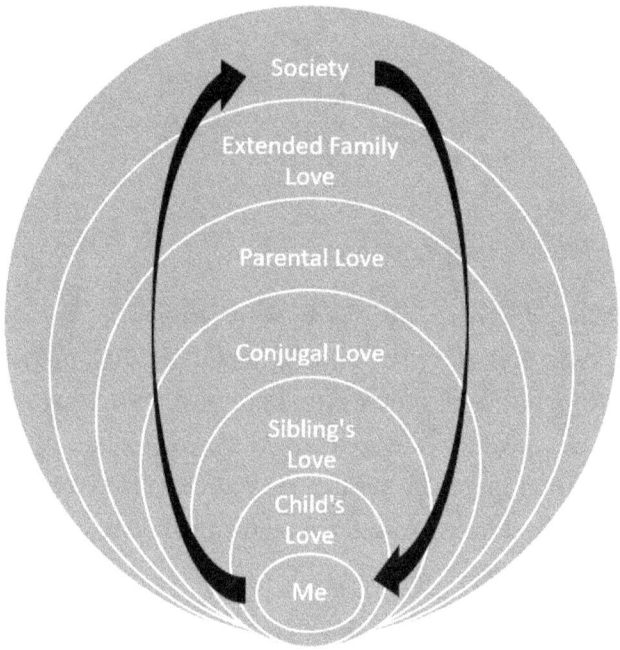

Figure 29 Spheres of Love and Developmental Assets

Our identity, self-esteem and resilience are deeply rooted in all these relationships. It takes a village to raise a child, which means that an entire community needs to interact with children for them to grow into well-adjusted, thriving individuals. These spheres of love and support not only help children grow into happy, functional adults but also establish the standard by which they relate to others in society. This interdependence and reciprocity are indicated by the two arrows in Figure 28.

A peaceful society and world mirror the dynamics of a functional family. A child learns to love by first being loved. To truly love one's neighbour as yourself, one must learn self-love – a foundation laid in the early years of life, when nurturing love shapes a child's ability to extend love to others.[201]

Our hope as parents is to raise children who can contribute to the welfare of others, their nation and the world. When families focus only on their own interests, society loses the kindness and altruism that naturally flow from loving homes. Living for the sake of others means recognising that our wellbeing is interconnected – the individual contributes to the family, the family supports the community, the community strengthens the nation, and the nation serves the wider world (see Figure 29).

Noted Professor of Sociology Brigitte Berger[202] observed that families create culture; good family members become good citizens in their nations and the world. When such individuals leave their homes, they are appreciated by others in society for their values. When they meet older people, they have a kind attitude towards them, and when they meet younger people, they have the heart of an older sibling or parent towards them.

The four spheres of love will be discussed more in ensuing chapters.

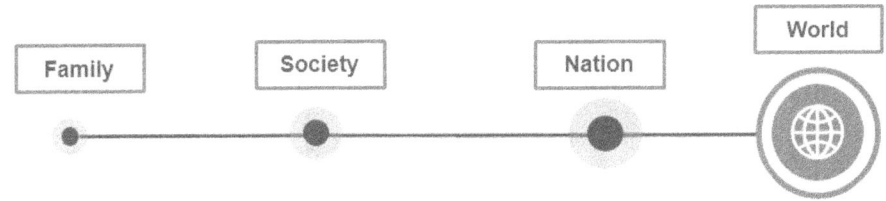

Figure 30 The global layers of support

Activity #62: Mapping your support network

Write in your journal and share with another:

1. Describe how the relationships and support structures in your extended family, friendships, community and society have contributed to your growth and wellbeing.

2. How has your family values shaped the way you treat others in society?

3. Write your name in the middle of the spiderweb. Write down the people and structures that supported you and made you who you are. Also, write down how you support others in this web.

Debrief:

- How easy is it for you to ask for help when you need it?
- If it feels easy, what experiences or relationships have helped you feel safe to do so?
- If it feels difficult, what thoughts or feelings arise when you consider asking for help?

1. How does it feel to ask your parent, sibling or spouse for support in particular? What makes it easier or harder with them?

2. What might help you feel more comfortable in receiving care and support from others?

Dysfunctional Families

While many families function as nurturing schools of love and morality, others may fall short. Unfortunately, families can sometimes become 'dysfunctional schools', where unhealthy values and a lack of love create lasting emotional damage. Many of our insecurities, prejudices and emotional struggles originate from these toxic family dynamics. When love is absent and relationships deteriorate, individuals can learn and perpetuate harmful patterns, shaping their future interactions and relationships.

For example, parent–child relationship research shows that early experiences, such as rejection by parents, contribute to the formation of dysfunctional core beliefs such as 'Unless I am loved, I am worthless'. These can deeply impact a child's self-esteem and the way they form relationships later in life.[41] This is why at the start of this book, I wrote that you should take a mature approach to personal growth, starting with the fundamental realisation that you are inherently a good person with intrinsic worth. Parents need to foster this sense of intrinsic worth in their children.

> ...you are inherently a good person with intrinsic worth

Additionally, adolescents who witness their parents fighting often feel anxious when it comes to forming their own relationships and may find it harder to connect with others outside the family. Children also tend to learn and model their parents' behaviours, especially when it comes to conflict resolution. They adopt these patterns of behaviour and methods of dealing with conflict, which can carry over into their peer and romantic relationships.[203]

Research suggests that a history of childhood abuse and exposure to spousal violence are significant risk factors for perpetrating child abuse.[204] Therefore, many adults who abuse children have themselves been abused. An Australian report found that children with harmful sexual behaviours are often victims or survivors themselves, and may have been affected by one or more adverse childhood experiences such as sexual, physical and emotional abuse; neglect; exposure to family violence; or exposure to and use of pornography.[205]

A significant percentage of sexual abuse is committed by family members or other caregivers who are close to the child. The closer the emotional bond between the perpetrator and the victim, the greater the potential for harm, as the trust and dependency within these relationships can make the abuse even more damaging.(206) There are no closer relationships than family ones, so the harm can be profound.

The absence of love, particularly in childhood, can have disastrous effects. The anthropologist Ashley Montagu(201) maintained that love is without question the most important experience in the life of a human being. The newborn baby is extraordinarily sensitive to love and relies on it for normal development. The baby behaves as if it expects to be loved, and when this expectation is not met, reacts in a grievously disappointed manner.

There is strong evidence suggesting that not only does a baby need love, but it also has an innate desire *to* love. All drives are oriented towards both receiving and giving love. If a baby doesn't receive love, it is unable to give love in return. This pattern extends from infancy into adulthood. From the moment of birth, a baby requires a reciprocal exchange of love with its mother. It has been universally acknowledged that the mother-infant relationship, more than any other, defines the very essence of love. The infant suffers no greater loss than the deprivation of a mother's love, and maternal rejection is often seen as a contributing factor to neurotic or behavioural issues in children.(201)

> ... the mother-infant relationship, more than any other, defines the very essence of love.

Children who experience maternal rejection may develop externalising behaviours as a way of acting out or seeking attention. For example, a child who feels neglected might become aggressive towards peers, exhibit oppositional defiance or engage in delinquent behaviour.(207) Maternal rejection is also strongly linked to internalising problems such as anxiety, depression and low self-esteem. A child who feels unloved may adopt this belief, leading to a profound sense of unworthiness and a negative self-image.

Research has found a link between insecure attachment between parents and children to delinquent behaviours in youth. These young people often have problems with attachment to parents and in parental communication and satisfaction. Attachment deficits may also influence the degree of control over inappropriate sexual urges. Additionally, youth attachment to parents influences the quality of friendships. Interventions with troubled youth can begin by targeting family attachment and enhancing communication skills with parents and reducing feelings of anger and alienation.[208]

Activity #63: Layers of connection

Write your name in the centre of a web and write down in the surrounding sections the layers of connections that have undermined you, and how.

'In a great romance, each person plays a part the other really likes.'
—*Elizabeth Ashley*

12

Conjugal Love
(Sphere 1)
Dr John Bellavance and Dr Rafia Naz

To fully understand the positive impact of the four love dimensions, we begin with the first sphere – the bond between spouses, the love of our life partner. The cornerstone of a healthy family is a couple united by love, grounded in sound values and personal qualities. This subsystem ideally exists prior to the birth of children and continues throughout childhood and adolescence. This union is crucial for building flourishing families and, consequently, a harmonious society, given the interconnectedness of family and social life.

However, the relationship between a man and a woman is not simple or easy. It is influenced by a complex interplay of biological, psychological and social factors that shape their ways of thinking, communicating and interacting. Building a great marriage requires ongoing work; like a garden, it must be cultivated regularly. When two adults with shared values, mature love and psychological affinity meet, romantic love can become a pathway not only to sexual and emotional happiness but also to personal growth. Two people dedicated to personal growth can stimulate personal development in each other.[209]

The Benefits of Marriage
Dr John Bellavance

People are searching for 'the one true love'. Some may ask, why is marriage important in this pursuit? I once asked a young woman I know, 'What are you doing on the weekend?' She replied, 'I am watching *Bachelorettes* on TV, on my own with a bottle of wine.' I thought to myself: *It is a deep human aspiration to find our prince charming or our princess.*

I saw this question posted on Quora:

> 'Depression is killing me after my breakup. I lost passion and purpose in everything. I feel that I need someone I can love and who loves me back, and to share our life moments together. I can't live without it. What should I do?'

This reminded me that we all need someone to love and who loves us in return. Parents' greatest wish is that their children will find someone they can love and be loved in return.

Throughout history and across cultures, people have consistently formed long-term intimate relationships. This pattern suggests that such relationships offer essential benefits, including the reliable support of an intimate partner for both themselves and their children.[210]

With increasing public recognition of the vital role that couple relationships play in health, work productivity and parent–child wellbeing, research into understanding, predicting and enhancing relationship quality has surged. Marriage is linked to numerous benefits, including better physical and mental health, economic wellbeing and improved academic performance in children.[210]

Marriage is linked to numerous benefits...

Marriage significantly contributes to the wellbeing of both spouses. It provides social support that aids stress management, fosters a sense of purpose, and creates a sense of obligation that discourages risky behaviours while promoting healthy ones. Furthermore, marriage offers tangible advantages, including enhanced material wellbeing, improved health, greater educational opportunities and increased safety.[174, 210] It also expands social networks, connecting individuals to supportive in-laws and other social groups.[191]

Young adults who feel confident in their social and romantic abilities also report higher self-esteem and fewer depressive symptoms.[203] In stark contrast, unhappy marriages are linked to a cascade of negative stress-related effects, including poor physical health, high blood pressure, weakened immunity, increased mortality and mental health issues. Moreover, low marital quality negatively impacts work productivity and children's wellbeing.[211]

Children raised in families where the relationship between husband and wife is stable are generally healthier, better educated and more likely to avoid poverty than those who experience family transitions. According to the US Census Bureau, one in four children live without a biological, step or adoptive father in the home.[212] Research shows that a father's absence affects children in numerous unfortunate ways such as increased likelihood of behavioural problems, while a father's presence makes a positive difference in the lives of both children and mothers.[213]

> *This is not to discredit single-parent families or divorced parents but to acknowledge the role both parents play in the lives of children. Many examples exist of successful single parenting.*

Is there a difference between cohabiting parents and married ones, particularly when it comes to stability and outcomes for their children?

Research shows that married parents are more likely to stay together than cohabiting ones. Two-thirds of cohabiting parents split up before their child reaches age 12, compared with one-quarter of married parents. The fact that married couples are more likely to stay together is an important finding with respect to the importance of marriage commitment.[214]

Activity #64: Personal benefits of marriage

Explain how your marriage, your parents' marriage or your long-term relationship has benefited you and your family?

Core Values and Qualities of a Good Marriage
Dr John Bellavance

Marriage is a journey, not a destination. It is a journey of love that can create life, expand values and cultivate love in the family and society. This relationship plays an important role in our happiness, our capacity to love our children and even our effectiveness as leaders. Understanding the characteristics that underpin a positive relationship in a couple, and what undermines these, is needed.

Many single adults turn to online dating sites to find a future partner. Observing these platforms, physical attraction and shared interests and hobbies often appear as key markers of a successful match, which can be a good starting point. While initial attraction can be powerful, personal interests and desires often shift over time.

Studies indicate that college students using dating apps are more likely to engage in risky sexual behaviours. Specifically, they are twice as likely to have had multiple sexual partners in the past year and are 1.4 times more likely to have engaged in sex under the influence of alcohol.[215] These findings suggest that while online dating platforms can facilitate connection, they do may not consistently facilitate the formation of stable, long-term relationships.

Becoming the right person

So how do you find your true love, and once you do, what are the qualities that underpin that relationship? In short, it is about finding the right person but also *becoming* the right person.

Recent research suggests that while the compatibility of personal characteristics in couples is important, the effort made by each spouse to make the relationship work is the most important factor[216] – becoming the right person. The partnership you build and how appreciative you are of your partner says more about the quality of your relationship than either of your personalities.

Abilities: Making love work

Don't focus so much on whether a person fits your type or whether they tick all your boxes. Instead, think about how you're engaging with each other and whether the relationship feels satisfying. The lesson is that each of us creates compatibility, attachment and romance. Making relationships work relies primarily on considering the needs of the other and striving to improve oneself for the other.

This brings us to consider how to become the right person and the qualities we bring to the relationships. Key qualities that contribute to a healthy relationship include:

- love
- appreciation for one another
- responsiveness
- commitment
- emotional regulation
- effective communication
- support for each other's goals
- conflict resolution skills
- gender-equitable behaviours.

Research shows that out of these abilities, females outscore males in communication, knowledge of partner and self-management, while males outscore women in conflict resolution.[217]

Given the powerful impact of relationships on health and happiness, relationship science seeks to understand why some partnerships thrive more than others. We need to know what predicts how satisfied and committed we will be with our partner. Research shows that risk factors include conflict, depression and insecure attachment. Yet, when couples establish appreciation for each other, sexual satisfaction, low conflict and perceived commitment, these individual risk factors may have less influence.[211] Gottman's research shows that day-to-day interactions – small bids to connect with one's partner – also play a vital role.[218]

Activity #65: Making relationships work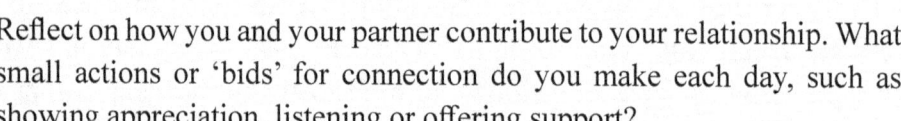

Reflect on how you and your partner contribute to your relationship. What small actions or 'bids' for connection do you make each day, such as showing appreciation, listening or offering support?

Using a Y-Chart, describe how these efforts look like (e.g. attentive body language, small acts of care, staying present), sound like (e.g. warm tone, appreciative words, open communication) and feel like (e.g. connection, reassurance, calmness, trust).

You could also *'think, pair and share'* with another person or couple to exchange ideas on the qualities that help relationship grow in alignment with your values and shared purpose.

Note for those not currently in a relationship:

You can still complete this activity by reflecting on past relationships, or by considering close friendships, family connections or work partnerships where mutual effort and communication are important. Alternatively, use this reflection to imagine the kind of relationship you would like to build in the future. *Ask yourself:*

- What would healthy connection *look, sound* and *feel* like for me?
- What qualities would I want to bring to a future relationship?
- What values would guide how I give and receive care?

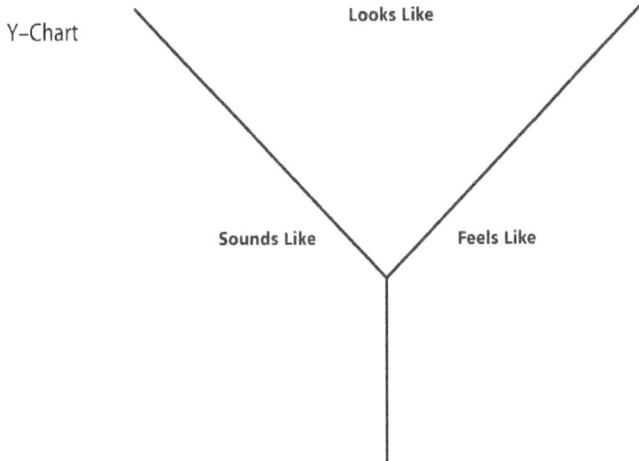

Treating your spouse with care

One of the biggest rewards of a long-term relationship is feeling deeply loved and cared for.[219] Love can be expressed through acts of service, respect, giving each other time and attention (taking notice and acknowledging what the other is saying and doing), and sexual intimacy.

Love is also about caring about how to improve and even change yourself for your partner. Each person contributes something the other values and cherishes. If you don't know how to go about that, inquire. Ask him/her. How to please one's partner sexually and remaining attractive to them is also important. My wife often said that to become a good couple, we must each be willing to change for the other and act in ways that are pleasing to them. Make time for intimacy. 'Treat your wife like a princess,' my wife and I used to tell our sons. I love doing this at least once a day. I bring her a cup of tea on a nice tray or make her lunch, and I tell her she is beautiful and how much I love her. She responds with a smile.

In his article, 'The Gentleman's Guide to Dating: How to Be a Man in a Sea of Boys', James Michael Sama[220] maintains that to set yourself apart, show a woman that you are genuinely interested in her and are willing to put in the consistent effort – not just during the first few dates, but over time, potentially for life. If this sounds like a lot of work, consider this: a woman who loves and cares for you will always match or exceed your efforts.

Activity #66: Nurting your spousal relationship

Write in your journal and share with another:

1. How do you consider the needs of your spouse?

2. How do you strive to improve yourself for your spouse?

Photograph By Raja (Khalsa Studio) Own work, CC BY-SA 4.0,

https://commons.wikimedia.org/w/index.php?curid=107394062

Being committed to the relationship

While romantic love is a strong motivator to form personal relationships, it can fade when those relationships encounter challenges. For many today, marriage is not a popular option, or it is considered an outdated institution where it is unreasonable to expect couples to stay together for a lifetime. There is more social pressure than ever before to be individually happy, and this may outweigh the need to make a marriage work. Society has accepted that life partners need not be for life anymore.

> ...the family institution carries an ethical obligation that contributes to the collective good of society [3]

However, although a percentage of marriages end in divorce, this doesn't mean a lack of faith in marriage as an institution.

Cohabitation has become a common pathway to marriage for many couples, and the outcomes of these relationships are complex and depend on a variety of factors. While there are potential risks, data show that many cohabiting couples do transition to marriage or form long-term, stable unions. However, it doesn't generally imply a lifetime commitment to stay together. Cohabitating couples seem to bring different, more individualistic values to the union than those who marry.[191]

A study published in *Evolutionary Psychology* reports that being in a committed relationship allows participants to experience more positive emotions, such as love and passion, while reducing feelings of loneliness. [219] In most cultures, marriage is celebrated publicly, with family and friends witnessing the couple's union. This public recognition reflects the longstanding value placed on marriage as the bedrock for the couple's life together and for future generations. Regardless of the level of commitment between a couple, society continues to recognise marriage as an institution that provides the greatest stability.

Despite its diverse forms, the family as an institution carries an ethical obligation that contributes to the collective good of society.[3] As a social institution, marriage is underpinned by moral obligations that form the foundation of families, foster social stability, and provide resilience amidst emotional fluctuations and challenges. We seek a partner with an unwavering desire for exclusive commitment – someone who loves us for our intrinsic selves. This profound love is the source of the loyalty essential for both partnership and parenting.[184]

Lutz [3] maintains that understanding marriage as a social institution requires understanding love as both an emotion and a virtue – expressed through consistent behaviours. Emotion alone is too unstable a base upon which to build a permanent relationship. Romantic-based marriages may end when romantic love or sexual attraction fades. A virtuous society requires an understanding of marriage as a social institution that perseveres through both bad times and good.

Love means living for the sake of others in good times and in hard times.

As societies have transitioned from traditional to liberal structures, marriage has undergone a corresponding transformation, moving from an institutional model to a romantic one. Liberal societies characterised by individualism and liberty (implying freedom from authority) have played a key role in this shift.

The 'soulmate model' of marriage prioritises a strong romantic or emotional bond, with its longevity contingent on personal happiness and fulfillment. This model introduces an inherent tension between marriage as a foundation for social stability and the pursuit of individual freedom and emotional satisfaction.[3]

If love is considered temporary in society, a strong foundation, such as a committed marriage, becomes even more important to hold couples together. Love, friendship, support, trust and commitment are vital to a couple's wellbeing. We can't encourage couples to live a more relaxed relationship, particularly when children are involved, because parents are responsible for a child's welfare.

Commitment remains a crucial value and practice for a successful relationship. Research indicates that a strong commitment to the institution of marriage significantly reduces the likelihood of marital breakdown.[188] Furthermore, relationship and marriage education programs have proven effective in improving relationship satisfaction and communication, but only for couples who are already committed. Notably, these programs show minimal benefit for unmarried couples, highlighting the necessity of pre-existing commitment before marriage or starting a family.[189]

Despite its numerous benefits, marriage rates have declined for several reasons:[191]

1. High divorce rates have eroded public confidence in marriage's long-term stability, discouraging investment in it.
2. Evolving divorce laws have increased the potential negative financial consequences of separation.

3. In a high-divorce environment, men are less inclined towards marriage and parenthood, fearing the potential loss of contact with their children.

4. Public policies supporting single mothers, coupled with shifting societal attitudes towards premarital sex and unmarried childbearing, have also contributed to this decline.

These trends reflect broader cultural shifts away from collective values of commitment and responsibility towards more individualistic notions of freedom and personal fulfilment. As the institution of marriage weakens, so too does one of society's most vital frameworks for nurturing love, stability and moral development within families.

The virtue of love

While love is a powerful emotion, it can change. A successful, lasting marriage needs more than that. The emotion of love is like the spark that starts a fire, but the virtue of love – the conscious decision to act with kindness, patience and commitment even when you don't feel like it – is the steady fuel that keeps it burning. Marriage, as a social institution, is built on this foundation of commitment and shared values, not just fleeting feelings.

...the virtue of love – the conscious decision to act with kindness, patience and commitment ...

Activity #67: Layers of connection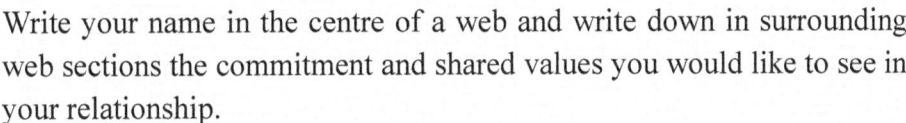

Write your name in the centre of a web and write down in surrounding web sections the commitment and shared values you would like to see in your relationship.

Managing yourself well

Knowing and managing yourself well is essential to building and sustaining a loving, trustworthy relationship. For example, managing your sexual impulses is critical. Sexual infidelity is a major source of conflict in relationships and leads to a decline in wellbeing. Unfaithful partners feel confused and ashamed. Betrayed partners feel hurt and angry, lose trust, have decreased confidence in relationships, feel abandoned and have lower self-esteem.

Additionally, infidelity is the most frequently reported reason for divorce, while sterility is second and abuse is third.[200] Most of us don't approve of infidelity, yet studies suggest around 30% to 40% of unmarried relationships and 18% to 20% of marriages see at least one incident of sexual infidelity.[221] Also, watching pornography may be considered a form of infidelity.

If opportunities arise for sexual encounters outside a committed relationship, commitment and managing ourselves is vital. We need to be clear on our values and aware that sexual impulses can affect how we think or behave in certain situations. Impulse control is important to not hurt the ones we love.

Activity #68: Managing yourself

Use a Y-Chart to describe what managing yourself well for your spouse or future spouse sounds like, looks like and feels like.

For example:

- **Sounds** like – honest conversations, calm tone, taking responsibility for your feelings.
- **Looks** like – setting boundaries, avoiding situations that test your commitment.
- **Feels** like – self-respect, peace, trust, confidence.

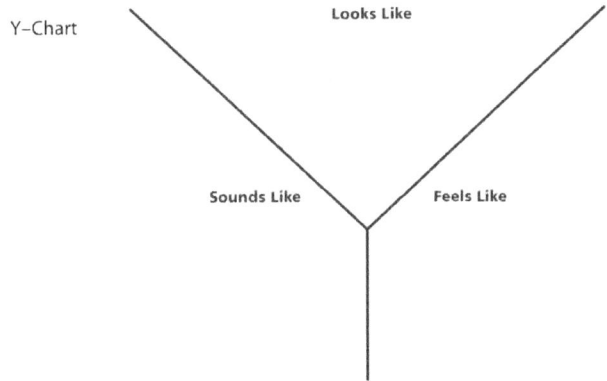

Communication – know your spouse and support their aspirations

Communication breakdowns inevitably lead to relationship difficulties. Effective and respectful communication is paramount for a thriving marriage. Crucial to this is the ability to actively listen to one's partner with empathy and understanding. Deeply understanding each other's core needs, values, thoughts, feelings, aspirations and preferences is a significant predictor of relationship satisfaction. Notably, in one study couples who remained married turned towards each other for genuine communication and connection 86% of the time, compared to only 33% for those who later divorced.[218]

Additionally, a relationship becomes the strongest when two people discover they have shared values and aspirations. Values such as commitment to the marriage, trust and the willingness to see another's viewpoint are important. Research also suggests that faith-based values and cultural and family practices in marriage, such as having children, reduce rates of divorce.[188]

Researchers found that nearly 93% of participants identified support as a significant benefit of being in a relationship. This can include having someone who provides comfort during difficult times, shares daily responsibilities and offers encouragement in pursuing goals.[219]

Based on our love for each other, my wife and I found our shared values and came to know each other's aspirations. This allowed us to support each other's goals and aspirations. To support this process, we listen deeply – striving even to be aware of the unspoken.

Activity #69: Love in practice

Write in your journal and share with others:

1. Have I paid enough attention to my actions and reactions with respect to my spouse/partner today?
2. Have I practised acting in a loving way towards them?
3. How has my relationship with my spouse/partner helped me to grow in positive ways?
4. How have I helped my partner to grow?

Conflict resolution

Adolescents' social skills and their ability to effectively resolve interpersonal conflicts are associated with the development and maintenance of peer and romantic relationships. Handling conflict situations well is a good indicator of the future success of a marriage. We often want to be right and put our views forward, expecting others to listen and accept these. There is a lot to say about being able to think deeply and listen before speaking and acting. We need to be patient in a relationship, ready to forgive and apologise when needed. The best way to improve our relationships is to accept feedback and use that information to improve oneself. If we can't do this in our relationship, it will be hard to do with others. Instead of getting upset when we get criticised, it is better to be thankful that our partner is honest with us.

Activity #70: Active listening and self-reflection in relationships

Write in your journal and share with others:

1. Do you listen to your partner before speaking and acting?

2. Do you accept feedback and use that information to improve yourself?

Gender-equitable beliefs and behaviours

Promoting equitable gender beliefs and practices is essential for healthy marriages, effective child rearing, and the cultivation of positive values that children carry into their future families and society. An Australian report suggests that gender inequality is an important underlying causal factor in domestic, family and sexual violence.[205]

A marriage counsellor I know with many years of experience shared that marriage is a partnership of equals. The UN maintains that equality will not be achievable without greater equality in families.[222] In some family seminars that I have attended, the conversation about who is the 'boss' at home and 'who wears the pants' often comes up. A friend of mine shed new light on this and told me that we should not put focus on power relations between men and women, but on understanding what constitutes a positive and mutually beneficial relationship. We need to foster and practise gender-equitable beliefs and behaviours and combat rigid gender role stereotypes.

Positive male and female relationships need to be modelled in the family. I have found that my four sons respect and serve their wives, and I believe this is partly because I modelled this with my wife. Actions speak louder than words. I had seen how my father served and respected my mother and did his share of cooking and household work. Family life today is often based on both partners sharing in paid and unpaid work and constantly negotiating arrangements that suit their mutual needs. It is up to all of us to model serving and egalitarian relationships at home and in society.

Activity #71: A gender lens

Write in your journal and share with another:

This activity encourages you to examine your own perspectives. Imagine viewing the world through a gender lens, like wearing spectacles. One lens reveals the viewpoints, needs and realities of women, while the other reveals those of men. Your resulting vision is a synthesis of both perspectives.

1. What do you perceive when you look through this combined lens?
2. What are the attitudes and beliefs that justify, excuse, conceal or minimise improper male and female relationships?
3. What does it mean to be a man and what does it means to be a woman, for you?

The Impact of Respectful Communication on Spouse Relations and Marriage Satisfaction
Dr Rafia Naz

Exploring the link between respectful communication and enhanced spouse relations, this section highlights its impact on marriage satisfaction. Marriage is a fundamental institution across religions and cultures, and effective communication is vital for its success and the creation of a happy family life.[223]

Respectful communication enhances affection between couples.[224-226] Culture influences the quality of socialisation, which shapes behaviours. [227] Thus, good communication strengthens relationship ties.[228] Crucially, both the amount of time couples spend together and the quality of that time significantly impact marital wellbeing and the development of emotional honesty.[229]

Respectful communication between couples is a strong predictor of marriage satisfaction. Studies indicate that negative communications and interactions are intertwined with inferior marriage relationship satisfaction, while affirmative communications and interactions lead to higher marriage satisfaction. A lack of respectful communication can contribute to marital breakdown.[230] Research consistently demonstrates that respectful communication between couples is a strong predictor of immediate marriage satisfaction.[231-233] Studies also reveal a clear link between negative communication patterns and lower marital satisfaction, while positive communication and interactions correlate with higher satisfaction levels.[234, 235]

Respectful and open communication

Marriage can be understood as an institution or culturally constructed. Culturally, how spouses relate to each other will invariably differ; however, the common denominator is respectable communication. I come from an extended family, raised by a single mother. I entered an intermarriage with my husband, who was from a different religious and cultural background. The best part of our relationship has been our honest dialogue about all issues from the outset. I was very privileged to find a spouse who decided to convert to my faith, Islam. The level of disagreement in our relationship has been low because our communication is open and our friendship grounded. We never let disagreements reach a point that becomes unbearable. For me, respectful communication has always been about opening up, sharing, empathising and expressing what is felt.

Values and building trust

The transparent nature of our relationship gave us the platform to sidestep any mind or blame games, which continues today. We gradually worked with each other in trust and on each other's strengths and value systems, even when we differed as individuals. Our value system is something we have always reflected on in our spousal relationship. This has facilitated our comfort level with each other and our relationship satisfaction.

Throughout my six years of marriage, I have focused greatly on verbal and non-verbal communication, on listening and on feedback. My husband, in turn, has offered a great deal of responsiveness. Respectful communication requires that I understand myself and have a high level of awareness about my spouse – his likes and preferences – and this is reciprocal. Marriage satisfaction arises from enhanced understanding, interaction, intimacy, and a bond that enables us to relate and put across our messages clearly. It also depends on being able to talk about important matters and focus on issues even when differences arise – whether these involve career, parenting roles and responsibilities, or other concerns. Respectful communication has been the core of trust-building and appreciation in our relationship.

I know marriage is a two-way street. As individuals coming from differing backgrounds and cultures, working through our differences with respectful communication has enabled us to share a united dream. It has been the key enabler for peace, conflict resolution, problem solving, being a devil's advocate, listening, feedback, empathy, bonding, self-actualisation, self-awareness, self-control, mindful meditation, self-regulation, emotional intelligence (EI) and spiritual intelligence (SI).

From both my studies and personal life, respectful communication plays a decisive role in marriage and significantly influences marital satisfaction. Couples may experience discord simply due to a lack of respectful communication. The lasting strength of a spousal connection, which is heavily reliant on communication, ultimately shapes the relationship.

Activity #72: Respectful communication reflection

Write in your diary and share with another:

1. What does respectful communication mean for you, and how do you see others doing this?
2. If you are married, or in a committed relationship, explain with an example how respectful communication has strengthened your spousal relationship.
3. If you are not married or in a committed relationship, reflect on how you see yourself practising respectful communication in your future marriage or relationship.

The problem with pornography

There are several potential problems associated with teenagers viewing pornography, which can impact their mental, emotional and social development. These issues range from distorted views of sex and relationships to the potential for addiction.

Viewing pornography can affect young people's sexual attitudes, expectations and practices. In Australia, research shows that 90% of boys under the age of 16 have visited a pornography site online, with around 60% of girls doing the same.[236] Other research found that one in four boys and one in 20 girls watch pornography weekly.[237] Recent research suggests that 53% of young men watch pornography once a week, 12% watch it daily, and the average age for young people – boys and girls – to be exposed to pornography for the first time was 13.6 years of age.[205]

What is concerning about viewing pornography is the wrong message of control, pleasure and physical aggression it can give to young people about sexuality. Pornography often presents unrealistic and idealised portrayals of sex that are not representative of healthy, real-world intimacy. Research has shown that boys who view pornography are more likely to engage in verbal and physical sexual aggression, and adolescents who are exposed to violent sexually explicit material were six times more likely to be sexually aggressive than those who were not. Additionally, exposure to pornography was associated with greater acceptance of sexist attitudes about gender and sexual roles, including notions of women as sexual objects.[237, 238] Teenagers' expectations of their first intercourse were more disappointing than the expectations of youth who viewed less sexual content.[239]

A study of 18 to 35 year olds reveals that pornography was the most common avenue for people first hearing about choking during sex (35%), and concluded that 'sexual strangulation has become a mainstream sexual behaviour that is commonly seen in media such as pornography and movies and discussed among friends'.[205]

Pornography, particularly the intense and varied content available online, can tap into the brain's reward system. This can also lead to a desensitisation where less stimulating, real-life sexual experiences become less appealing.

Pornography typically separates sex from emotional intimacy and connection. This can lead to the belief that physical gratification is the primary goal of a relationship, rather than mutual respect, communication and emotional closeness. With respect to adults, a recent report shows that 1 in 3 men, whether married or in a committed dating relationship, said they viewed pornography at least weekly, compared to 1 in 8 of the women who were dating, and 1 in 16 for married women.

- Why is this a problem?

The study found that a third of the women were worried their partner could be more attracted to pornography than to them and might be thinking about pornography during sex. Additionally, the highest levels of relationship stability, commitment and satisfaction were reported by couples in which both partners said they don't view pornography. As frequency of pornography viewing climbed, relationship stability, commitment and satisfaction declined.[240]

In my book *Values in the Digital World*, I conclude that the best solution is to focus on the minds of young people because trying to control the internet use of young people by technical means alone will not work. As a high school IT teacher of 24 years, I can tell you that this does not work. We cannot let young people get their relationship and sex education advice from pornography. Despite much interest shown by national and state governments with respect to values education, research is at a beginning stage with respect to understanding the role of moral values and abilities in the use of Information and Communication Technologies (ICTs) by young people.

Additionally, less is known about how young people conceive moral responsibilities with respect to their uses of ICTs. I have seen some parents and teachers approaching unethical practices with the attitude of either 'putting up with it' or responding with a 'knee jerk' reaction to the 'evils' of technology. Media panics tend to construct most youth activity as risky and ignore the positive ways teens interact online.

Activity #73: Media, sexualisation and its impact

Behind sexualised images in advertising, entertainment and pornography are powerful messages about manhood and womanhood.

- What are these messages?
- How do they shape ideas about gender, relationships and sexual expectations?

In the web below, write a real or fictional teenagers' name in the centre. Around the name, in the surround web sections, write down the potential effects of exposure to sexualised media e.g. changes in body image, relationship expectations, self-esteem, emotional wellbeing and attitudes towards intimacy and respect.

Fostering Sexual Ethics and Healthy Sexual Development

Instead of sexualising young people, adults can help them develop a healthy and positive self-image by:

- focusing on their character, skills and accomplishments
- encouraging them to make their own choices about their bodies, clothing and boundaries
- modelling healthy and respectful relationships in their own life.

The goal is to help young people feel safe and respected, not judged or valued for their physical appearance. It's about empowering them to develop their own identity in a way that is healthy and age appropriate. Two decades ago, the American National Commission on Adolescent Sexual Health wrote the following definition of sexual health:

> *'Sexual health encompasses sexual development and reproductive health, as well as such characteristics as the ability to develop and maintain meaningful interpersonal relationships; appreciate one's own body; interact with both genders in respectful and appropriate ways; and express affection, love and intimacy in ways consistent with one's own values.' (cited in* [241]*)*

Any attempts to foster healthy sexuality need to acknowledge that sexuality is not devoid of values. It can be void of genuine love and care. You can have sex, but it may not be out of love but a sexual urge. Without love and intimacy, sex can become empty, self-serving, ungratifying or even abusive. When sexuality is imbued with love, responsibility and commitment, however, it deeply enhances our happiness. Quality sex education provides young people with opportunities to explore their own values, along with the values and beliefs of their families and communities.

Sexual ethics for teenagers refers to the moral principles that guide their decisions and behaviours regarding sex, intimacy and relationships. It's about more than just a list of rules; it's a framework for making responsible choices that respect themselves and others. By focusing on respect, consent and communication, it helps teenagers build relationships based on trust and mutual care rather than pressure or manipulation. Learning to make ethical choices empowers teenagers and helps them avoid regret, emotional distress and potential harm. It encourages self-respect and the ability to stand up for their own boundaries. Additionally, sexual ethics seek to foster sexual behaviours that are appropriate within the norm for their age and level of development. This is vital for adults to understand that we cannot impose an adult sexual identity on a child or young person.

Sexual ethics can be used to encourage abstinence until a certain level of maturity is reached or marriage. Some sexual ethics approaches may focus on a harm-reduction model, emphasising that sex is a normal part of human development if it is consensual and safe. The key is for teenagers to understand the different perspectives and understand the values they want to guide their personal choices.

As young people move from early to late adolescence, they experience and explore different feelings and behaviours with respect to sexuality. This is an important period for young people's healthy psychosocial, moral and physiological sexual development. The role families and society play in helping adolescents set values and grow up to be healthy adults with responsible approaches to sexuality, consent and sexual behaviour is vital.

During this period, teenagers receive different information about sex from parents, peers and popular culture. This information shapes their attitudes and behaviours. For example, there may be some pressure on boys to pursue girls sexually, while girls are expected to be sexually attractive and available. Their attitudes about sex can affect the risks they take and how they treat others.

For healthy sexual development into adulthood, encompassing personal ethics, relationships and physiological understanding, it's crucial for young people to understand their own sexuality and make informed behavioural decisions. While most school programs adequately address the physiological aspects and consent, other dimensions of sexual ethics are often significantly overlooked, creating a gap in comprehensive sexual education. This includes the importance of open and honest communication with a partner about topics such as risky sexual behaviours, early-onset intercourse, abstinence, substance abuse and sexuality. Talking about boundaries, desires and health history is an essential part of building trust and mutual respect. Without clear communication, genuine consent and healthy intimacy are difficult to achieve.

Risky sexual behaviours

Discussing risky sexual behaviours as part of sexual ethics is crucial because it helps young people understand and prepare for the potential consequences of their actions for themselves and others. Sexual ethics rooted in risk awareness teaches young people to be responsible for themselves and their partners. It goes beyond simply saying 'Don't do this' and instead provides the knowledge and ethical framework to make informed, responsible choices. When teenagers understand the risks, they can make decisions based on facts rather than impulse, peer pressure or misinformation.

Risky sexual behaviours for teenagers include sexual activity with multiple sexual partners, without the use of contraceptives and while under the influence of drugs or alcohol. The social consequences of adolescent risky sexual behaviours can be long-lasting and costly to adolescents, their families and society at large. Early-onset sexual intercourse, sex with multiple partners and unprotected sex increase adolescents' susceptibility to sexually transmitted infections and unplanned pregnancies. Research suggests that the transition to sexual intercourse is associated with increases in levels of depression and anxiety, particularly for girls who initiate prior to age 16.[242]

> ...the transition to sexual intercourse is associated with increases in levels of depression and anxiety...

Australian research shows that by the age of 16, two-thirds of teenagers have had a romantic relationship and one-third have had sexual intercourse. Half of the girls and one-third of the boys said that they had experienced some form of unwanted sexual behaviour towards them in the past 12 months.[237] It is estimated that 16% of female college students experience sexual abuse before beginning college, which is associated with various psychological symptoms such as post-traumatic stress disorder, anxiety and depression.[243] All these factors suggest the importance of discussing early-onset sexual intercourse with teenagers so that they can make safe choices.

Studies have also linked sexual abuse to substance abuse issues, such as early alcohol use, regular tobacco use, illicit drug use and dependence, early injection drug use and higher rates of prescription drug abuse.[244] Additionally, frequent use of psychoactive substances strongly predicts earlier sexual initiation.[245]

Another study found that almost 20% of female undergraduates reported having a sexual debut due to wanting to be loyal to their boyfriends or under emotional coercion from them. Under these circumstances, the requirements for female safety and the ability to protect themselves are weakened.[246] Discussing unwanted sexual experiences and emotional harm and regret helps young people understand the need for consent, open communication and emotional readiness, not just physical readiness.

Activity #74: Avoiding risky sexual behaviours

Use a Y-Chart to describe the three aspects of the topic. How does avoiding risky sexual behaviours and pressure to have sex sound like, feel like and look like? For example:

- **Looks** like setting boundaries, making safe choices, steady body language
- **Sounds** like clear communication, firm but respectful tone
- **Feels** like confidence, self-respect or momentary discomfort when asserting boundaries.

You could also '*think, pair and share*' with another person about the personal qualities you think are needed to achieve your values and purposes with respect to sexual relations.

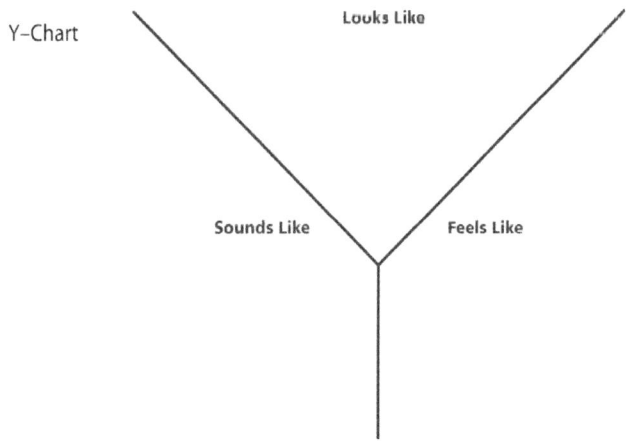

The case for sexual ethics

Schools and society make great efforts to educate young people about a broad range of topics related to human physiological development, such as puberty, anatomy and reproduction. Some programs also discuss risky sexual behaviours and romantic relationships. I maintain that a comprehensive and holistic program must also include sexual ethics in romantic relationships, an understanding of consent, gender ethics (fair gender beliefs) and healthy human physiological development (see Figure 30). Additionally, research shows that distinct strategies may be necessary to support boys and girls through tailored sex education.[245]

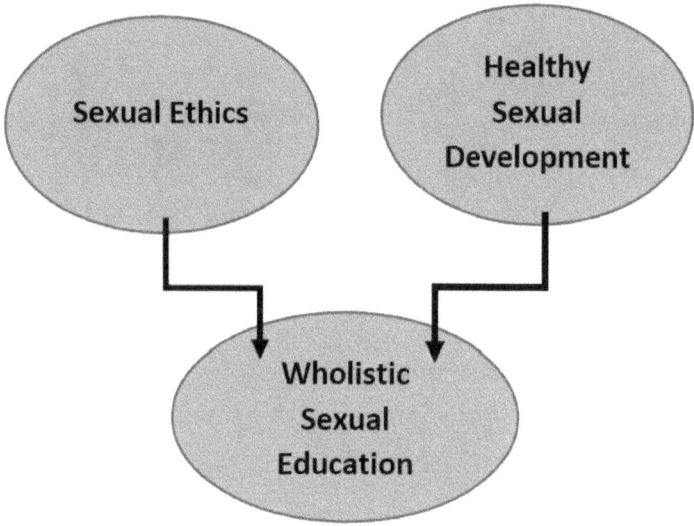

Figure 31 A holistic sexual education program

The importance of fostering sexual ethics is strong when considering that one in nine girls and one in 53 boys under the age of 18 experience sexual abuse or assault at the hands of an adult. Moreover, sexual abuse prior to age 18 may put some women at risk of engaging in sexual risk taking.[247] Early and risky sexual behaviours can establish unhealthy sexual patterns. These alarming statistics underline the need for prevention programs that target risk factors long before the onset of risky and inappropriate behaviours. Parents, the extended family and the community all play a vital role in fostering ethical and healthy sexuality.

In addition, research shows that quality sex education programs can help young people delay the onset of sexual activity, reduce the frequency of sexual activity, reduce their number of sexual partners and lower sexual risk-taking behaviour.[248]

So where will young people learn about ethical and respectful relationships and have open conversations about the positive nature of sexuality and ethical values and practices? From popular culture, peers or the media? Because teenagers exist and develop in relation to others, their sexual understanding and behaviours are shaped by the interactions between their own individual characteristics, family, peers and the media.

The importance of parental guidance

Parents play a pivotal role in shaping their children's understanding of sexuality, ethics and relationships. The social and emotional skills required for ethical and healthy sexuality – including the ability to resist peer influences related to risky sexual behaviours – are often developed through interactions with parents. For example, good academic performance and strong family support tend to delay young people's decisions to engage in sexual activity. [245] Parents also play a vital role in guiding young people's use of social media.[23]

Many studies show that the family environment influences adolescent psychosocial maturity. Teens raised in homes with authoritative parenting – which combines warmth with firm boundaries – are more mature and less likely to engage in risky or antisocial behaviour.[249] Relationships with parents set the stage for young people's relationships with peers. Open communication between parents and children about sex, consistent parental monitoring and peer groups that promote ethical, healthy behaviours are all effective in helping young people avoid risky sexual behaviour and delay their first intercourse.[250]

When adolescents have poor relationships with their parents, with little support or communication, they're more likely to be influenced by peer pressure and adopt their peers' views and behaviours about sex. Having a caring, open and communicative relationship with parents can help protect teens from peer pressure and guide their sexual choices. Peer influences don't replace parental influences; rather, parental guidance continues to play an important role, either directly predicting sexual behaviour or moderating the link between peer attitudes and sexual behaviour.[199]

The parent–child relationship and parenting styles also shape youth experiences with peers, including now much they are influenced by their peers' problematic behaviours. Young people whose parents are overly controlling are more likely to have close friends who accept early sexual behaviour. Adolescents who fail to establish autonomy in parental relationships – where they are nurtured to make their own choices and develop their own values – are less likely to exhibit autonomy with peers and may be vulnerable to adopting inappropriate values. Teens with overly controlling parents might tend to move away from those parents and conform more to peer relationships. However, when parents are more communicative and emotionally supportive, adolescents whose close friends were accepting of early sex are less likely to engage in risky sexual behaviour.[199]

Parenting well in sexual ethics involves open communication, consistent values and providing a safe space for teenagers to ask questions without judgement. It's about guiding them towards responsible and respectful choices, rather than simply enforcing rules. Open communication is the foundation.

Building on this foundation, the following practical suggestions can help parents guide their teenagers towards ethical and healthy sexuality, model positive values and set clear expectations in a supportive way.

Abilities: Guiding teens towards ethical sexuality
Open and ongoing communication

- **Start conversations early and keep them going:** Open dialogue helps normalise the topic and builds trust over time.
- **Be a source of information:** Don't let your child learn everything from the internet or their peers. Be proactive in providing

accurate, age-appropriate information about anatomy, puberty and relationships.

- **Create a safe space:** Make it clear that your child can come to you with any questions or concerns without fear of judgement. This builds trust, and it ensures that they feel comfortable discussing sensitive topics.
- **Use the right language:** Use proper anatomical terms and talk about sex and relationships in a healthy, respectful way. This helps normalise the topic and reduces **embarrassment.**

Modelling and teaching values

Your actions and words are the most powerful teaching tools:

- **Show your child what a respectful and loving relationship looks like:** This provides a real-life example of the ethical principles you are teaching.
- **Discuss core values:** Talk about what values are important to your family, and explain that these values apply to all relationships, including romantic and sexual ones.
- **Discuss the 'why':** Instead of simply saying 'Don't do that,' explain *why* certain behaviours can be harmful. For example, casual sex can lead to emotional hurt, and consent is vital for every person's dignity and safety.

Practical guidance and boundaries

While the conversation is important, teenagers also need practical advice and clear boundaries:

- **Set clear expectations:** Discuss your family's expectations regarding sexual activity. Whether you advocate for abstinence or harm reduction, be clear about your position and the reasons behind it.
- **Address media and peer pressure:** Help your child critically analyse what they see in media and discuss ways to handle peer pressure. Encourage them to trust their own judgement and to respect their personal boundaries.

Peer influence

During early adolescence, peers significantly shape one's social behaviour – both positively and negatively. One key factor is role modelling. Adolescents tend to adopt behaviours when a larger number of peers engage in them, especially if doing so leads to social rewards like acceptance, respect or popularity. Social Norm Theory shows that individuals tend to adapt or modify their own behaviours to align with what they perceive as popular, prevalent or socially accepted within their social circles.[251]

Negative peer influence is linked to both substance use and earlier initiation of sexual behaviour. Friendships with peers who hold more conservative attitudes about sex are linked to delayed sexual activity. Conversely, friendships with peers who approve of sex at early ages are linked to increased risky sexual behaviour. Supportive parents, as discussed previously, can help mitigate these effects. Greater peer acceptance of early sex at age 13 was significantly associated with greater risky sexual behaviour before age 16.[199]

Peer-resistance skill-based interventions have been proven effective in helping adolescents manage peer pressure related to both substance use and sexual behaviour. One effective approach is the REAL model, which teaches four primary strategies:

1. Refuse
2. Explain
3. Avoid
4. Leave

These strategies empower young people to strengthen their own sense of agency and make healthy values-based decisions in the face of peer pressure. In one study, 74% of young girls demonstrated communication competence in applying the REAL model to resist pressure towards early sexual activity. [250]

Activity #75: Pair and share

Try to answer the following questions:

1. What would you say or do if a person you liked wanted to do sexual things with you that you did not want to do?
2. As a friend, what advice would you give them?
3. As a parent, what would you say?

Activity #76: Avoiding risky sexual behaviours

Use a Y-Chart to describe the three aspects of the topic. How does saying no to sexual advances sound like, feel like and look like? For example:

- **Looks like** – steady eye contact, confident posture, clear physical boundaries
- **Sounds like** – firm but respectful tone, direct and honest words
- **Feels like** – confidence, calmness, occasional discomfort or nervousness.

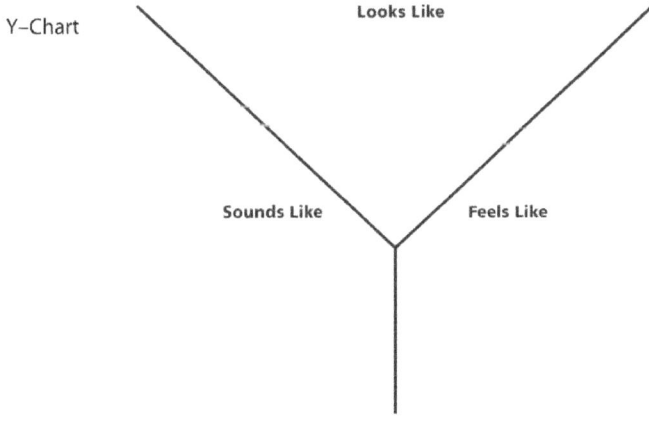

Sexual Ethics Guidance

Sexual curiosity during adolescence often leads to engagement in sexual activities or the consumption of sexual content. At this stage, many critical biological and psychological changes occur, for which many teenagers are not sufficiently prepared, often exposing them to stress.[245] The psychologist Archibald Hart[252] suggested that having sex is healthiest when it occurs at an appropriate time, with the right partner, under the right circumstances, while Devine et al.[52] added that it is important for sexual activity to be guided by appropriate motives and values.

My wife and I recognised these challenges, so we wanted to provide our four boys with some guidance about what healthy and responsible sexuality looks like and how to build healthy male and female relationships. This is the type of message we did our best to communicate to our boys.

The right time

- When is the right time for youth to start having sex?

There are many opinions on this. I suggest not until marriage or months into a mature relationship. Premature sexual experiences – often defined as a young age at first sexual intercourse – have been linked by numerous studies to a range of potential social and health problems. This is a well-documented area of research in public health, psychology and sociology. Research done by UNESCO found overwhelming support among both adults and adolescents for sending teens a clear message about abstaining from sex until they are at least out of high school. This perspective has led to strong interest in identifying programs that are effective in postponing sexual initiation (intercourse) among youth.[253]

Some researchers argued that consensual adolescent sexuality is good for personal development.[241] However, other research suggested that premature sexual experiences can lead to social and health problems. For example, men who begin sexual activity at an early age are more likely to experience

> ...sex is not necessarily positive or healthy when done under the wrong conditions and time.

sexual behavioural risks and sexual arousal/orgasm problems. Similarly, women who initiate sex early show an increased likelihood of reporting sexual behavioural risks.[254] For example, risky sexual behaviour for young women is often associated with sexual coercion. Hence, sex is not necessarily positive or healthy when done under the wrong conditions and time.

The first advice my wife and I gave to our boys was to delay sexual activities until the appropriate time. We suggested not until marriage, yet we knew that in the end, this would be their choice. Sexual abstinence is a sexual choice that may be the healthiest choice for an individual at a particular time. Evidence from studies conducted in the USA showed adolescent perceptions of parental disapproval of early intercourse are associated with a delay in the onset of sexual activity.[255]

You may ask, what's wrong with young people exploring their sexuality as teenagers?

We wanted our sons to learn to control their sexual urges, to create the right conditions and timing for their first sexual encounter. Unlike adults, young people find it hard to delay gratification. This is a well-established concept in developmental psychology, and research points to the still-developing nature of the adolescent brain, particularly the imbalance between the reward system and the prefrontal cortex, which contributes to risk-taking behaviour and a reduced capacity for delaying gratification.[256] We told them, 'Controlling urges is important for relationships. How will you stay in a committed relationship if you can't control your sexual urges?'

EI has taught us that self-discipline is learned when we are young. Young people who delay gratification are able to be more successful at school, in their careers and in their relationships.[39] Having impulse control with respect to sexuality is important in maintaining a long-term relationship. At this stage of their lives, adolescents are in a conflict between forming intimate, loving relationships and avoiding committed relationships.[257] Hence, we thought taking it slower was good advice.

Research conducted in China suggested that females initiating sex earlier were more likely to have their first sexual intercourse with men who were not their 'boyfriends'; less likely to use contraception; more likely to have multiple lifetimes and concurrent sexual partners; to report pregnancy; and be diagnosed with sexually transmitted diseases. Additionally, after their sexual debut, 40.6% of students felt regret and unease, 29.1% had a sense of loss, 26.1% felt guilty, 12.5% felt hateful and only 23.8% reported feeling happy.[246] Psychological factors such as feeling regret or not feeling ready are more common among individuals who initiate sexual intercourse early.[242]

Research suggests that those who abstain from sexual intimacy during the early part of their relationships allow communication and other social processes, such as shared values, to become the foundation of their mutual attraction rather than just sex. Compared with those in the early sex group, those who waited until marriage rated their relationship stability and satisfaction higher, and their sexual relations and communication better.[258]

However, another study showed that those having sex later than the norm (usually 18) were no more satisfied with their sexual relationships than those who had started at an earlier age.[254] Note that sexual satisfaction doesn't necessarily mean an emotional bond and satisfaction in the relationship.

I remember one day talking to teachers in our staffroom about dating. Since I had sons at my school, they asked me whom my sons were dating. I told them that my wife and I encouraged our sons not to have sex before marriage and discouraged dating until the right time. They must have thought, *This man is a throwback from the 50's*. The room became silent and the atmosphere awkward – why? In our society, it is considered cute by most people for teenagers to date and explore their sexuality. Well, when you put two young people together with hormones rushing and the desire to be loved (mostly insecure), what do we expect will happen?

The right person

We also suggested to our sons that a premature sexual relationship may cause them to be stuck in a relationship that may be wrong for them. Early

> Early sexual activity can create strong emotional bonds that make it harder to judge whether a relationship is truly compatible.

sexual activity can create strong emotional bonds that make it harder to judge whether a relationship is truly compatible.

If couples become sexually active too early, this rewarding area of the relationship may overwhelm good decision making and keep couples in a relationship that might not be in their best long-term interest. Many parents worry about this one because they want their children to mature and be with the right person.

Research shows that younger married couples have higher rates of infidelity.[200] So, we suggested to our sons that having transient sexual relationships would make it harder for them to bond with 'the one' later.

The right motives and values

Studies on hormones and behaviour highlight the role of different hormonal systems in driving sexual desire versus feelings of love and attachment. These findings support the idea that sex and love aren't necessarily the same thing[259] – something we also advised our sons.

It is important that love and sex come together, and for this to occur you need to be a bit more mature. Research suggests that most people find it hard to imagine passionate love absent of sexual desire. However, this doesn't mean that sexual desire and love are the same. For example, males report having fewer problems imagining sex without love than females do. However, when people are asked to think about love, they start thinking about long-term attachment and commitment and the positive aspects of their partner. Conversely, sexual desire focuses on the 'here and now', not the long-term prospects of the relationship.[260]

The right conditions

We also suggested to our sons that sexuality is wonderful when one is in a loving, respectful and mature relationship. Sex fosters intimacy, bonding and shared pleasure. In this context, people can be free to explore their sexuality. You may ask, what does maturity have to do with sexuality? Can we expect teenagers to have this? Most of us would say, no. Neuroscience highlights the potential for adolescents to engage in risky sexual behaviours due to incomplete brain development. This of course doesn't tell the whole story.

Sex is compelling, and when sexual desire is not managed well, it can diminish our ability to love and be loved in a deeply emotional way. Think about it… When you are aroused, does it mean you want to love the other person, or are you expecting something from them for yourself? Arousal needs to be paired with love – an ethic of love. We need to harmonise other-centred love with passionate sexuality.

Research shows that two-thirds of sexually experienced teenagers (ages 12 to 19) say they wish they had waited longer before having sexual intercourse for the first time (61% of females and 39% of males). Their reasons included:

- being too young
- not feeling ready
- not being in a close relationship or with the right person
- the experience being unplanned or unprotected
- unrealistic expectations about what the first sexual experience would be like.

What most strongly influenced these feelings of regret were a younger age at first intercourse and lower parental guidance and monitoring.[239]

We shared the advice above with our boys, knowing that, ultimately, their choices were their own and that no set of guidelines can guarantee smooth or uncomplicated relationships.

Is this any different for adults? Do people in monogamous, committed relationships commonly feel frustrated by their commitments? Most would say, 'No, it's wonderful.' My wife and I feel we made the right choice in offering this guidance because our sons may have been spared some of the regrets and pressures that young people often face around early sexual activity.

In conclusion, we must be mindful that as adults and as a society not to sell the wrong messages and sexualise our youth at a very early age. Research is telling us that there is a strong link between the messages kids get at home and from the media and their attitudes about sex and relationships between men and women. Research suggests the need for an intervention that includes reaching out to parents and teens. Parents could discuss sexual messages in popular culture with their children and offer a broader perspective on sexuality to compensate for the skewed portrayals in the media. Youth could be made aware of the ways in which sex is depicted and perhaps distorted. [239] It is incumbent on adults to help young people with a 'reality check' with respect to sexuality.

Activity #77: Postponing sex: making values-based choices

Write in your journal and share with another:

1. What advice would you give to a teenager with respect to sex and that it should be done:
   - at the right time and with the right person
   - when the right conditions are fulfilled
   - with the right motives and values?

2. List the strategies that would allow you or teen/young adults in general to resist pressure to have sex too early. List some delay statements you could tell another.

3. Using the Y-Chart, describe what postponing sex means for you or controlling your sexual desire means for you
   - **Looks** like (e.g. setting clear boundaries, confidently saying no, avoiding risky situations)
   - **Sounds** like (e.g. firm but respectful words, honest explanations, calm tone)
   - **Feels** like (e.g. self-respect, patience, occasional discomfort or pressure, inner strength)

You could also *'think, pair and share'* with another person about the qualities that make a relationship healthy. Suggest tips to the other person for waiting.

LIVING WITH PURPOSE

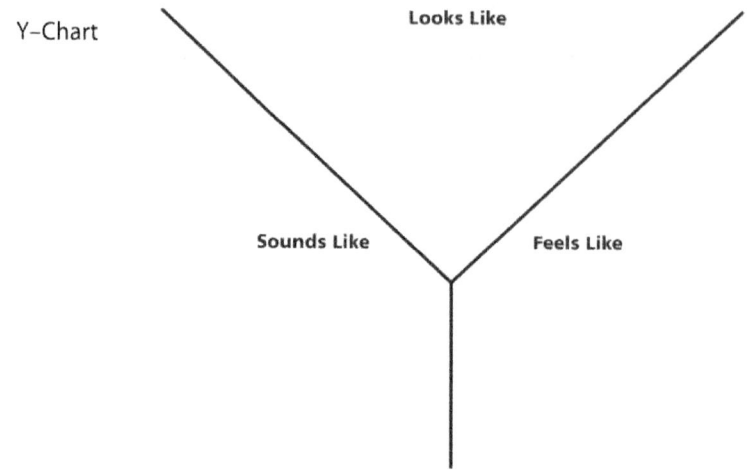

'Sexual ethics are not just about avoiding harm but about pursuing what is truly good for ourselves and others.'
—*Dr Paul TP Wong*

13

The Need for Sexual Ethics in Sexual Education
(Sphere 1)
Dr Tuong Thi Phan

Most countries around the world are providing sex education (SE) to students in both private and public schools. Understandingly, SE programs aren't uniformly developed, even within the same geographic boundaries, but depend on the political, socio-economic structures and educational policies of each nation, region, education ministry or school. It is acknowledged worldwide that the cultural and ethnic diversity within any society significantly shapes the formation and delivery of SE programs.

> SE must also teach what constitutes a good relationship

Another major factor influencing SE is religion. Parallel to mainstream educational institutions, SE is commonly delivered by religious organisations. There are many religions in the world, and each have a unique viewpoint on sexuality. This adds considerable complexity so how SE is conceptualised and implemented.

This chapter reviews the relevance and effectiveness of Western-based SE. Pros and cons of this education will be highlighted, progressing to suggestions for improvements.

Comprehensive Sexuality Education (CSE) is the UN's technical guidance framework for SE. Its primary aim is to provide young people with accurate and age-appropriate information about sexuality. CSE is considered critical for the physical health, safety and overall wellbeing and survival of young individuals.

Developed collaboratively by the UNESCO, the United Nations Population Fund (UNFPA), the United Nations International Children's Emergency Fund (UNICEF), UN Women, the Joint United Nations Programme on HIV/AIDS (UNAIDS) and the World Health Organization (WHO), the CSE, framework recommends that SE curriculum should be science-based and age appropriate. The contents should be comprehensive, addressing a broad range of topics related to sexuality, as well as sexual and reproductive health, throughout childhood and adolescence.

While the specific curriculum may vary between religions or school, SE should aim to equip children and adolescents not only with health-related knowledge and skills, but also – and more importantly – with the attitudes, moral values and legal principles required to engage in respectful and safe social and sexual relationships. For young people's long-term happiness and wellbeing, it's vital that they can make responsible choices that respect and protect their own autonomy and rights, as well as those of others.

The positive outcomes of SE have been collectively agreed upon and documented. The WHO reported that evidence consistently shows that high-quality sexuality education delivers positive health outcomes, with lifelong impacts.[261] An extensive review of sexual education in Australia reveals that literature from the past three decades strongly supports the delivery of comprehensive SE across various topics and grade levels.[262]

Assessing High-Quality Sexual Education

Attention should be paid to the emphasis on 'high-quality' and 'comprehensive' when it comes to SE and identify which teaching elements are of high-quality or comprehensive and those that aren't.

The United Nations CSE framework recommends that SE be understood as a lifelong, incremental learning process. It recommends beginning as early as age five and continuing through high school, with age-appropriate content tailored to different age groups.

For instance, at ages five to eight, children might learn about identifying the different needs and roles of family members, as well as understand the roles and responsibilities of each family member. During adolescence, the conversation broadens to include puberty and the expected changes in bodily parts and functions, and then extends to relationship topics such as autonomy, consent, sexual diseases, pregnancy and pregnancy prevention.

Armed with such knowledge, young individuals are better equipped to protect themselves from sexual violence, exploitation and abuse, while also becoming dependable and responsive partners capable of forming loving and equitable relationship.[263]

Bianca Fileborn argues that current SE often fails to address essential topics such as sexual consent and how to navigate romantic or sexual relationships. Despite legal prohibitions against sexual violence and coercion, which are regarded as crimes, young women aged 18 to 24 remain the predominant victims of sexual violence in Australia.[262]

Fileborn maintains that an ethical approach to SE prepares young people with skills to recognise sexual signals and respond appropriately. In general, it can be challenging to distinguish between signals of physical desire and expressions of love, especially for youths who are new to sexual relationships. However, knowledge of sexual ethics helps empower young people to not accept sexual violence and disrespect, to seek protection from such abuse criminal behaviour, and to negotiate mutual and compassionate agreement.

A publication from the Harvard Graduate School of Education's reinforces this perspective. Grace Tatter[264] observed that while effective SE programs can significantly reduce rates of sexually transmitted diseases, teen pregnancies and pregnancy-related dropouts, the focus should extend beyond physical health outcomes. According to Tatter, SE must also teach what constitutes a good relationship – one grounded in respect, empathy and mutual understanding.

Tatter also broadens the meaning of consent in SE beyond its legal definition, reframing it as a moral and relational responsibility, namely, what we owe to one another. This moral dimension deepens students' understanding of interpersonal respect and accountability within intimate contexts.

The preventative power of ethical sexual education

This book and program support an approach to SE in which young people are educated about healthy sexual relationships that are caring, respectful and just. This addition to SE is crucial because helping young people understand and accept what constitutes a healthy relationship empowers them to manage their own sexual urges and tendencies towards sexual violence, recognise coercion, and protect themselves from becoming victims, or perpetrators, of sexual violence.

This approach is a valuable preventative strategy, as statistics reveal that most sexual assault and violence in schools are perpetrated by individuals known to the victim – whether dating partners, friends or classmates. Ethical sexual education, therefore, does more than prevent disease and unwanted pregnancy; it cultivates empathy, accountability and mutual care. The end outcome is preparing young people for more meaningful lives.

Strengths and weaknesses of current sex education

Goldfarb and Lieberman[265] conducted a systematic review of 8,058 SE-related articles published over three decades to search for evidence of SE's effectiveness. They started with US-based research and later expanded to international studies. Alarmingly, they found that around 80% of these articles focused solely on pregnancy and disease prevention. While these are undeniably important topics, the emphasis on biological and risk-reduction content overlooks the most pressing need for the inclusion of sexual ethics in any comprehensive SE program.

By learning and practising sexual ethics, young people can build accountable and equitable sexual relationships and partnerships. They can also develop awareness, moral reasoning and skills for self-protection from sexual abuse and sexual violence tendencies.

Sexual ethics and morality

Sexuality refers to the capacity to practise and experience sexual activity, including physical and emotional pleasure, companionship and reproduction. Sexual ethics comprise the legal, moral, cultural and religious values that govern sexual behaviour and relationships.

The legal aspects of sexuality ensure that everyone has the right to:

- make decisions about their own body and sexual choices
- be treated equally in partnerships and sexual relationships, regardless of gender, ethnicity or appearance
- express their sexual preferences
- give autonomous consent to sexual activity
- protect themselves from sexual violence or coercion.

Existing SE programs often emphasise legal rights but give little attention to moral, cultural and religious aspects of sexuality, which are equally crucial in guiding responsible sexual behaviour.

The moral aspects of sexuality encompass values derived from cultures, norms, protocols, beliefs, habits and attitudes. Moral values are almost always inseparable from family upbringing and religious values. When a couple decides to get married, they might prefer to follow religious protocol for their engagement and/or wedding ceremony. The religious protocols are conformed to either religious beliefs or social appearances.

Western-based SE is rooted in Western morality, which is grounded in individualism. Each person has the autonomy to search for a partner, including exploring sexual compatibility and companionship. This approach encourages individuals to seek like-minded sexual partners, starting with affection or love and progressing to compatibility. Compatibility refers to equality or similarity in key aspects of a relationship, such as intellectual level, physical attraction, life choices, earning capacity, sexual preferences and more. While individuals may seek advice from friends, family members or parents if they choose, these parties have neither the right nor the duty to provide such advice.

Western-based perspectives and multicultural influences

In addition, the Western culture of sexual relationships and partnerships has also been shaped by Freudianism. From the cultural perspective, individuals who are familiar with a Freudian theoretical framework may use psychological impairments and disorders to justify their own inappropriate sexual behaviours. By using justification, a person may intentionally shift responsibility for their objectionable sexual behaviours onto their parents or caregivers, blaming past maltreatment during earlier stages of life.

Moreover, Western countries have been exposed to various cultures and have implemented multiculturalism over the last four to five decades since the wave of immigrants and refugees from many continents, including Asia, Eastern Asia, Middle East, Africa, South America and the Caribbean. These immigrants and refugees brought with them their respective cultures and religious beliefs including those related to sexual relationship and marriage. These cultures and beliefs are different from those practised by the Anglo-Celtic and English community.

Religious and cultural ethics of sexuality

Religions provide distinct codes of sexual ethics based on which sexual activities are regulated, and which normative values are mandated. For sexual ethics to be taught effectively to students, curriculum developers and educators of SE need to understand the regulations and values of major religions.

Importantly, this knowledge would allow educators to acknowledge that students come from diverse cultural, religious and family backgrounds, which means they may not all view sexual ethics in the same way. Even students of the same age and from the same place of origin might respond differently to SE.

Conclusion

A sexual relationship is a long and complex journey for young people, one that comes with physical and emotional baggage that evolves over time. They may face difficult transitions along the way. The challenges they encounter can stem from a variety of factors, including physical, mental, social and financial struggles, which complicate their experiences of sexual interaction, partnership or marriage. These issues aren't exclusive to students of non-Anglo-Celtic backgrounds living in Western countries. Interracial marriages and partnerships are common in other parts of the world as young people travel, work, migrate and live away from their countries of origin.

Given the complexity and fluidity of cultural and religious ethics surrounding sexuality, SE content needs to go beyond just physio-biology, encompassing sexual characteristics and ethics, including cultural and religious perspectives. This broader approach is essential for conflict resolution and serves a preventative purpose, helping students understand and navigate diverse views on sexuality.

Current literature acknowledged the key role of SE in preparing students for harmonious sexual relationships and partnerships as well as preventing risks to sexual activities. The reviewed literature pointed out that current SE has been successful in introducing the biological aspect of sexuality and prevention of accidental or unwanted pregnancy. Nevertheless, to assist young people in having an established, safe, fair and enjoyable sexual relationship, it is important that SE place a stronger emphasis on legal, moral, cultural and religious notions of sexual activities and relationship.

Students need to be aware of the relevant laws that uphold their rights to make decisions about their own bodies, including the right to consent to or refuse sexual contact and relationships, while respecting the rights of others. The ability to negotiate the terms of sexual experiences is crucial for fostering just and respectful relationships. Recognising these legal rights can empower individuals with the confidence to advocate for themselves in such situations.

Understanding broader cultural systems can provide insight into how expectations around sexuality and sexual companionships are shaped.

Cultural variation is evidenced across observable sexual behaviours, sexual interactions and marriage planning. Some cultural practices might not be perceived as friendly but threatening to Western-based approaches of sexuality and sexual alliance.

For example, arranged marriage is criticised as imprudent by those who practise individualism-based sexual partnership and matrimony, of which autonomy and love are fundamental building materials. In contrast, societies with extended family structures see arranged marriage as positive. Supporters of arranged marriage view this setting as culturally and socially sensitive, constructed on the foundation of parental wisdom, family trust and respect, and societal coordination. On such a footing, the essence of love is said to not be missing but rather is intrinsically developed as the husband-wife relationship progresses.

Sacred rules and doctrines shape how religious communities respond to sexual relationships and marriage. Religious perspectives on sexuality, relationships and matrimony are highly complex, influenced by diverse cultural origins and centuries-old doctrinal codes unique to each faith. Even devoted scholars may find these rules and their applications challenging to interpret. However, SE can help students develop an awareness of religious viewpoints, which may have both positive and negative implications. Recognising the complexity of religious and cultural attitudes towards sexuality, partnership and marriage can serve as an essential foundation for students, aiding in conflict resolution and the prevention of exploitation, deception, abuse and health risks.

'The love of a parent for a child is the only love that is truly unconditional.'
—Unknown

14

Parental Love, Attachment and Effective Parenting Styles (Sphere 2)
Dr John Bellavance and Dr Rafia Naz

Since the 1980s, the important role of the family has increasingly gained attention from the international community. The UN General Assembly (UNGA) adopted several resolutions and proclaimed the International Year of the Family and the International Day of Families. The UN emphasised the critical role of parents in raising children, recognising that families have the primary responsibility for nurturing and protecting children. For the full and harmonious development of personality and health, children benefit most when they grow up in a family environment characterised by happiness, love and understanding.

> You want to make the world a better place? Be a good parent.

In keeping with the spirit of the Convention on the Rights of the Child, family and parenting support is increasingly recognised as a key part of national social policies and social investment packages, aimed at reducing poverty, decreasing inequality, and promoting positive parental and child wellbeing.

Once a couple has children, they become parents, bringing love, joy and challenges. This sphere of love allows parents to grow in their capacity to love. They experience the love a parent feels for their child and the joy and love a child gives in return. We come to better understand our parents' love when we ourselves become parents.[52]

The primary job of parents is to love and care for their children, prioritising their wellbeing over their careers, income or other considerations. This is not easy. Love takes effort, and it means living for the sake of the child.

You want to make the world a better place? Be a good parent. You want to mess up the world? Be a bad parent.

The family is the school of values and love, and parents are its first teachers.

How do we become good parents? What lessons are we teaching our children? This brings us to think about what we learned from our own parents about parenting and how their parenting affected us for good or for ill. The research is clear about the critical role parents play in child development. Parental attachment impacts children's personality development and social relationships.[24, 266]

Parental Attachment and Personality Development
Dr John Bellavance

Psychological research consistently supports that children who did not receive sufficient love, care and attachment from their parents may struggle with trusting others and rely heavily on themselves. Attachment Theory, a foundational concept in developmental psychology, shows that a child who receives consistent, loving and responsive care develops a secure attachment. This allows them to see the world as safe and to trust that others will be there for them when they need them.

The most important task in the first years of life is the creation of a secure emotional bond with a primary caregiver. Long before infants can speak, they adjust their actions and judge whether others will attend to their needs and make them feel safe.

If, as a child, you cried when you were hungry and received love and care, you most likely developed a sense that you deserve and are worthy of love. If you were unloved, neglected or abused, you most likely developed a sense that you are unworthy to be cared for by others. You learned to rely on yourself and not trust others. These types of positive or negative responses are etched in unconscious memories, influencing lifelong habits and behaviours.[267]

When caregivers do not provide adequate care, a child's brain may not develop properly, affecting emotional regulation in adulthood, moral development and learning ability. Without this security, the body, brain and behaviour may default to fear and defensive retreat.[24, 266] Physiologically and psychologically, infants depend on caregivers to foster their sociality and their ability to communicate, relate and connect with others. Conversely, inadequate or poor early care can lower the threshold for activating stress-response systems (that is, make them more sensitive to stress) in social situations, undermining social bonding – a pattern that can persist throughout life. Human babies are born with only 25% of the brain complete, thus the caregiver's training in a baby's self-regulation is vital in managing stress responses. Care-deprived infants develop abnormal brain structures and behavioural disorders that lead to greater hostility towards others.[266]

Activity #78: Your personal attachments

Reflect, write in your journal and share with another:

1. Reflect on your memories of parental attachment, such as playing with a parent. How did this impact your personality development?
2. When someone is unloved, neglected or abused, they can develop a sense that they are unworthy of care and must rely on themselves. Is that true for you or someone you know?

Parental Attachment and Social Development
Dr John Bellavance

Parental love for children is foundational for future quality relationships. A child who experiences inconsistent, neglectful or emotionally distant parenting may develop insecure attachments. For instance, adults who described their early parental relationships as cold or neglectful are more likely to report feeling uncomfortable with intimacy and have difficulty trusting their partners, mirroring the avoidant attachment style. Secure attachment at one year old also predicts peer and social competence in the pre-school years. Parental attachment and values shown by parents also affect how siblings relate to each other.

Parental influence doesn't decline as children mature into adolescence. Social skills, emotional adjustment and relational competence in young adults are also greatly influenced by parental attachment. Young people who have a good attachment to their parents tend to report better self-esteem and a lower occurrence of depressive moods. According to Attachment Theory, the child constructs internal working models of the self (how they see themselves) and what she or he can expect from relationships based on her or his first relationship with their parents. These models form the basis for peer and romantic relationships, operating as a template by which to appraise and interpret subsequent relational interactions.[203]

The quality of adolescent intimate relationships with parents is linked to a positive self-concept, psychological adjustment and physical health. Conversely, diminished quality of relationships is associated with an increase in depression and lower self-esteem.[268] Poor attachment in childhood can also lead to being less empathetic and receptive to others.[266]

According to continuity models of family-peer linkages, the quality of peer relationships will mirror the quality of family relationships.[199] Positive or negative maternal caregiving at 18 months can predict a child's positive or negative attachment style 20 years later.

Additionally, a child's attachment experiences with parents affect his or her subsequent functioning in peer and romantic relationships.[268] Relationships between infants and caregivers share similar features with adult romantic partners. For example, both feel safe when the other is nearby and responsive. Anxiety and avoidance in romantic relationships were found to be positively correlated with early caregiving.[267]

Children who have an insecure attachment to their parents have more instances of sibling conflict.[257] Stronger parental attachment is positively linked to better conflict resolution skills in young people. Conversely, inter-parental conflict adversely affects the parent–child bond and children's social skills and emotional adjustment, influencing their own relationship behaviours.[269] Parental relationships provide a model for negotiating conflict. When parents display poor conflict-based behaviours, it can negatively influence how children resolve conflict with peers and in romantic relationships.[270]

Adolescents exposed to marital conflict often experience anxiety about forming their own relationships and may struggle to engage socially outside their family.

Activity #79: How family shapes me

Write in your journal and share with another:

1. Did parental attachment and values shown by your parents affect how you related to your siblings?
2. Did your family relationships influence how you relate to your friends?
3. Did your parents impact how you resolve conflicts? If not, why?

Parenting Styles and Their Influence
Dr John Bellavance and Dr Rafia Naz

Even though parents may not always be aware of it, children naturally learn from and resemble their parents (kids are always watching), and this also applies to how they parent their own children. Different parenting styles contribute to differing degrees of social competence in children. For example, oppositional defiant disorder in children has been associated with a harsh, inconsistent and neglectful parenting style.[72]

Parenting and parent–child relationships impact sibling relationship quality, with harsh and authoritarian parenting linked to more conflictual sibling exchanges.[271] The way parents resolve their child's needs for both nurturance and limit-setting has a major impact on the child's degree of social competence and behavioural adjustment.

Challenges to parenting

One way adolescent–parent relationships can become problematic is when parents undermine their teenager's autonomy to handle their natural adolescent strivings for greater independence and control over personal decisions. When parents use guilt, anxiety, shame, withdrawal of love or other psychologically controlling tactics with their adolescent, they inhibit the development of autonomy. Adolescents exposed to such control are at increased risk of making decisions that are developmentally immature and poorly reasoned.[199]

Some common reasons parents struggle to raise children include a lack of social or practical support, high levels of stress and substance abuse, their own unrealistic expectations of the child, not knowing how to foster positive development and behaviour, doubts about their own ability to meet the child's needs and the lingering effects of the parents' own adverse childhood experiences.[272]

The four parenting styles

Parenting styles establish the emotional atmosphere in which parents express behaviours aimed at socialising their child.[273] The four primary parenting styles – authoritarian, indulgent, neglectful and authoritative – are outlined below.[274, 275] I focus primarily on the authoritative style, which I believe represents good parenting.

Authoritarian parenting

The authoritarian parenting style is characterised by strict and inflexible behaviours and rules, high demands and emotional unresponsiveness (being emotionally cold). The emphasis is on obedience, respect for authority and an expectation that rules are followed without question or explanation.

Indulgent parenting

Indulgent parenting is characterised by low demands and high responsiveness. These parents are warm and accepting but exercise little authority, make few behavioural demands, and allow considerable self-regulation by the child or adolescent.

This reminds me of teachers who want to be friends with their students. This doesn't work for teachers or for parents because adults will often sacrifice standards and respect to create 'friendship'. As a teacher, I know that students may not like me when I discipline them, such as when I point out their behaviour in class, but in the long run, it is better for them, and with time they do come to respect and appreciate this. After disciplining my students, I always show them that I believe in them, reinforcing their good qualities. Adults need to reward the attitudes and behaviours that underpin young people's success in the world.

Neglectful parenting

A neglectful parenting style is neither demanding nor responsive. These parents do not monitor their children's behaviours nor support their interests, and parents are often disengaged from their parental responsibilities. Neglected adolescents are the most disadvantaged with respect to social competence, academic achievement and psychosocial adjustment.

Authoritative parenting

The authoritative parenting style, which was first defined by psychologist Diana Baumrind, takes a middle route in parenting, being warm and approachable. This style circumvents punitive measures while allowing room for the child's independence. The focus is on administering standards and expectations through guidance and reasoning, with the child's cooperation. [276] In short, this style acknowledges that raising children is a *collaborative effort* between both the parents and the child.

Consistent parenting style

One of the keys to parenting is that both parents adopt a similar parenting style and support each other in that style. Inconsistent parenting between mothers and fathers was related to anxiety and depression in adolescents. Mothers have traditionally been the caregiver, socialised to provide care for their children, while fathers have been socialised to be the provider and disciplinarian. Consequently, mothers and fathers have often adopted different parenting styles. Mothers more often use an *authoritative* parenting style, while fathers use an *authoritarian* parenting style. With women increasingly joining the workforce and fathers spending more time with their children, fathers are now mostly adopting authoritative or permissive styles of parenting.[275]

Activity #80: What is your parenting style?

Use a Y-Chart to describe the three aspects of the topic. What parenting style do you use, or would use if you were a parent? What does this sound like, feel like and look like? Examples:

- **Looks like** – setting consistent rules, showing warmth, active listening
- **Sounds like** – kind but firm tone, encouraging words, clear communication
- **Feels like** – patience, confidence, empathy, calmness

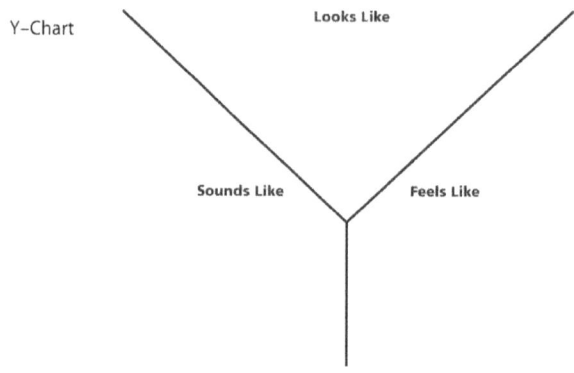

Authoritative Parenting and Inductive Discipline
Dr John Bellavance

A key feature of authoritative parenting is the use of inductive discipline, where parents guide children to understand the impact of their actions on others. Both authoritative parenting and inductive discipline are consistently linked to enhanced moral reasoning and prosocial behaviour in children and adolescents. When young people are raised in authoritative homes – and perceive inductive discipline as fair and appropriate – they are more likely to pay attention, accept and internalise their parents' values and guidance, developing a strong moral identity.[23, 187]

Authoritative parenting effectively balances high expectations and supervision with responsiveness and warmth. These parents consistently monitor their children's behaviour while providing warmth and support. Research indicates that adolescents raised with this style demonstrate higher levels of psychosocial competence and school achievement and lower levels of emotional distress, behavioural problems and enhanced prosocial behaviours.[23, 274]

This parenting style helps children balance the need for autonomous and active thinking with other-oriented and rule-following tendencies. Parental warmth and responsiveness involve promoting individuality, self-regulation and self-assertion by being aware, supportive and understanding of children's unique needs and demands, allowing them to grow in their autonomy and responsibility. Parents who are responsive to children's signals and needs have a warm and loving relationship with their children.

Parental control and strong expectations involve setting standards that support children in integrating into the family. This fosters a mindset in which children learn to consider the wellbeing of others, not just their own. Parents must supervise, discipline and address disobedience. Children suffer when caregivers avoid conflict and fail to provide guidance. Guiding a child through inductive discipline is an act of responsibility and love.[40]

We must remember that a common developmental characteristic of childhood and adolescents is egocentrism, which gradually decreases with maturity. Parents who set high expectations tend to raise children who develop stronger high self-control, altruism and self-esteem. When parents use induction – praising or disciplining with explanations with a focus on the consequences of the child's behaviour on others – children are more likely to grow in empathy, conscience, altruism and moral reasoning.[6, 275]

During my PhD studies into students' behaviours on social media, 14-year-old student, Baba, gave an example of the importance of parental guidance and influence by explaining, 'I have the rule: if my mum would see it and be like, "Oh my God, it's terrible," I won't post it.'

Some parents I interviewed also suggested that parental supervision and clearly communicated expectations are vital for their children's online behaviour.

Activity #81: Communicating with your child

Clear expectations and positive reinforcement build trust, cooperation and a stronger parent–child bond.

Reflection:

1. How can you strengthen communication with your child in everyday situations?
2. Write down your family rules. Are they clear and age appropriate?
3. Consider how you give positive feedback (praise, hugs, affection).

Debrief (optional):

- Share your reflections with someone you trust and discuss strategies to improve communication.

Parental modelling of values and behaviours

Children mimic what they see in their daily lives. Research suggests that parents who model self-control and altruism raise children who develop higher self-control and altruism themselves. A critical key to setting children up for a happy adult life is treating them – and others – with love and respect from the start. Children will come to understand this respectful behaviour in relationships as not only normal, but the best way to be and to communicate with others. Then when they encounter abusive behaviour, they will see it as unacceptable.[277, 278]

Showing love in front of the children

Husband and wife expressing love for each other in front of their children helps model healthy relationships. In my experience, children love seeing mummy and daddy show affection to each other. My father was not a person who expressed affection, but he was a good and loving man. I remember when I was eight and he had not come home in the middle of the night. It was a 20 below zero night in Canada. (Remember, no mobile phones in 1963.) I woke up late in the night, peeked my head out of my room and saw my mother placing a blanket on my dad, coddling him, trying to warm him up. I never forgot this scene. It touched my heart deeply. I knew at that moment that my mum loved my dad. It turns out his car had broken down on the highway, and he was not dressed for it. The police had found him and brought him home.

With respect to my own family, my sons did not need my wife and I to preach about the value and wonders of marriage. I suspect that when they saw us show affection for each other, they said to themselves, consciously or not, 'I want this too.'

The unique contributions of mothers and fathers

The distinct dynamics of mother-daughter, father-daughter, mother-son and father-son relationships profoundly influence child development. Research indicates that father attachment predicts better social skills, leading to improved relational competence and emotional adjustment. Fathers often play a crucial role in children's exploration of new environments and social situations. Furthermore, a father's involvement in education positively impacts student achievement. Father-child physical play, affection and engaging father-son interactions are linked to later popularity in school, lower depression rates and higher marital satisfaction in adulthood.[275]

Similarly, attachment to mothers has been shown to predict better conflict resolution skills, which fosters relational competence and emotional adjustment. Mothers often serve as a secure base during times of distress, and the ability to re-establish attachment with them models the skills required to maintain healthy connections in adulthood.[203]

Research clearly shows how attachment to both fathers and mothers shapes children's ability to manage relationships, resolve conflict and develop emotional resilience. Beyond the data, lived experience offers a complementary perspective. In the next section, Dr Rafia Naz shares her personal upbringing and parenting journey, illustrating how these principles of attachment and authoritative parenting unfold in daily life.

The Benefit of Authoritative Parents: A Personal Reflection
Dr Rafia Naz

> *'Authoritative parents are assertive, but not intrusive and restrictive. Their disciplinary methods are supportive, rather than punitive. They want their children to be assertive as well as socially responsible and self-regulated as well as cooperative.'*
> **—Diana Baumrind.**

Upon reflecting on my experience as a daughter raised by a responsive, nurturing, and engaged mother who consistently demonstrated respect throughout my upbringing, I recognise that her parenting style aligns with the *authoritative* approach.

Our daily life was timetabled and scheduled – from getting up on time to mealtimes, sleeping times, study periods or even time set aside to watch TV. I sometimes wondered why we were so scheduled.

My mum constantly *explained* why managing our time, scheduling activities and prioritising work was important. This instilled in me early on the significance of time management and being methodical, ensuring that work was scheduled and planned out well. I never knew this was an authoritative parenting style until I became a parent.

When I'd ask for something that I desired – not a necessity but simply something I loved – my single mother, with limited income, would patiently explain why she couldn't provide it at that moment. She would clarify that she needed to work overtime first. Life was undeniably a struggle, but I appreciated my hardworking mum, who was continuously educating me to understand why I couldn't receive a particular 'want'. When I finally received it, I truly understood the effort, hard work and value of money she had invested.

My mum wouldn't let us get away with bad behaviour or language. She always taught us to behave responsibly and offered advice, warmth, counselling and guidance.

She was loving, caring and supportive. She would save her pay increments and bonuses to take us on family get-aways, and she involved us in planning those trips, taking our preferences into account. It felt wonderful to be asked where we wanted to go and what we wanted to do. I felt part of the process and valued.

Our relationship was open and transparent, almost like friends. She taught us to share our true thoughts and feelings. I believe this kind of parent–child relationship strengthened my bond with my mum and created trust and closeness.

Because my mum taught me to share my feelings openly, if I had any issues in school or at work, she was always a listening ear to whisper in. I felt so comfortable and secure knowing I had my mum to share with. She was a responsive parent who always taught me the need for problem solving and encouraged me to deal with issues. This boosted my self-confidence.

Mum encouraged us to make our own career decisions, which helped us become independent thinkers. As I grew older, I was so disciplined in life, organising events in general, managing life overall. It was because of the discipline I was taught from an early age.

Adopting authoritative parenting with my children

Having experienced an authoritative parenting style in my childhood, I naturally adopted the same style with my kids when I became a parent.

I remember a moment when my son told me not to be angry with my daughter when she was naughty, but instead to talk with her. At first, I was stunned and a little angry when he said that to me. But I knew he was right. So, I respected my son's opinion, gave my daughter the chance to explain what was wrong, and why she had done something I felt not right. The conversation went well, and I could see both were happy. They felt good that mummy was talking to them respectfully; they felt heard and understood.

I now feel that *being responsive* to my kids and their needs has built a stronger and healthier bond between us. They have felt appreciated and listened to, and it has given them internal security.

Another example is during Salaah (Prayer) times. At first, I was flexible when my kids wanted to watch TV or use their phone or iPad, saying nothing. But gradually, I set the ground rules and expectations of 'what can be done' and 'what was not permissible' during prayer times. Over time, they learned the importance of behaving appropriately during this time.

I also set parental controls on their devices to monitor screen time and content. This has really helped the kids. Now, they often ask me whether something is worth watching, which shows they are beginning to understand the logic behind those controls.

I always consult with them on what they prefer to eat and where they would like to go on vacation – just like my mother did with me. I can see that they love having some input in our family plans. This reaffirms our bond, communication and trust, as well as warmth and sense of belongingness. I strongly feel that our parent–child relationship is enhanced through this

Observing growth, and evidence of authoritative parenting

Through my own parenting experience, I have seen how children develop self-regulation, autonomy and decision-making skills under authoritative guidance. For example, when I work with my children in planning daily activities – such as study, eating, play and prayer – they feel empowered and consulted. (I love doing this!)

Over time, they have taken initiative in their learning to download educational apps and games for learning purposes and manage tasks independently – which I find amazing.

I have also started to ensure that they pray along with me. I can see that they are starting to engage in and ask question about prayer times. As I model the way prayer is performed and how chanting is done, I see learned behaviour in my kids as they imitate me. This is again fascinating. Observation, reflection and learning are taking place. So many questions and answers; logical reasoning is kicking in.

When I teach them Urdu and Arabic using technology, I observe their growing independence and self-regulated behaviour as they search their tutorials and study online. I find this enthralling because they are taking charge of their learning. This boosts their self-confidence and morale and ability to reflect on what they are learning. In the beginning, I provided guidance and took them through their online training. But over time, I saw them gradually take the lead.

Witnessing all this growth has been very rewarding as a parent. I can see that encouraging independence has helped my children develop self-regulated behaviour, critical thinking and decision-making skills, a sense of autonomy, empowerment and confidence, and it has also boosted their academic performance.

Research evidence supporting authoritative parenting

Research consistently shows that authoritative parents supports positive moral development and reduces the chances of a child engaging in destructive or disobedient behaviour.[103, 279] It has an authoritative parenting style can have a noteworthy influence on a child's psychological and social growth and social behaviour.[280, 281] Studies confirm improved self-control and emotional regulation in children as a result of this style,[282] as well as self-efficacy and the development of personal responsibility.[283]

The warmth and responsiveness deployed by the parents assists in nurturing internal security as well and leads to rarer chances of anxiety and depression in children. Authoritative parenting creates a bond where children feel a sense of intimacy with their parents and siblings.[284] [285] This style promotes compromise, negotiation and cooperation among children, and there is confirmed evidence throughout the world that aggression is reduced.[286-289] Research also promotes the findings that problematic children are more likely to recover if their parents show cordiality and avoid punitive measures.[290-292] Parents utilising this style apparently feel less strained by their children' challenging behaviours.[292]

Authoritative parenting endorses self-reliance, better problem solving and resourcefulness.[293, 294]

Finally, authoritative parenting promotes self-reliance, better problem solving and resourcefulness, demonstrating its wide-ranging and lasting benefits for children's development.

In conclusion, the authoritative parenting style has its share of benefits. For parents, respect and communication are key. This builds empathy and understanding with your child. Positive discipline promotes rules and guidance, enhancing self-regulation in your child. Structure and clear expectations guide children effectively.

Activity #82: Exploring your parenting style

1. Are you a parent presently? Yes, or no?

2. If yes, have you ever used authoritative parenting with your child? Provide examples.

3. Has it benefited you and your child in any way?

4. If not, do you see yourself as an authoritative parent in the future? Yes, or no? Why?

5. What parenting style would you prefer and why?

6. What was your parents' parenting style and what impact did this have on you as a young person?

'To the outside world, we all grow old. But not to brothers and sisters. We know each other as we always were. We know each other's hearts. We share private family jokes. We remember family feuds and secrets, family griefs and joys. We live outside the touch of time.'
—Clara Ortega

15

Sibling Love and Children's Love for Parents
(Spheres 3 & 4)
Dr John Bellavance

This chapter focuses on two connected expressions of love in the family: the love between siblings and the love children develop for their parents. Sibling relationships offer an early space to practise empathy, cooperation and conflict resolution. In turn, a child's love for their parents grows from the care they receive, forming the basis for responsibility, gratitude and emotional maturity. Together, these bonds show how love circulates within the family, shaping character and lifelong relationships.

Sibling Love

The third sphere or expression of love is sibling love. Sibling relationships play a profound role in shaping personality and social skills. They influence how children resolve conflicts and form intimate bonds. The unique dynamic of growing up with siblings provides a training ground for life. Its lessons are particularly relevant for navigating adult relationships, including marriage. Close, supportive sibling relationships promote the qualities and skills needed for successful friendships and romantic partnerships. They can also buffer youth from the impact of stressful life events.[271]

Conversely, the quality of sibling interactions influences the whole family system, affecting both parent–child and inter-parental relationships. Conflictual and coercive sibling interaction patterns can be substantial stressors for parents and diminish their psychological wellbeing. Sibling violence occurs more frequently than other forms of child abuse. It is also significantly related to substance use, depression, delinquency and aggression.

Despite longstanding awareness of the destructive and constructive powers of sibling bonds, prevention and intervention programs have generally ignored them.[271] Yet relationships can play a significant role in preventing mental health problems and are an important component of values education.

Time spent with siblings is also important. Children in the US today are more likely to grow up with a sibling than with a father and children. In fact, they spend more free time with siblings than with anyone else. In groups that emphasis the family, siblings play an even stronger role as companions.[271]

Sibling interventions and conflict resolution

Reduced coercive exchanges and enhanced positive interactions between siblings should lead to reduced levels of siblings' antisocial tendencies and foster wellbeing. Siblings can help each other learn about the world, feel secure about exploring it, learn how to behave in certain situations and foster empathy.

If a younger sibling views an older sibling as an attachment figure, it gives them a model for how they can relate to others. Older siblings, due to their position within the family and their role as supporters and advisers, are often seen as both powerful and nurturing.[271] When a new child enters the family, parents often ask the older sibling to care for the younger one. This teaches altruism and care.

Sibling warmth and support are linked to improved emotional regulation, peer acceptance, social competence, academic engagement and educational attainment. The quality of sibling relationships is also one of the most important long-term predictors of mental health in old age.[271]

> ...siblings can provide crucial support during family conflict and stress

Furthermore, siblings can provide crucial support during family conflict and stress. For instance, siblings close to each other during parental divorce experience fewer negative effects from the divorce. Conversely, aggressive sibling interactions can translate into aggressive behaviour with peers.[257]

Research suggests that a warm sibling relationship teaches the sharing of intimate thoughts, how to understand others' feelings and how to resolve conflicts.[271] Siblings are often each other's first and most frequent source of conflict. This has advantages. Learning to argue, compromise and forgive with a sibling teaches valuable lessons in conflict resolution. These experiences, whether positive or negative, lay the groundwork for how a person will handle disagreements with friends and future partners.

Guided intervention where parents teach their children to handle conflicts with their siblings, instead of resorting to anger and aggression, have proven effective. For example, mothers who received 90 minutes of conflict mediation training learned how to guide their children in resolving sibling disputes independently.[271]

This shows that parents acting as mediators, rather than simply arbiters, can shift sibling dynamics. Children gain tools for collaborative conflict resolution and develop healthier family relationships.

How siblings shape personality and perspective

Sibling relationships foster empathy and perspective-taking. Being a sibling requires considering another's perspective, whether it's understanding a younger sibling's needs or negotiating with an older one. This practice in empathy is crucial for developing emotional intelligence (EI) and the ability to understand and validate others' feelings.

Birth order and family dynamics often shape a person's personality traits. For example, older siblings may be more responsible and assertive, while younger ones might be more sociable or creative. These roles, while not a rigid template, help a person form their identity and understand how they fit into a social group.

Preparation for marriage

Sibling relationships are often the first peer-like relationship children experience and can be influential in establishing the capacity to form secure bonds. The skills learned in these relationship – such as negotiation, compromise and communication – can be transferable to marriage. Findings suggest that close sibling relationships may enhance interpersonal skills and social confidence, which are advantageous in forming romantic relationships. (295)

Like marriage, a sibling relationship is a shared life with constant demands for compromise, whether it involves sharing a room, a bathroom or a television remote. These experiences prepare people for the give-and-take necessary to build a life together.

Sibling relationships combine deep levels of intimacy with occasional conflict. They offer a safe space to practise communication skills, express anger constructively and understand that love can endure despite frequent arguments. This provides a realistic foundation for the ups and downs of a marital relationship.

Despite their fights, most siblings share a deep, unconditional bond. This kind of love, rooted in security rather than performance or conditional affection, is a crucial lesson for a successful marriage. The ability to forgive and move on after a fight, trusting that the relationship remains secure, is a skill often honed in sibling dynamics and is essential for sustaining lifelong partnerships.

Activity #83: Reflecting on sibling bonds

Write in your journal and share with another:

1. How was your relationship with your sibling(s)?
2. How has that relationship been important for you?

One must give to grow

Parents who help their children offer significant psychological benefits for children, contributing to their emotional, social and cognitive development. This practice is linked to a stronger sense of self-worth, increased empathy and improved family relationships. Conversely, by helping their parents, children learn to think beyond their own needs and consider the wellbeing of others. This is a foundational step in developing empathy.[296]

When it comes to parental love, it is first given to the child, but it is eventually returned as children's love or filial piety. Children grow by giving back to their parents and siblings. If we only receive love without learning to give it, we can't progress and mature. Loving in return is what nurtures human development.

Research shows that being given responsibility helps children feel capable and valued. Contributing to household tasks or assisting parents gives them a sense of purpose and competence. One study found that children who had regular household chores from an early age had higher levels of self-esteem and a greater sense of mastery in life.[296] Moreover, adolescents who regularly helped their parents with tasks are more likely to have better academic outcomes and be more responsible in their later lives.[297]

As parents, we move from caring for our children (childcare) to, ideally, being cared for by them (parental care). The model of parental care in collectivistic cultures tends to thrive more compared to individualist traditions of developed countries. In developed countries, the emphasis is on individual development and self-fulfilment. Viktor Frankl[19] said that Western societies are obsessed with youth and accomplishments, while less emphasis is put on appreciating the wisdom and contributions of elders. Responsibility for the care of parents by their children has diminished, and governments and other institutions have stepped in to fill the gaps. However, in OECD countries, the elderly are becoming the new poor.

In this context, it becomes urgent for us to consider what it means to love our parents.

Love comes full circle: couples love each other, parents love their children, siblings love each other, and children love their parents.

Abilities: How to love your parents

Here are some meaningful ways to show love and appreciation for your parents[298]:

1. Visit them with family members.
2. Spend holidays together.
3. Celebrate their birthdays with a special gathering.
4. Cook meals for them.
5. Call them on weekends to check in.

6. Listen sincerely to their life stories.
7. Express your love for them with affection or according to their love language.
8. Encourage and support their hobbies.
9. Help them achieve their unfulfilled dreams.
10. Take them for regular health check-ups.
11. Share your thoughts and feelings with them.
12. Include them in important events.
13. Show them your workplace.
14. Travel together and create new memories.
15. Exercise with them for a healthier lifestyle.
16. Join them in their social activities.
17. Watch movies together and enjoy quality time.

Activity #84: The love you give and the love you receive

Write in your journal and share with another:

1. List two times in your life when you could have helped your parents but did not. What do you feel about that now?
2. List two times when your parents or caregivers did something for you, even if they did not have to. How did it make you feel?

PILLAR 3:

Managing Our Natural Environment and Sustainable Development

Pillar 3 examines how societies can responsibly manage the natural environment while pursuing sustainable development. It explores the paradigms that shape our technological age, the relationship between science, economics and ecological stewardship, and the consequences of separating values from development. This pillar highlights the importance of academic and family values, calls for transdisciplinary approaches, and considers the practical challenges of effective implementation and governance. Ultimately, it emphasises how organisations and individuals can adopt sustainable practices that support the wellbeing of both people and the planet.

Related UN Sustainable Development Goals (SDGs)
Goal 4: Quality Education

- Target 4.7: By 2030, ensure that all learners acquire the knowledge and skills needed to promote sustainable development.

Goal 7: Affordable and Clean Energy

- Target 7.2: By 2030, substantially increase the share of renewable energy in the global energy mix.

Goal 11: Sustainable Cities and Communities

- Target 11: Make cities and human settlements inclusive, safe, resilient and sustainable.
- Target 11.4: Strengthen efforts to protect and safeguard the world's cultural and natural heritage.
- Target 11.a: Support positive economic, social, and environmental links between urban, peri-urban, and rural areas by strengthening national and regional development planning.

Goal 12: Responsible Consumption and Production

- Target 12: Ensure sustainable consumption and production patterns.
- Target 12.5: By 2030, substantially reduce waste generation through prevention, reduction, recycling, and reuse.
- Target 12.6: Encourage companies, especially large and transnational corporations, to adopt sustainable practices and integrate sustainability information into their reporting cycle.
- Target 12.8: By 2030, ensure that people everywhere have the relevant information and awareness for sustainable development and lifestyles in harmony with nature.

Goal 13: Climate Action

- Target 13: Take urgent action to combat climate change and its impacts.
- Target 13.2: Integrate climate change measures into national policies, strategies, and planning.
- Target 13.3: Improve education, awareness, and institutional capacity on climate change mitigation, adaptation, impact reduction, and early warning.

Goal 14: Life Below Water

- Target 14: Conserve and sustainably use the oceans, seas, and marine resources for sustainable development.

- Target 14.1: By 2025, prevent and significantly reduce marine pollution of all kinds, particularly from land-based activities, including marine debris and nutrient pollution.
- Target 14.4: By 2020, effectively regulate harvesting and end overfishing, illegal, unreported, and unregulated fishing, as well as destructive fishing practices.

Goal 15: Life on Land

- Target 15: Protect, restore, and promote the sustainable use of terrestrial ecosystems, manage forests sustainably, combat desertification, halt and reverse land degradation, and stop biodiversity loss.
- Target 15.5: Take urgent and significant action to reduce the degradation of natural habitats, halt biodiversity loss, and by 2020, protect and prevent the extinction of threatened species.

'You cannot get through a single day without having an impact on the world around you. What you do makes a difference, and you have to decide what kind of a difference you want to make.'

—Jane Goodall

16

Managing and Caring for Our Natural Environment

Dr John Bellavance

The UN suggests that a healthy society gives equal attention to economic development, ecological sustainability and social justice as these three pillars are deeply interconnected and mutually reinforcing. When one is neglected, the others are neg-

...what we do impacts nature and nature in turn impacts us.

atively impacted, leading to instability and imbalance. Environmental issues have a direct and significant impacts on peace and security.

With this broader picture in mind, the central focus of this chapter is caring for, managing, protecting and restoring our natural environment. Restoration involves repairing damage to ecosystems so that they can heal and return to a healthy state. For this to occur, education must equip learners with the knowledge, values and skills needed to promote sustainable development. Many of humanity's current existential risks stem from the mismanagement and exploitation of our natural environment.

This values education program doesn't condemn economic prosperity or technological development. But it does emphasise the critical importance of their responsible management. We must create new models for how to sustainably harmonise technological development with the ecology of the natural world for the benefit of humanity and the Earth. As stated in the UN preamble for 'Transforming Our World: The 2030 Agenda for Sustainable Development':

> *'This Agenda is a plan of action for people, planet and prosperity.'*(299)

Preserving our natural environment is one of the defining tasks of the 21st century.(300) The UN maintains that there is growing international recognition that Education for Sustainable Development is an integral element of quality education and a key enabler for sustainable development.(301)

Paradigms for a Technological Society

The modern era is often described as a 'technological society' that promises the attainment of the 'good life'. Most scientific and technological development has been driven by the desire to improve the human condition. Unparalleled advances in public health, education and digital technologies have brought great benefits to human wellbeing that have become defining features of our contemporary civilisation.

This section explores various views on how humans understand their relationship with technology. This is important as it sets the tone for this program's perspective on how we can best manage our relationship with the natural world.

The instrumental paradigm

The instrumental paradigm suggests that technologies are neutral, value-free tools; they are a means to an end determined by humans. Under this paradigm, the natural environment is seen primarily as a resource to be used for human benefit.

Technology as a neutral tool that can be used for good or evil, much like a hammer. The hammer itself is not inherently moral or immoral; its value depends entirely on the wielder's intent. Will it be used for good, such as to construct a shelter, or to cause harm? Its ethical meaning is shaped by the wielder.

This view holds that technology is shaped by and serves the values established within society. It focuses on the implementation of technology through valuing effectiveness, control and economic utility. This is considered the dominant view adopted by modern governments and policy sciences and thus impacts how we use natural resources. By viewing nature as a collection of neutral, value-free tools, this perspective can lead to its exploitation.

The substantive paradigm

The substantive paradigm argues that we should be wary of the instrumental paradigm because no tool is neutral since technologies have inbuilt biases that affect the social dimension and natural environment. Technologies are shaped by the interests, goals and biases of the people who produce and control them, and these 'interests' are embedded in the design, deployment and uses of technologies. Under this paradigm, technology transforms everything, including human life and nature, into means to human ends. We are more interested in technical efficiency and effectiveness – saving time and that things work well – than in how this affects humans and the environment.[302]

Understanding these paradigms helps us recognise that caring for the environment is not only a technical or policy problem; it is a *values and worldview* problem.

Activity #85: Technology, values and our relationship with nature

Write in your journal and share with others:

1. The instrumental paradigm posits that technologies are neutral tools and values-free. How does that sit with you?

2. The substantive paradigm argues that no tool is neutral since technologies have inbuilt biases (techniques) that affect the social dimension and the natural environment. How does that sit with you?

3. How do these views affect our relationship with nature?

The systems paradigm

The systems paradigm is the view that human values and goals shape our technologies, and our technologies also shape us (a system) for good or for ill. We can view the relationship between our technologies and nature as a **coupled human–natural system**. A systems approach views life on Earth as a complex web of natural and social systems that are interconnected and reciprocally affect each other.[171, 172] This applies also to interactions between human social systems and all other ecosystems.[303]

This is the view that this program puts forward as vital for the wellbeing of humans and the natural world.

Coupled human–natural systems

According to a coupled human–natural system perspective, education on the existence and nature of systems can foster system sensitivity and a desire for healthy environments.[266] This is why this values education program places so much importance on the principle of giving and receiving and the circularity of life: what we do impacts nature and nature in turn impacts us. All life is connected.

An open system is a system that has external interactions with its environment. It has input and output flows, exchanging matter, energy or information with its surroundings. System components impact each other, which creates a feedback loop – the process by which an effect (an output) feeds back (an input) onto its very cause.[173] Biological organisms (such as humans) and ecosystems in the natural environment (such as forests or planet Earth) are open systems. Humans and the natural environment are thus two interacting open systems that affect and feed back onto one another.

In the study of human ecology, human actions generate effects that reverberate throughout ecosystems and human social systems. The system in Figure 31 represents the feedback loop between humans and our natural environment. For example, if we input pollution from our technologies into our environment, it will impact us in the form of poor air quality (the output).

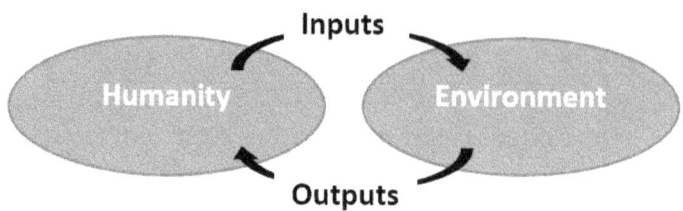

Figure 32 Feedback loop between humans and their natural environments

Human impacts on ecosystems

Human ecology is an interdisciplinary field that studies the relationships between humans and their natural, social and built environments. In human ecology, an environment is everything within a specified area – the air, soil, water, living organisms and everything built by humans. Human ecology analyses the consequences of human activities as a chain of effects through the ecosystem and human social system.

People affect ecosystems when they use resources such as water, fish, timber and livestock grazing land. In most cases, after using materials from ecosystems, people return the materials as waste.[303]

For example, the ocean is a coupled human–natural systems. It directly supports human livelihoods through food, industry and cultural identity. However, human pollutants and the overexploitation of marine resources is increasingly challenging the ocean's capacity to provide benefits, disrupting this relationship.

Another example of human impact on ecosystems can be seen in the inputs we make – such as pollution and resource depletion – which then feed back onto us in the form of climatic change, ocean acidification, land degradation, water scarcity, and fisheries and biodiversity loss (the outputs). All these outputs affect the quality of human life on Earth. For example, by the year 2000, human beings had cleared more than 2.3 million km^2 of primary forest, and 90% of global fisheries were being harvested at or near maximum sustainable yield. Humans have driven species to extinction at rates estimated to be more than 100 times those observed in the fossil record. Vertebrate species have, on average, experienced a 50% decline in population over the past 45 years.

The concentrations of major greenhouse gases in the atmosphere are now at their highest levels in at least 800,000 years.(304)

The beneficial outputs we receive from our natural environments are enormous. The atmosphere, oceans and key ecosystems such as forests, wetlands and tundra work together to sustain life on earth. They help maintain a stable climate, provide clean air, recycle nutrients such as nitrogen and phosphorus, and regulate the world's water cycle, ensuring a supply of freshwater. In addition, the land, seas and rivers – and the plants and animals they contain – provide us with vital resources, chiefly food, fuel, timber and medicinal compounds.(304)

Activity #86: Sustainability issues and solutions

Write in your journal and share with others:

1. Brainstorm some of the major issues surrounding sustainability such as water, non-renewable and renewable energy, recycling, landfill and fisheries.
2. Select one issue from the list and write a short narrative about this issue and what could be done.

Planetary health

The Earth is aching and sick; we need to care for it. Many of us are so concerned about our own health, but are we as concerned about the health of the Earth?

Humans play an important role in managing the planet's systems and reducing damage to them. One solution is the concept of 'planetary health'. This is an emerging field of study connecting human health, civilisation and the natural systems on which humans depend. This approach suggests that health and environmental policies need to be harmonised.(304)

Changes to the structure and function of the Earth's natural systems represent a growing threat to human health. Research shows that a quarter of the global disease burden is attributable to human-modifiable environmental factors. For example, three out of every four new infectious diseases in people come from animals, including HIV, Ebola, Zika, Hendra, SARS, MERS and COVID-19. [304] Hunting and selling wildlife, often endangered, increases the risk of disease transmission from animals to humans. Ambient air pollution from fine particulates causes around 3.6 million deaths per year, mostly as a result of fossil fuel combustion.[304] Our health and survival are interdependent with the health of our planet.

Managing Science, Technology, Economics and the Environment

'Let us not forget that human knowledge and skills alone cannot lead humanity to a happy and dignified life.' — **Albert Einstein**

Science and technology have been used for the conquest and exploitation of nature. As a result, we have become desensitised to the destruction of nature, seeing its exploitation as normal. This has caused us to lose sight of our responsibility to care for it.

Humanity has traded off many of the Earth's supportive and regulating processes to feed and fuel human population growth and development. However, we can no longer take for granted the planet's ecosystem's ability to sustain future generations. In a world still plagued with unsustainable exploitation of natural resources, famine, conflict, inequity and disease, it is evident that science and technology are not being used as ethically and effectively as they could be. Humans have always been better at building tools than using them wisely. We gained the power to manipulate the world, but not the wisdom or the will to manage the complexity of the global ecology.

> Humans have always been better at building tools than using them wisely.

To effectively manage science, technology and economics – and by extension, our environment – four critical dimensions must be addressed:

- **Separation of values from development** – Ensuring that ethical, social and environmental values are integrated into technological and economic progress

- **The need for transdisciplinary research** – Encouraging collaboration across multiple disciplines to develop holistic and innovative solutions
- **Implementation and governance challenges** – Addressing gaps in policy enforcement, regulatory oversight and accountability in decision making
- **Sustainable practices of organisations and individuals** – Promoting responsible consumption, corporate sustainability and individual action towards environmental stewardship.

The following sections will discuss each of their dimensions.

The Separation of Values from Development

The first critical challenge to achieving sustainable development is the separation of values from development. This has several components.

First, **values have become separated from scientific, technological and economic development**. For example, corruption and misuse taint all aspects of the fishing industry. Illegal practices undermine conservation efforts; corrupt officials may accept bribes to issue fishing licences to unauthorised vessels, and illegal, unreported, and unregulated (IUU) fishing damages fisheries and marine ecosystems. Science is also a human activity that can be constructive or destructive. For example, mathematics can be used to guide instruments capable of killing on a mass scale.[305]

The assumption that science and values occupy two competing areas has contributed to many environmental and social disasters in the 20th and 21st centuries. When science excludes values, it diminishes the importance of ethical responsibility in human decision making and technological applications. Science doesn't need moral indifference to maintain its neutrality for the sake of scientific objectivity.[14]

Yet when scientific and technological development is pursued solely through a lens of utility or efficiency, nature is reduced to a decontextualised and objectified resource, open to exploitation.[306-308]

The ethical desire to use development for humanity's prosperity and peace is being sidelined or undermined by a lack of values perspective. The misuse of scientific knowledge by various political and economic interests has contributed to equity and environmental problems.[5] Scientific and technological development has often marginalised the role of values in development. It is therefore critical that we cooperate across academic, social, political, national and industry boundaries when it comes to economic and scientific development.

Activity #87: Mapping how you use nature

Write your name in the middle of the spiderweb. Around it, list examples of how you, and people around you, use natural resources primarily for personal or immediate benefit. Consider both everyday activities and larger-scale uses. Reflect on any patterns you notice and how these uses impact the environment.

The second problem associated with a lack of values perspective is **the growth of selfish individualism and a materialist values perspective**. In industrialised nations, self-fulfilment, consumerism, free enterprise and continuous economic growth have become major components of our worldview. Such value perspectives have negative consequences for humans and the natural environment. The deployment of technology shaped primarily by commercial interests affects social and ecological systems, and the demand for consumer goods now extends far beyond that required for a decent life. (303)

As development progresses, we are gradually losing our ability to control it. We are not taking responsibility for the detrimental effects on the health of humans and the natural environment. If this continues, it will have destructive consequences, which will be difficult for us to remedy.

The third problem associated with a lack of values perspective is the absence of a global worldview or consciousness. We need to consider alternatives to the current modern paradigm. This means adopting affirmative attitudes such as valuing universal values, multiculturalism, spirituality, the dignity and wellbeing of all people, and environmental conservation. Yet we are facing global problems without a truly functioning global community. No single discipline or local prescription can solve the problems facing humanity.[4, 5] When it comes to climate change and the threat of nuclear weapons, countries are no longer sovereign in any meaningful sense. These issues require global solutions, based on a global worldview. A failure to reach agreement between countries, or to act decisively, remains a significant barrier to the success of environmental management.(309)

> No single discipline or local prescription can solve the problems facing humanity.(4, 5)

The fourth problem associated with the absence of a values perspective concerns **inequality and greed and their link to environmental issues**. We have not upheld human dignity nor demonstrated adequate care for our environment.[5] Human welfare and environmental harms are frequently disregarded for the sake of present-day economic gains.(304) Hence, equity issues need to be considered in development and climate policies.

The impacts of climate change are unevenly weighted against the world's poor and vulnerable people, who have the least resources to withstand climate stresses. The interplay between climate change, conflict, hunger and poverty creates increasingly complex emergencies. The former President of the World Bank argued that if we don't confront climate change, we won't end extreme poverty.[310] For example, air pollution continues to kill millions of people around the world, often the poorest.[309]

Damaged ecosystems that lose their capacity to meet basic human needs also limit opportunities for economic development and social justice. [303] For example, developing countries that lack policies or technology struggle to regulate biofuels, which adversely impacts both food security and biodiversity.[309] The annual report by the UN High Commission for Refugees acknowledges that climate change is a significant factor driving people to flee their homes and preventing many from returning.[311] Furthermore, climate change drives conflict in areas where scarce resources heighten tensions.

The failure to achieve environmental sustainability has prompted discussions on the need for new economic paradigms.[309] A healthy society gives equal attention to economic development, ecological sustainability and social justice because they are mutually reinforcing.[303]

Linking values with development

Environmental problems are primarily rooted in selfish human behaviour. Hence, adopting the right values is essential to change behaviour and drive sustainable development. UNESCO maintains that the values and attitudes we hold significantly influence how we engage with the environment, shaping our prospects for achieving a sustainable future.[282] Values and knowledge determine how we process and interpret information and translate it into action, while science and technology provide tools to support those actions. [303] A moral orientation in economics and science, centred on shared values, will help foster equitable and sustainable development (see Figure 32). To advance human dignity, a shared standard of values must guide our economic and scientific analyses and policies. Sustainable development depends on such a holistic approach.

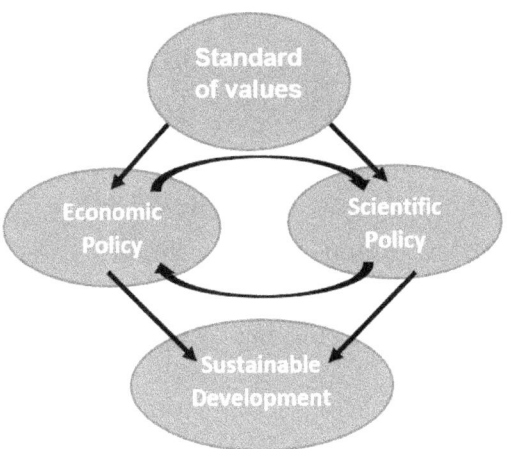

Figure 33 Values and sustainable development

Academic values and sustainable development

In the sphere of values, scholars play a vital role in promoting sustainable development through three key contributions. First, they need to be pioneers in the realm of conscience, inspiring humanity to follow an ethical path in addressing the world's problems and pursuing human ideals. Conveying appropriate values to the wider world is as important as conducting research and theoretical teaching. Had science and technology been underpinned by human dignity and environmental care, many of the formidable problems of environmental destruction could have been prevented.[4, 5]

Second, scholars need to contribute their knowledge to address corruption and immorality by engaging in public debates and voicing moral concerns. Their knowledge can be pivotal in challenging unethical practices and advocating for responsible development.

Family values and sustainable development

What values can underpin sustainable development? Fundamentally, it is the love within families and the care for the environment that is expressed both in families and throughout society.

In many traditional societies, humans are considered children of nature, with Mother Nature deeply respected. Indigenous peoples, who have had longstanding connections to their lands, emphasise that everything in nature is connected. Their cultures promote treating the environment with care and respect to avoid adverse consequences.

For example, Indigenous Australians hold a spiritual and emotional attachment to the land on which they live and to all living things, seeing people, plants and animals as sharing common ancestors. Similarly, many Native American traditions regard land formations, plants and animals as possessing spirits, viewing them as sacred and deserving of respect. As one Native American traditional owner stated:

> 'We are indigenous people to this land. We are like a conscience. We are small, but we aren't a minority. We are the landholders; we are the land keepers; we are not a minority. For our brothers are all the natural world, and by that, we are by far the majority.'[312]

More broadly, a growing number of people feel a strong spiritual connection with the natural world regardless of their involvement in organised religion.[303]

Activity #88: Connecting with nature

Write in your journal and share with others:

1. Do you feel a connection to nature? If so, how?
2. What can we learn from traditional owners about their connection to the land?

The Need for Transdisciplinary Research

The second major challenge in achieving sustainable development is the urgent need for transdisciplinary research activities and capacity.[304] Transdisciplinary research is an approach that integrates knowledge and methods from diverse disciplines to address complex, real-world problems. It actively seeks to create a new, overarching framework that transcends the boundaries of traditional disciplines, often involving non-academic participants such as community members and policymakers in the research process.

The complicated problems of the world can't be fully understood from the narrow perspectives of individual fields of knowledge. In the twentieth century, we created ministries and UN agencies to deal with individual, collective and environmental problems. Similarly, academia created dedicated university departments, scholarly journals and professional career paths to address each problem. Today we realise that this siloed approach – dealing with one problem cluster at a time – is *not working*. On the contrary, it seems to be part of the problem,[16] contributing to worsening the challenges we face.

Solutions to global problems are beyond the capacity of any single specialised society of scholars. Cooperation among scholars is no less important than individual research in specialised fields. The fragmentation of academic disciplines is preventing the fulfilment of its collective work. Each discipline offers its own unique but partial view of reality. For example, there is a lack of transdisciplinary research into problems and solutions with respect to energy production, irrigation, food security, carbon dependence and biosecurity.[309] Additionally, although a vast majority of scientists concur that climate change is a fact, there is no consensus regarding the best economic response to this threat.

For transdisciplinary research to be conducted, it must be guided by a well-understood purpose and shared values. Various fields need to be brought together through complementary relationships that prioritise cooperation and the common good. An ideal society can only be realised when every field of science and technology is unified for the benefit of humankind.[5]

> An ideal society can only be realised when every field of science and technology is unified for the benefit of humankind

Activity #89: Collaborating for a sustainable future

Write in your journal and share with others:

1. List the organisations and people that you believe should be involved in solving climate change and pollution.
2. What can these organisations and people learn from each other?

Implementation and Governance Challenges

A significant third challenge to achieving sustainable development lies in implementation and governance. Key obstacles include 'implementation traps' such as prioritising economic growth at the expense of other concerns, a lack of political will, poor governance and long-term planning, insufficient capacity and inadequate legal frameworks.

Academics

Challenge arises when policy papers are developed with incomplete specifications. This is one of the implementation traps. Conflicting objectives, policy goals being too vague or broad to be converted into actions, terms within policies not clearly defined, a lack of guidance on how policies and objectives can be achieved, and a lack of coherence between policies and objectives all prevent successful implementation.[309]

Another common implementation barrier on the local level is a lack of coordination between central and local governments. Fragmented central-local connections hinder environmental initiatives from being implemented effectively. Local political resistance can also be a barrier when imposed central policies routinely face backlash due to local government concerns that environmental measures will undermine growth and employment. Another challenge is when short-term results drive the agenda over long-term sustainability.[313]

Other examples of implementation and governance problems include: how governments and institutions delay recognition and responses to threats;

and the lack of implementation of environmental policies and practices in manufacturing, agriculture, transport and energy.[304] Additionally, a lack of accountability due to inadequate monitoring, reporting and verification mechanisms and authoritarian governments are barriers to international environmental cooperation.[313]

Economics

Economic policies also present implementation and governance challenges. Many governments continue to provide economic incentives that encourage private and public sectors to exploit natural resources without considering environmental damage. For example, European Union fisheries subsidies have fuelled the growth of the EU fleet to levels estimated to be two to three times above sustainable capacity.

Conversely, poorly designed regulations are causing market failure by discouraging investment in, and development of, innovative environmentally sustainable solutions. The disconnection between economic markets and environmental sustainability – often described as the decoupling of economic growth from environmental degradation – is the result of failures in values and policies. For example, the failure to pass the Canada Endangered Species Protection Act was due to debates being framed entirely in economic and commercial terms, prioritising economics over species protection.[309] By contrast, when economic development is balanced with consideration for the depreciation of natural resources, sustainable development becomes achievable.[304]

Governance

Another implementation and governance challenge is when governments don't have the capacity and/or political will to implement sustainable policies. The absence of appropriate laws is a concern, as is the presence of laws that hinder progress towards environmental targets. Case studies indicate that failure may result when environmental legislation is not implemented fully, are not politically popular or go against a prevailing political agenda.[309]

These implementation and governance failures point to the need for education. The seriousness of sustainability issues and the urgent need for change have not been effectively communicated to key stakeholders or fully understood. This suggests that there has been a failure to convince decision-makers that sustainable development offers a realistic pathway to a prosperous economy, a better society and a healthy environment.[309] Moreover, partisan political divides have prevented the development of a coherent long-term plan that integrates both economic and environmental perspectives of both the left and the right.

Sustainable Practices and Policies of Organisations and Individuals

> *'Never doubt that a small group of thoughtful, committed citizens can change the world; indeed, it is the only thing that ever has.'*
> *—Margaret Mead*

The fourth major issue in achieving sustainable development is the lack of sustainable practices of organisations and individuals. The natural environment is the foundation for human flourishing. However, there is growing evidence that the current pattern of consumption and production can't continue without overstepping planetary boundaries – the safe operating space for humanity.[314] We now risk our wellbeing and health because of the ongoing degradation of nature's life support systems. In effect, we are mortgaging the wellbeing of future generations to secure short-term economic and development gains in the present. These gains are driven by inequitable, inefficient and unsustainable patterns of resource consumption and technological development.[304]

Deloitte Australia chief economist Chris Richardson says the COVID pandemic showed the cost of failing to anticipate and prepare for catastrophic risks. This was a wake-up call for us to get ahead of that other big risk, climate change. Climate change is no longer a distant possibility but a present reality, and its economic and social costs are rising each year. Doing nothing is now the costliest policy choice. It is predicted that by 2050, Australia will experience economic losses on par with those experienced during COVID every single year if we don't address climate change.

Despite the global reach of policies to protect the environment originating from the 1992 Rio Earth Summit, the state of the global environment has continued to deteriorate. This international commitment was supported by domestic policies at the national and local levels of government. There have been some patchy improvements in selected indicators for a few locations; however, the overall decline in environmental quality has continued unabated. The world's ecological footprint (which measures resource use) exceeded the sustainable capacity of the planet in 1970, and emissions of greenhouse gases are rising.[309]

Sustainable practices

Sustainable development policies and practices are primarily concerned with how best to govern the relationship between humans and the natural environment for the benefit of both.[303, 304]

There is hope for a sustainable future if we aim for sustainable development that meets the needs of the present without compromising the capacity of future generations to meet their own needs. If policymakers and individuals can learn from past failures and address these issues, we will still be able to set the world on a sustainable development path.

Opportunities now exist to improve governance, harness new knowledge, and exploit a range of technologies that can improve health and reduce environmental damage.[304] To address the climate emergency, the UN Secretary-General outlined three critical actions[300]:

1. Achieving global carbon neutrality within 30 years
2. Aligning global finance with the Paris Agreement
3. Prioritising adaptation to protect vulnerable populations and nations from climate impacts.

Sustainability is inherently a holistic systems approach, and the business sector is a major part of both the problem and the solution. We need to first reevaluate change in the value system that underpins scientific and economic development. Sustainable development includes three interdependent and mutually reinforcing values/pillars[314, 315]:

1. Social development (which was discussed with respect to values)
2. Economic development
3. Environmental protection

Circular economy system

One sustainable practice is the circular economy system, which keeps products in use for as long as possible by repairing goods and recycling end products. Figure 33 represents a circular economy of inputs and outputs with respect to manufacturing, consumption and recycling. This includes the reduction of waste through the production of goods that are more durable and require lower quantities of materials and less energy to manufacture. To achieve this, we need to incentivise recycling, reuse, repair and better manufacturing practices.[304]

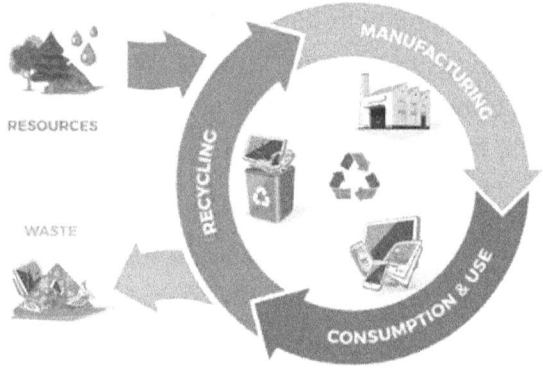

Figure 34 Circular Economy

Sustainable practices of individuals

Sustainable development is more likely to be successful if it gains social backing and people feel a personal sense of responsibility for it. That means each of us must become informed and be part of the solution. Why?

There are several key reasons why sustainable development struggles to gain widespread public support [309]:

- Lack of public demand for stronger action on climate change and sustainability.

- Attitudes towards science influencing behaviour; for example, a study of fishermen in the European Union found that a lack of trust in scientific estimates of fish stock depletion contributed to overfishing.
- Environmental issues are highly politicised, leading to polarisation, misinformation and public doubt that action is necessary.
- Community opposition to environmentally sustainable policies and initiatives is widespread.
- Limited awareness and understanding of sustainability issues, often due to ineffective communication strategies.

The other problem with respect to individual responsibility is the promotion of commercialisation and consumption to children and adults. I remember sitting in a school assembly during the 2008 Global Financial Crisis. A Year 12 student leader stood up in front of 300 senior students and told them to buy a new phone to alleviate the impact of the financial crisis. I thought, *'There must be a better way.'*

Sustainability begins with prioritising it in our daily lives. We can all make a conscious decision to be more sustainable today, even by taking small steps like reducing water and electricity usage. The following practices will help you make small daily changes that will help our shared planet.

Abilities: daily sustainability practices

Be aware of your eco footprint

To better understand your impact, try calculating your ecological footprint using online eco footprint, carbon footprint and water footprint calculators. These are a great starting point to raise awareness of your use of resources.

Connect with others

Once you become intentional about your environmental footprint, it is a good idea to **connect with others or with community organisations** that support sustainability by exchanging products and sharing practices. Who knows, you might make friends with people who share similar values to yours. You can find out about collaborative movements in your community and connect with them. In this way, you will learn a lot.

Reduce purchases and simplify your life

Before you buy any product, consider asking: **'Do I really need this?'** or **'How did the production of this product impact the environment** and what further impacts will there be with the disposal of the product?'

To curb impulse buying, try implementing a **10-day waiting period**. After initially desiring an item, you delay your purchase decision for 10 days. The dopamine release during 'retail therapy' creates a desire for further purchases to replicate the experience. To counteract this psychological mechanism, repeat the phrase: **'Don't buy this; I don't need it.'**

Another strategy is to **evaluate prices before purchasing**. Think rationally about the cost. A neuroscientific study, using brain scans, showed that the pleasure centre is activated when people consider products, but the prefrontal cortex, associated with decision making, activates when prices are revealed. Subjects with more active prefrontal cortices were less likely to buy. This supports the strategy of evaluating price before purchase.

Another way to reduce is to **simplify your life**. Only keep belongings that you use or enjoy on a regular basis. By making the effort to reduce what you own, you will be more inclined to purchase less, hence creating less waste. (316)

Push businesses to reduce waste, and reduce your own consumption

- Advocate for supermarkets to sell more 'seconds' produce. Currently, 30% to 50% of all food production is wasted due to inefficiencies in harvesting, storage, transportation, marketing and consumption. (304) Food insecurity affected 11% of US households in 2018. Food waste also contributes to methane production in landfills, a significant environmental concern. Economically, US food loss and waste is estimated at $161 billion. Alarmingly, 13% of household food is discarded before its use-by-date.[317]

- Buy no more food than what you expect to use. You will be more likely to keep it fresh and use it all up.
- Freeze and preserve surplus fruits and vegetables.
- Prepare perishable foods soon after shopping.
- Be mindful of old ingredients and leftovers you need to use up.

Making small, conscious choices can lead to significant environmental impact.

Reduce consumptions of energy and resources
- Reduce energy consumption: aim to use 10% less energy each month.
- Switch to LED lighting: LEDs offer the greatest energy savings
- Use a clothesline: reduce dryer use to save electricity.
- Fix leaks quickly: prevent water waste from dripping taps.
- Avoid single-use packaging: buy in bulk and store in reusable containers.
- Pack waste-free lunches: use reusable wraps and containers.
- Carry a reusable mug: reduce disposable cup waste.
- Support waste reduction efforts: advocate for businesses to minimise waste.
- Hold companies accountable: for example, McDonald's globally recycled only 10% of guest packaging as of 2020.[318]

Adopt the circular economy

The circular economy focuses on reusing, repurposing and creating by finding new uses for old items. Here's how you can adopt this practice:

- Repurpose and reuse: get creative with upcycling! Pinterest is a great source of inspiration.
- Choose reusable over disposable: swap single-use products for sustainable alternatives.

- Buy and sell second-hand: shop online for used products and hold garage sales.
- Borrow instead of buying. Share equipment with family and friends for temporary needs.
- Donate unused items: support those in need by giving away functional equipment, like computers. My wife, for example, sends used sewing machines to Pacific Island women to help them start micro-businesses.
- Compost organic waste: turn food scraps and yard trimmings into nutrient-rich compost.
- Join or start a Fixers' Collective: work with your community to repair appliances and household items, shifting away from a 'throw-away' mindset.

By adopting these practices, we can extend the life of products, reduce waste and contribute to a more sustainable world!

Refuse
Refuse and reject programs and products that produce waste as often as you can.

Increase physical activities
Incorporating more physical activity into daily life benefits both personal health and the environment.

- Active travel: walk or cycle whenever possible to reduce greenhouse gas emissions and improve fitness.
- Health benefits: physical inactivity is linked to over 3 million deaths annually, contributing to conditions like heart disease, diabetes, cancer, Alzheimer's and depression.
- Small changes matter: instead of spending five minutes searching for the closest parking spot, park further away and walk.

By choosing active travel and making small adjustments, we can boost health while protecting the planet!

Diversify your diet

Major proportions of the world's crops are being fed to animals or used for biofuels, resulting in 41% of the calories available from global crop production being lost. Allocating more crops from animal feed and biofuels to direct human consumption could substantially increase global food availability.[304] A UN report concludes that the livestock sector (primarily cows, chickens and pigs) is one of the largest sources of greenhouse gases.[316]

We cannot change the past, but we can change the future.

Activity #90: Planning for a smaller eco footprint

Write in your journal and share it with others:

1. Plan how you will reduce your eco footprint.
2. Add this to your journal and share your plan with another person or a small group.

'It's time to challenge the concept that human nature is inherently conflict-driven and to recognise that a better life and a better world are possible when our values and worldview shift.'
—*Dr John Bellavance*

17

Conclusion

Our hope with the text you just read in this values education program is firstly that you will have found some powerful, knowledge-based keys to assist you in cultivating lifelong skills for managing yourself, your relationships and your environment effectively.

Our holistic approach to education integrates cognitive and intellectual development with personal meaning, emotions and motivation. The aim is to foster individuals who have self-esteem, tolerance, responsibility and the capacity to form meaningful goals, all within a supportive framework of ethical values.

Whatever role you play in society – educator, policy maker, business leader, student, parent and so on – we hope that you will draw on this text to support and guide those in your care, as well as yourself. This may be through your work, the programs you create, the policies you promote, or the curriculum you help shape. And, importantly, it may also be expressed in the everyday life of your family and community.

Education is never values-neutral. A holistic, values-based approach, such as the one presented in this program, is crucial for wellbeing, social and emotional development, healthy relationships and community harmony. Our worldviews and values serve as guiding principles; they shape our identity and how we engage with the world around us. This text has presented a critical societal challenge: how to integrate new understandings and values while still honouring and preserving the traditions that genuinely nourish us.

We need to move beyond 'us versus them' thinking, polarisation, distrust and pessimism, and instead promote – and action – much-needed values education. It's time to challenge the concept that human nature is inherently conflict-driven and to recognise that a better life and a better world are possible when our values and worldview shift.

This program invites us to open our minds to new possibilities and to prioritise meaning, connection and service to others over external measures of success such as wealth and power. True happiness and fulfilment arise from purpose that reaches beyond oneself – and even beyond one's immediate family, society or nation. We need a global worldview.

We can't emphasise enough that **love is the central value of life** – the connecting force that binds us and enables self-transcendence and unity. Love is also foundational to mental wellbeing. Now more than ever, humanity needs a renewed focus on the social foundations of happiness: love, values, meaning, and connection with others and with the natural world.

To overcome what we describe as the 'Great Human Contradiction' where individuals and society collectively create undesirable outcomes – we must address the spiritual, social and ecological divisions at the root of these challenges. This book and program therefore advocate for prioritising the wellbeing of the whole.

The *Six Pillars Framework for Wellbeing, Positive Relationships and a Sustainable and Peaceful Future* provides a comprehensive approach to education with this goal in mind. It nurtures ethical individuals and relationships, responsible businesses, effective governance and engaged global citizens. In this volume, we have focused on the first three pillars. Here's a quick recap:

Pillar One: Managing Ourselves and Self-Actualisation

We explored how meaning and purpose, conscious living, personal responsibility and understanding mind–body relations shape wellbeing. We emphasised the importance of knowing oneself, managing one's inner life through mindfulness and emotional intelligence, and recognising the cultural influences that support or constrain self-actualisation and self-development.

Pillar Two: Managing Our relationships and Self-actualisation

We examined love as the central value of life, and the family as the foundational school of love and values. We discussed how shared values, reflective listening and living for the sake of others nurture harmonious relationships. We highlighted the four spheres of love within families – conjugal, parental, sibling and filial – and their importance in healthy development and social stability. We also addressed the impact of popular culture on relationships and affirmed the importance of lifelong, comprehensive sexuality education.

Pillar Three: Managing our Natural Environment and Sustainable Development

We considered the interconnectedness of human and natural systems, and how human activities shape ecosystems. We examined the consequences of resource use, waste generation and environmental degradation, and advocated for balancing economic development with the preservation of natural systems. We highlighted the need for transdisciplinary research, government commitment, circular economic models and individual sustainable practices.

This book and program advocates for a values-based approach to life – one that emphasises self-management, fosters positive relationships rooted in love and communication, and promotes sustainable practices for our natural environment. It argues that true happiness and a peaceful future arise when we align our lives with meaningful purpose, genuine connection, and responsible action towards ourselves, others and the planet.

Achieving this requires an *open mind, an open heart and an open will* – qualities essential for learning, leading and innovating. Aligning with the right values and focusing on what truly matters is critical for personal wellbeing, happiness and positive change.

In our next volume of works, we will explore the remaining three pillars of global citizenship within the Six Pillar Framework: **universal values,**

interdependence and **mutual prosperity.** These pillars are vital for cultivating national and global citizens who embrace our shared humanity, common values and collective future.

— Dr John Bellavance, Dr Tuong Thi Phan and Dr Rafia Naz

– COMING SOON –

Three Pillars of Global Citizenship:
Universal Values, Interdependence and Mutual Prosperity

The second book in the *Six Pillars Framework for Wellbeing, Positive Relationships, and a Sustainable and Peaceful Future* series is *Three Pillars of Global Citizenship*.

Dr John Bellavance, Dr Tuong Thi Phan and Dr Rafia Naz and other distinguished academics and community leaders, authored this work, drawing on their extensive experience in peacebuilding, education, health and management.

This book delves into the three pillars of global citizenship – universal values, interdependence, and mutual prosperity, which are essential for cultivating national and global citizens who embrace our common humanity and shared values.

The authors define a global citizen as someone who understands the deep interconnectedness between individuals, communities and the natural environment. This sense of interdependence and shared identity is the foundation for social justice and meaningful relationships and is essential for a thriving and just society.

The book emphasises that embracing the values and ethics of global citizenship is no longer an ideal but a necessity for humanity in the 21st century. This requires individuals with a global mindset, respecting all people as neighbours within this global community, and recognising their equal dignity and right to a peaceful and prosperous life on our shared planet.

The authors identify several challenges to achieving positive peace, including the ruins of failed systems, threats to peace and human and planetary wellbeing, and the lack of shared understanding and values. They stress the need to move beyond the mere absence of war (negative peace) towards a holistic state encompassing harmony justice, and mutual prosperity (positive peace).

The book highlights the interconnectedness of the 17 UN Sustainable Development Goals (SDGs) with positive peace, and the potential for the absence of positive peace to undermine political, social and economic stability. Other challenges include poverty, inequality, unemployment, global health threats, natural disasters, forced displacement, natural resource depletion, environmental degradation and climate change.

The authors call for a global, holistic systems approach to peace building, based on universal values, interdependence and mutual prosperity. This approach integrates the social, economic and environmental dimensions of sustainable development, and aligns with the UN Sustainable Development Goals (SDGs).

Each pillar is explored in detail, examining the key concepts, challenges and solutions, and providing practical activities to foster the development of related values and abilities.

The first pillar, **universal values**, emphasises the importance of establishing a common ethical ground that transcends diverse cultural, religious and political perspectives. The authors discuss the need for shared values to address global problems, promote ethical behaviour, and foster cooperation and trust. They also acknowledge the obstacles to achieving universal values, such as human selfishness, the challenge of formulating a compelling values framework, the misconception that value-free choices are possible, and the absence of a strong global consciousness.

The second pillar, **interdependence**, explores the interconnectedness of individuals, communities and the natural world. It emphasises the need to move beyond self-interest and embrace a sense of 'we', recognising our shared responsibility for each other and the planet. The authors explore the challenges of individualism, tribalism and the tragedy of the commons, and highlight the importance of cooperation, reciprocity and a global mindset.

The third pillar, **mutual prosperity**, addresses the need to rethink our models for economic prosperity to ensure that they benefit all of humanity and the planet. The authors critique the shortcomings of current economic systems, such as free market capitalism and globalisation, and propose alternative models based on principles of co-ownership, equitable distribution of wealth and technology, and sustainable development. They also discuss the importance of good governance, food security, and addressing the needs of the poor and marginalised.

The second book, *Three Pillars of Global Citizenship*, hopes to equip readers with the ethical framework and systems perspective necessary to shift from passive recognition of global issues to proactive co-creation of positive peace. Its purpose is to foster a global mindset rooted in universal values, interdependence and mutual prosperity, thereby enabling individuals and organisations to implement holistic, sustainable solutions that align with the UN SDGs and address the fundamental challenges facing humanity.

References

1. Branden N. Six Pillars of Self-Esteem: The Definitive Work on Self-Esteem by the Leading Pioneer in the Field: Bantam Books; 1995.

2. Nagel T. Mind & Cosmos. New York: Oxford Universaty Press; 2012.

3. Lutz D. THE INSTITUTION OF THE FAMILY AND THE VIRTUOUS SOCIETY. Journal of Dharma. 2020;45(3).

4. Moon SM. Professors World Peace Academy and Our Resolution. First International Congress of the Professors World Peace Academy; Seoul, Korea: Family Federation for World Peace and Unification; 1983. p. 699.

5. Moon SM. Absolute Values and the New Cultural Revolution. Thirteenth International Conference on the Unity of the Sciences; Washington, DC, USA: Family Federation for World Peace and Unification; 1984. p. 699.

6. Berkowitz MW, Colby A, Kristol I, Power C, Schwartz AJ, Sherman N, et al. Bringing in a New Era in Character Education. Damon W, editor. Stanford: Hoover Institution Press; 2002.

7. Educating with Values: A Holistic Approach to Integrating Values in Education. Melbourne, Australia; 2023.

8. Karvelas P. A Survey about how we see the future should worry politicians: ABC News Australia; 2025 [Available from: https://www.abc.net.au/news/2025-03-10/the-survey-that-should-worry-politicians/105027738.

9. Trubshaw D, Turfus C. The Just Society: Equality or Freedom? Freedom and Belonging: Societal Values Publications; 2021.

10. McGilchrist I. The Matter with Things - Our Brains, our Delusions, and the Unmasking of the World. London, UK: Pespectiva Press; 2021.

11. Dyer W. The Power of Intention: Hay House; 2006.

12. Holden R. Higher Purpose. New York: Hay House Inc.; 2022.

13. Radhakrishnan N. Foreword. In: Swarup A, editor. Give Nonkilling a Chance. New Delhi: Konark Publishers Pvt. Ltd; 2019.

14. Sponsel LE. Reflections on the Possibilities of a Nonkilling Society and Nonkilling Anthropology. In: Swarup A, editor. Give Nonkilling a Chance. New Delhi: Konark Publishers Pvt. Ltd; 2019.

15. Helliwell J, Layard R, Sachs J. WORLD HAPPINESS REPORT 2017. 2017.

16. Scharmer O, Kaufer K. Leading From the Emerging Future From Ego-System to Eco-System Economies. San Francisco, California: Berrett-Koehler Publishers; 2013.

17. Lee SH. Explaining Unification Thought. New York, N.Y.: Unification Thought Institute; 1981.

18. Kyrios M. 2016 Presidential Initiative - THE CONTRIBUTIONS OF PSYCHOLOGY TO THE BIG ISSUES OF THE 21ST CENTURY. Melbourne, Australia: The Australian Psychological Society Limited; 2017.

19. Frankl V. Man's Search for Meaning. New York, NY: Simon & Schuster; 1984.

20. Jin S-B. New Essentials of Unification Thought Head-Wing Thought. Tokyo. Japan: Kogensha; 2006.

21. Singleton J. HEAD, HEART AND HANDS MODEL FOR TRANSFORMATIVE LEARNING: PLACE AS CONTEXT FOR CHANGING SUSTAINABILITY VALUES. Journal of Sustainability Education. 2015.

22. OECD. OECD Economic Outlook November 2019. OECD Publishing; 2019.

23. Bellavance J. A digital moral framework for Australian secondary schools. Melbourne, Australia: Monash University; 2018.

24. Hart T. Interiority and Education - Exploring the Neurophenomenology of Contemplation and Its Potential Role in Learning. Journal of Transformative Education. 2008;6(4).

25. Schlein L. More People Die from Suicide Than From Wars, Natural Disasters Combined: SCIENCE & HEALTH; 2014 [

26. Colby A, Damon W. The Power of Ideals The Real Story of Moral Choice. New York, NY: Oxford University Press; 2015.

27. Hart D, Atkins R, Ford D. Urban America as a Context for the Development of Moral Identity in Adolescence. Journal of Social Issues. 1998;54(3):513-30.

28. Frankl V. Man's Search for Meaning. Boston USA: Beacon Press; 2006.

29. Hosier SAS. Trauma in the Mind and Pain in the Body Mind-Body Interactions in Psychogenic Pain. HUMAN ARCHITECTURE: JOURNAL OF THE SOCIOLOGY OF SELF-KNOWLEDGE. 2011;9(1).

30. A Call for Connection: Understanding and Addressing Youth Loneliness in Australia. Sydney, Australia: Ending Loneliness Together; 2025.

31. Damon W. Noble Purpose: The Joy of Living a Meaningful Life. USA: Templeton Press; 2003.

32. Combs A. Consciouness Explained Better. Saint-Paul, MN: Paragon House; 2009.

33. Carnegie JSPCJ. Heroes - a guide to realising your dreams. Australia2003.

34. Moon SM. PERSEVERANCE AND CONTEMPLATION London, England: Family Federation for World Peace and Unification; 1978 [699].

35. Greenleaf RK. Servant Leadership. New York: Paulist Press; 2002.

36. Malti T, Latzko B. Moral Emotions. Encyclopedia of Human Behavior (Second Edition): 2 Elsevier Inc.; 2012. p. 644-9.

37. Allegory of the cave: Wikipedia; 2022 [Available from: https://en.wikipedia.org/wiki/Allegory_of_the_cave.

38. Griffith J. Freedom The End of the Human Condition. Sydney, Australia: WTM Publishing and Communications Pyy Ltd; 2019.

39. Goleman D. Emotional Intelligence and Working With Emotional Intelligence. London: Bloomsbury Publishing; 2004.

40. Peterson JB. 12 Rules for Life An Antidote To Chaos. Canada: Penguin Random House; 2018.

41. Fenn K, Byrne M. The key principles of cognitive behavioural therapy. InnovAiT. 2013;6(9).

42. Alberts SFPH. 3 Positive CBT Exercises. Positive Spychology.com; 2022.

43. Branden N. Answering Misconceptions about Self-Esteem: nathanielbranden.com; 2013 [Available from: https://nathanielbranden.com/answering-misconceptions-about-selfesteem/.

44. Tolle E. The Power of Now - A Guide to Spiritual Enlightment. Novat, California: Namaste Publishing; 1999.

45. King ML. "Mental and Spiritual Slavery," Sermon at Dexter Avenue Baptist Church: Stanford University; 1954 [Available from: https://kinginstitute.stanford.edu/king-papers/documents/mental-and-spiritual-slavery-sermon-dexter-avenue-baptist-church.

46. Greaney MD. Why "Binary"? The Just Third Way.org: The Just Third Way; 2024 [Available from: https://just3rdway.blogspot.com/2024/11/why-binary.html.

47. Haden J. Why You Should Stop Complaining Today, Backed by Neuroscience: Inc. Australia; 2024 [Available from: https://www.inc-aus.com/jeff-haden/why-you-should-stop-complaining-today-backed-by-neuroscience.html.

48. Gruber J, Mauss IB, Tamir M. A Dark Side of Happiness? How, When, and Why Happiness Is Not Always Good. Perspectives on Psychological Science. 2011;6(3).

49. Okan N, Ekşi H. Spirituality in Logotherapy. SPIRITUAL PSYCHOLOGY AND COUNSELING. 2017;2(2):143–64.

50. Our Definition of Self Esteem: The National Association for Self-Esteem; 2016 [Available from: https://healthyselfesteem.org/about-self-esteem/.

51. Reasoner R. POSITION PAPER ON THE MEANING OF SELF-ESTEEM: The National Association for Self-Esteem; 2016 [Available from: https://healthyselfesteem.org/about-self-esteem/meaning-of-self-esteem/.

52. Devine T, Saunders JHJ, Wilson JRWA. Educating for Life's True Purpose - Fostering Character, Love and Service. New York, NY: International Education Foundation; 2001.

53. Berkowitz MW, Grych JH. Fostering Goodness: Teaching Parents to Facilitate Children's Moral Development: Marquette University; 1998 [Available

from: http://tigger.uic.edu/~lnucci/MoralEd/articles/berkowitzfostering.html.

54. Zimberoff DHD. The hero's journey of self-transformation: models of higher development from mythology. Journal of Heart Centered Therapies. 2009;12(2).

55. Villate VM. Qualitative research as a hero's journey: six archetypes to draw on. The Qualitative Report. 2012.

56. Lawson G. The hero's journey as a developmental metaphor in counseling. Journal of Humanistic Counseling, Education and Development. 2005;44(2).

57. Saver P. Your Guide To Discovering Your Own Unique Life Purpose. Goodna, QLD Australia: Mind Body Rich for World Peace; 2010.

58. Philosophy of mind: New World Encyclopedia; 2022 [Available from: https://www.newworldencyclopedia.org/entry/Philosophy_of_mind.

59. Freeborn A. The history of the brain and mind sciences. History of the Human Sciences. 2019; 32(3):145–54.

60. Reductionism: New World Encyclopedia; 2022 [Available from: https://www.newworldencyclopedia.org/entry/Reductionism.

61. Brigandt I, Love A. Reductionism in Biology: Stanford Encyclopedia of Philosophy; 2017 [cited 2022 27/09]. Available from: https://plato.stanford.edu/entries/reduction-biology/.

62. Baumeister RF, Masicampo EJ, Vohs KD. Do conscious thoughts cause behavior? Annual review of psychology. 2011;62:331–61.

63. Heller MA. Mind and Body: Psychology and Neuroscience. Perception. 2004;33(4):383-5.

64. Wu W. The Neuroscience of Consciousness: Stanford Encyclopedia of Philosophy; 2018 [

65. Fogg BJ. On the Journey to New Habits, Take Tiny Steps. Dow Jones & Company Inc; 2020.

66. Hu M, Wang X, Zhang W, Hu X, Chen A. Neural interactions mediating conflict control and its training-induced plasticity. NeuroImage. 2017;163:390-7.

67. Friedrich E, Wood G, Scherer R, Neuper C. Mind over brain, brain over mind: cognitive causes and consequences of controlling brain activity. Frontiers in Human Neuroscience. 2014.

68. Bueno D. Genetics and Learning: How the Genes Influence Educational Attainment. Front Psychol. 2019;10.

69. Pereira A. Triple-aspect monism: A conceptual framework for the science of human consciousness. In: Lehmann D, Junior AP, editors. The Unity of Mind, Brain and World: Current Perspectives on a Science of Consciousness: Cambridge University Press; 2015.

70. Covey SR. Foreword. Servant Leadership. New York: Paulist Press; 2002.

71. Smith N, Siegel E. DESDEMONA'S INNER CONFLICTS. Psychoanalytic Review. 2010;97(1):137.

72. Wagener D, Thomas S. Impulse Control Disorders and Substance Abuse: American Addiction Centers; 2019 [Available from: https://americanaddictioncenters.org/co-occurring-disorders/impulse-control-disorder.

73. Bonnstetter R. Book Review – Altered Traits: Science Reveals How Meditation Changes Your Mind, Brain, and Body. Neuro Regulation. 2018;5(3):103–4.

74. Goodwin GP. Moral Character in Person Perception. Current Directions in Psychological Science. 2015;24(1):38-44.

75. Eby RA, Hartley PL, Hodges PJ, Hoffpauir R, Newbanks S, Kelley JH. Moral Integrity and Moral Courage: Can You Teach It? The Journal of nursing education. 2013;52(4):229-33.

76. Laabs C. Perceptions of moral integrity: Contradictions in need of explanation. Nursing ethics. 2011;16(3):431-40.

77. Volkman R. Computer ethics beyond mere compliance. Journal of Information, Communication and Ethics in Society. 2015;13(3/4):176-89.

78. Durant W. The Story of Philosophy. Garden City, New York: Garden City Publishing; 1926.

79. Morales-Sánchez R, Cabello-Medina C. The Role of Four Universal Moral Competencies in Ethical Decision-Making. Journal of Business Ethics. 2013;116(4):717-34

80. Colman AM. A Dictionary of Psychology: Oxford University Press; 2015. Available from: http://www.oxfordreference.com.ezproxy.lib.monash.edu.au/view/10.1093/acref/9780199657681.001.0001/acref-9780199657681-e-4007.

81. Galla BM, Wood JJ. Trait Self‐Control Predicts Adolescents' Exposure and Reactivity to Daily Stressful Events. Journal of Personality. 2015;88(1):69-83.

82. Silva SD, Moreira B, Jr NDC. 2D:4D Digit Ratio Predicts Delay of Gratification in Preschoolers. PLoS ONE. 2014;9(12).

83. Johansson F, Rozental A, Edlund K, Côté P, Sundberg T, Onell C, et al. Associations Between Procrastination and Subsequent Health Outcomes Among University Students in Sweden. JAMA network open. 2023;6(1):e2249346.

84. Hassed C. Mindful Learning: why attention matters in education. Department of General Practice Mindfulness coordinator Monash University 2018.

85. Fogg B. Tiny Habits - The Small Changes That Change Everything. New York: Ebury Publishing; 2020.

86. Palmer SB, Wehmeyer ML. Promoting self-determination in early elementary school: Teaching self-regulated problem-solving and goal-setting skills. Remedial and Special Education. 2003;24(2):115-26.

87. Rouillard L. Goals and goal setting: achieving measured objectives. Oklahoma City, USA: Crisp Learning 2003.

88. Schutte NS, Malouff JM. The connection between mindfulness and flow: A meta-analysis. Personality and Individual Differences. 2023;200.

89. Schwab K. The Fourth Industrial Revolution. Geneva: World Economic Forum; 2016.

90. Bartunek JM. Contemplation and Organization Studies: Why contemplative activities are so crucial for our academic lives. Organization Studies. 2019;40(10):1463–79.

91. Mental Health [Internet]. World Health Organization 2020. Available from: https://www.who.int/news-room/fact-sheets/detail/mental-health-strengthening-our-response.

92. Kador T, Chatterjee H. Object-based learning and well-being: Exploring material connections: Routledge; 2020.

93. Anālayo B. Adding historical depth to definitions of mindfulness. Current Opinion in Psychology. 2019;28:11-4.

94. Schuman-Olivier Z, Trombka M, Lovas DA, Brewer JA, Vago DR, Gawande R, et al. Mindfulness and behavior change. Harvard Review of Psychiatry. 2020;28(6):371-94.

95. Baer RA. Mindfulness training as a clinical intervention: a conceptual and empirical review. Clinical Psychology: Science and Practice. 2003;10(2):125.

96. Brown KW, Ryan RM. The benefits of being present: mindfulness and its role in psychological well-being. Journal of Personality and Social Psychology. 2003;84(4):822.

97. Tang Y-Y, Hölzel BK, Posner MI. The neuroscience of mindfulness meditation. Nature Reviews Neuroscience. 2015;16(4):213-25.

98. Vasudevan S, Reddy JK. Mindfulness as the Key to Well-Being: A Review of Literature. The International Journal of Emotional Education. 2018;6:186-92.

99. Crane RS, Hecht FM. Intervention integrity in mindfulness-based research. Mindfulness. 2018;9:1370-80.

100. Matiz A, Fabbro F, Paschetto A, Cantone D, Paolone AR, Crescentini C. Positive impact of mindfulness meditation on mental health of female teachers during the COVID-19 outbreak in Italy. International Journal of Environmental Research and Public Health. 2020;17(18):6450.

101. Carlson LE, Ursuliak Z, Goodey E, Angen M, Speca M. The effects of a mindfulness meditation-based stress reduction program on mood and symptoms of stress in cancer outpatients: 6-month follow-up. Supportive care in Cancer. 2001;9:112-23.

102. Ghodspour Z, Najafi M, Rahimian Boogar I. Effectiveness of mindfulness-based cognitive therapy on psychological aspects of quality of life, depression, anxiety, and stress among patients with multiple sclerosis. Practice in Clinical Psychology. 2018;6(4):215-22.

103. Wang N. EFL teachers' mindfulness and emotion regulation in language context. Frontiers in Psychology. 2022;13:877108.

104. Wells CM, Klocko BA. Principal well-being and resilience: Mindfulness as a means to that end. NASSP Bulletin. 2018;102(2):161-73.

105. Gobout N, Morissette Harvey F, Cyr G, Bélanger C. Cumulative childhood trauma and couple satisfaction: Examining the mediating role of mindfulness. Mindfulness. 2020;11:1723-33.

106. Luberto CM, Hall DL, Park ER, Haramati A, Cotton S. A perspective on the similarities and differences between mindfulness and relaxation. Global Advances in Health and Medicine. 2020;9:2164956120905597.

107. Kostanski M, Hassed C. Mindfulness as a concept and a process. Australian Psychologist. 2008;43(1):15-21.

108. Sacchet MD, LaPlante RA, Wan Q, Pritchett DL, Lee AKC, Hämäläinen M, et al. Attention Drives Synchronization of Alpha and Beta Rhythms between Right Inferior Frontal and Primary Sensory Neocortex. Journal of Neuroscience. 2015;35(5):2074-82.

109. Haidt GLJ. The Codling of the American Mind. UK: Penguin Random House; 2019.

110. Olendzki A. The Fourth Foundation of Mindfulness: Barre Centre for Buddhist Studies; 2004 [Available from: https://www.buddhistinquiry.org/article/the-fourth-foundation-of-mindfulness/.

111. Weis R, Ray SD, Cohen TA. Mindfulness as a way to cope with COVID‐19‐related stress and anxiety. Counselling and Psychotherapy Research. 2021;21(1):8-18.

112. Klapproth F, Federkeil L, Heinschke F, Jungmann T. Teachers' Experiences of Stress and Their Coping Strategies during COVID-19 Induced Distance Teaching. Journal of Pedagogical Research. 2020;4(4):444-52.

113. Naz R. Migrating to e-Learning- Modeling the Framework. Journal of Samoan Studies. 2023;13(1):11-20.

114. Naz R, Khan MH, Peseta-Esau F. Education in Emergencies in Samoa. Journal of Samoan Studies. 2023;13(1):73-8.

115. Naz R, Khan MH, Tamanikaiyaroi LU, editors. COVID-19 Pandemic and Its Impact for Teaching and Learning: Systematic Review of the Literature. Samoa VPEC 2021 "Re-imagining Pacific Education Together for the New and Sustainable Normal" 2021 13-14 December, 2021. ; Le Papaigalagala Campus, Apia, Samoa.

116. Suárez-García Z, Álvarez-García D, García-Redondo P, Rodríguez C. The effect of a mindfulness-based intervention on attention, self-control, and aggressiveness in primary school pupils. International Journal of Environmental Research and Public Health. 2020;17(7):2447.

117. Zohar D. 12 Principles of SQ: Oxford Quantum Systems Dynamics Ltd; 2023 [

118. Martins EC, Osorio A, Verıssimo M, Martins C. Emotion understanding in preschool children: The role of executive functions. International Journal of Behavioral Development. 2016;40(1):1–10.

119. Goldstein AN, Greer SM, Saletin JM, Harvey AG, Nitschke JB, Walker MP. Tired and Apprehensive: Anxiety Amplifies the Impact of Sleep Loss on Aversive Brain Anticipation. Journal of Neuroscience. 2013;33(26).

120. Whitbourne SK. 5 Ways to Get Your Unwanted Emotions Under Control: Psychology Today; 2015 [Available from: https://www.psychologytoday.com/au/blog/fulfillment-any-age/201502/5-ways-get-your-unwanted-emotions-under-control.

121. Razzetti G. Your Success Depends on the Emotional Culture: Spychology Today; 2019 [Available from: https://www.psychologytoday.com/au/blog/the-adaptive-mind/201904/your-success-depends-the-emotional-culture.

122. Anwar MA, Osman-Gani AM. The Effects of Spiritual Intelligence and its Dimensions on Organizational Citizenship Behaviour. Journal of Industrial Engineering and Management. 2015;8(4):1162-78.

123. Mayer JD, Caruso D, R, Salovey P. Emotional Intelligence Meets Traditional Standards for an Intelligence. Intelligence. 2000;27(4):267-98.

124. Mayer JD, Salovey P, Caruso DR, Cherkasskiy L. Emotional intelligence: Cambridge University Press; 2011.

125. Salovey P, Mayer JD. Emotional Intelligence. Imagination, Cognition and Personality - Sage. 1990;9(3).

126. Greenberg J. Behaviour in Organizations, Second Canadian Edition. Instructor's Resource Manual with Video Guide: Scarborough, Ont.: Prentice Hall Canada Incorporated; 2000.

127. Johns G, Saks AM. Organizational Behaviour: Understanding and Managing Life at Work: Addison Wesley Longman; 2001.

128. Barling J, Slater F, Kelloway EK. Transformational leadership and emotional intelligence: An exploratory study. Leadership & Organization Development Journal. 2000;21(3):157-61.

129. George JM. Emotions and leadership: The role of emotional intelligence. Human Relations. 2000;53(8):1027-55.

130. Marshall-Mies JC, Fleishman EA, Martin JA, Zaccaro SJ, Baughman WA, McGee ML. Development and evaluation of cognitive and metacognitive measures for predicting leadership potential. The Leadership Quarterly. 2000;11(1):135-53.

131. Zaccaro SJ, Mumford MD, Connelly MS, Marks MA, Gilbert JA. Assessment of leader problem-solving capabilities. The Leadership Quarterly. 2000;11(1):37-64.

132. Görgens-Ekermans G, Roux C. Revisiting the emotional intelligence and transformational leadership debate:(How) does emotional intelligence matter to effective leadership? SA Journal of Human Resource Management. 2021;19:1279.

133. Prezerakos PE. Nurse managers' emotional intelligence and effective leadership: A review of the current evidence. The Open Nursing Journal. 2018;12:86.

134. Gill R. Towards an integrative theory of leadership: Leadership Trust Foundation; 2002.

135. Patterson SE. Primal Leadership: Realizing the Power of Emotional Intelligence [review]/Goleman, D., Boyatzis, R., & McKee, A. Journal of Applied Christian Leadership. 2008;2(2):76-80.

136. Yukl GA. Leadership in Organizations. 7. ed., global ed. ed. Upper Saddle River, NJ: Pearson.; 2010.

137. Yukl G. Leadership in Organizations, 9/e: Pearson Education India; 2006.

138. Rahim MA. Managing Conflict in Organizations: Routledge; 2023.

139. Gross MA, Guerrero LK. Managing conflict appropriately and effectively: An application of the competence model to Rahim's organizational conflict styles. International Journal of Conflict Management. 2000;11(3):200-26.

140. Jordan PJ, Troth AC. Emotional intelligence and conflict resolution: Implications for human resource development. Advances in Developing Human Resources. 2002;4(1):62-79.

141. Jordan PJ, Troth AC. Managing emotions during team problem solving: Emotional intelligence and conflict resolution. Emotion and Performance: CRC Press; 2021. p. 195-218.

142. Jordan PJ, Ashkanasy NM. Emotional intelligence, emotional self-awareness, and team effectiveness. Linking emotional intelligence and performance at work: Psychology Press; 2013. p. 145-64.

143. Declerck CH, Bogaert S. Social value orientation: Related to empathy and the ability to read the mind in the eyes. The Journal of Social Psychology. 2008;148(6):711-26.

144. Singer T, Fehr E. The neuroeconomics of mind reading and empathy. American Economic Review. 2005;95(2):340-5.

145. Kamdar D, McAllister DJ, Turban DB. " All in a day's work": how follower individual differences and justice perceptions predict OCB role definitions and behavior. Journal of Applied Psychology. 2006;91(4):841.

146. Sehrawat A, Sharma T. Emotional intelligence and leadership in Indian context. International Journal of Research in

Organizational Behavior and Human Resource Management. 2014;2(2):89-95.

147. Sehrawat A, Sharma T. Leadership and conflict management style among Indian managers. International Journal of Scientific and Engineering Research. 2014;5(5):145-52.

148. Rosete D, Ciarrochi J. Emotional intelligence and its relationship to workplace performance outcomes of leadership effectiveness. Leadership & Organization Development Journal. 2005;26(5):388-99.

149. Raeburn A. What is self-management? (7 skills to improve it): Asana; 2024 [Available from: https://asana.com/resources/self-management.

150. Suderman J. Leading Globally: Understanding Cultural Assertiveness: Suderman Solution; 2021 [Available from: https://jeffsuderman.com/leading-globally-understanding-cultural-assertiveness/.

151. Tan C. A Confucian perspective of self-cultivation in learning: Its implications for self-directed learning. Journal of Adult and Continuing Education. 2017;23(2).

152. Yan A, Zheng B. Chinese Wisdom and Modern Management: Cambridge Scholars Publishing; 2018.

153. Aritz J, Walker RC. Leadership Styles in Multicultural Groups: Americans and East Asians Working Together. International Journal of Business Communication. 2014;51(1).

154. Jalaluddin U, Stapley M. Three Holidays and a Wedding: Atlantic; 2023.

155. Popplewell J. What Jennifer Did. Netflix2024.

156. Spering M. Current Issues in Cross-Cultural Psychology: Research Topics, Applications, and Perspectives. Scientific Research. 2001.

157. Spering M. Current issues in cross-cultural psychology: Research topics, applications, and perspectives. Universität Heidelberg Unpublished paper Retrieved December. 2001;5:2012.

158. Richey J. Principles of Moral Thought and Action: Patheos; 2001 [Available from: https://www.patheos.com/library/confucianism/ethics-morality-community/principles-of-moral-thought-and-action.

159. Schwartz SJ, Unger JB, Zamboanga BL, Szapocznik J. Rethinking the concept of acculturation: Implications for theory and research. American Psychologist. 2010;65(4):237–51.

160. Jurkova S. Transcultural Competence Model: An Inclusive Path for Communication and Interaction. Journal of Transcultural Communication. 2021.

161. Muinde B. Difference Between Acculturation And Transculturation: A Comprehensive Overview: Geekbitz.com; 2024 [Available from: https://geekbitz.com/difference-between-acculturation-and-transculturation/.

162. Schwartz SJ, Unger JB, Zamboanga BL, Szapocznik J. Rethinking the Concept of Acculturation - Implications for Theory and Research. American Psychologist. 2010;65(4).

163. Kunst JR, Lefringhausen K, Zagefka H. Delineating the boundaries between genuine cultural change and cultural appropriation in majority-group acculturation. International Journal of Intercultural Relations. 2024.

164. Dhall M. Enculturation, Acculturation and Transculturation: Social Cultural Anthropology; 2022 [Available from: https://ebooks.inflibnet.ac.in/antp02/chapter/enculturation-acculturation-and-transculturation/#:~:text=Transculturation%20is%20a%20term%20coined,an%20individual%20or%20a%20group.

165. Tan C. A Confucian perspective of self-cultivation in learning: Its implications for self-directed learning. Journal of Adult and Continuing Education. 2017;23(1).

166. Chen S, Wu C. #StopAsianHate: Understanding the Global Rise of Anti-Asian Racism from a Transcultural Communication Perspective. Journal Journal of Transcultural Communication. 2021;1(1).

167. Lauber C, Falcato L, Nordt C, Rössler W. Lay beliefs about causes of depression. Acta Spychiatrica Scandinavica. 2003;108(418).

168. Goldsmith B. Top 10 Reasons for Relationship Break-Ups: Psychology Today; 2018 [Available from: https://www.psychologytoday.com/au/blog/emotional-fitness/201808/top-10-reasons-relationship-break-ups.

169. Normal differences and warning signs of a relationship breakdown: Relationships Australia; 2019 [Available from: http://www.relationships.org.au/relationship-advice/relationship-advice-sheets/relationship-difficulties-1/normal-differences-and-warning-signs-of-a-relationship-breakdown.

170. Salai S. More Americans prone to depression as they opt to live alone: CDC study. 2024.

171. Straussfogel D, Schilling CV. Systems Theory. Minneapolis, MN, USA: Elsevier Ltd.; 2009.

172. Seising R. Cybernetics, system(s) theory, information theory and Fuzzy Sets and Systems in the 1950s and 1960s. Information Sciences 2010;180(23):4459-76.

173. Heylighen F, Joslyn C. Encyclopedia of Physical Science & Technology (3rd ed.) Cybernetics and Second-Order Cybernetics. New York: Academic Press; 2001.

174. Mineo L. Good genes are nice, but joy is better: The Harvard Gazette; 2017 [Available from: https://news.harvard.edu/gazette/story/2017/04/over-nearly-80-years-harvard-study-has-been-showing-how-to-live-a-healthy-and-happy-life/.

175. Fuller A. 'Valuing Boys, Valuing Girls' www.andewfuller.com.au 2002 [Available from: http://www.andrewfuller.com.au/research.php.

176. Franzoso E. What Does 'Giving & Receiving' Mean In A Couple? 2025 [Available from: https://elisabettafranzoso.com/articles/givingandreceiving?utm_source=chatgpt.com.

177. The health benefits of strong relationships: Harvard Health Publishing; 2010 [

178. How Helping Others Benefits You! : New Jersey City University; 2024 [Available from: https://www.njcu.edu/student-life/campus-services-resources/counseling-center/additional-resources/articles/how-helping-others-benefits-you?utm_source=chatgpt.com.

179. Kittel R. GTA and Purpose of Life2018.

180. Hastwell C. Why Shared Values Triumph Over Rules and Policies in the Workplace: Great Place To Work Institute.; 2023 [Available from: https://www.greatplacetowork.com/resources/blog/why-shared-values-triumph-over-rules-and-policies-in-the-workplace?utm_source=chatgpt.com.

181. Lee P. Nonkilling Media: A Normative Framework. In: Swarup A, editor. Give Nonkilling a Chance. New Delhi: Konark Publishers Pvt. Ltd; 2019.

182. Matos PFFGd. Towards a Nonkilling Linguistics. In: Swarup A, editor. Give Nonkilling a Chance. New Delhi: Konark Publishers Pvt. Ltd; 2019.

183. Qu L. Couple Relationships. In: Studies AIoF, editor.: Australian Government; 2022.

184. Greene J. Moral Tribes - Emotion, Reason and the Gab Between us and Them. New York: The Penquin Press; 2013.

185. Kim H. Ownership as seen from the Perspective of Unification Political Thought: 'Joint Ownership' of the Principle of Interdependence and 'Public Ownership' of Modern Utopianism. In: Selover T, editor. Interdependence,

186. Wood D. RAFT 2035 - Roadmap to Abundance, Flourishing, and Transcendence, by 2035. London: Delta Wisdom; 2020.

187. Patrick RB, Gibbs JC. Inductive Discipline, Parental Expression of Disappointed Expectations, and Moral Identity in Adolescence. Journal of Youth and Adolescence. 2012;41(8).

188. Hewitt B. Marriage breakdown in Australia: social correlates, gender and initiator status. Commonwealth of Australia; 2008.

189. Wood RG, McConnell S, Moore Q, Clarkwest A, Hsueh J. The Effects of Building Strong Families: A Healthy Marriage and Relationship Skills Education Program for Unmarried Parents. Journal of Policy Analysis and Management. 2012;31(2):228–52.

190. Teens From Single-Parent Families Leave School Earlier: New York University; 2015 [Available from: https://www.nyu.edu/about/news-publications/news/2015/february/teens-from-single-parent-families-leave-school-earlier.html.

191. Waite LJ. The Case for Marriage. Contemporary Sociology. 2000;30(6).

192. Karhina K, Bøe T, Hysing M, Askeland KG, Nilsen SA. Parental separation and school dropout in adolescence. Scandinavian journal of public health. 2024;52(5):632-9.

193. Louden CEHLMSL. Grandmother–Grandchild Relationship Quality Predicts Psychological Adjustment Among Youth From Divorced Families. Journal of Family Issues. 2009;30(9):1245-64.

194. Desai A. The effects of divorce: Focus on the Family; 2019 [Available from: https://www.families.org.au/article/effects-divorce.

195. OECD. The Future of Families to 2030 - PROJECTIONS, POLICY CHALLENGES AND POLICY OPTIONS. ORGANISATION FOR ECONOMIC CO-OPERATION AND DEVELOPMENT; 2011.

196. Chen Q, Chi Q, Chen Y, Lyulyov O, Pimonenko T. Does Population Aging Impact China's Economic Growth? International Journal of Environmental Research and Public Health. 2022.

197. Swarup A. Give Nonkilling a Chance. New Delhi, Seatle: Konark Pubishers; 2019.

198. Ungar M, editor Nurturing Resilience: How Caregivers, Schools and Communities Can Help Young People Thrive. Strengthening Families; 2019.

199. Oudekerk BA, Allen JP, Hafen CA, Hessel ET, Szwedo DE, Spilker A. Maternal and Paternal Psychological Control as Moderators of the Link between Peer Attitudes and Adolescents' Risky Sexual Behavior. Journal of Early Adolescence. 2014;34(4):413–35.

200. Harwood K. Projecting infidelity: Does an individual's experiences with infidelity affect their perception of their partner's infidelity? : California State University; 2009.

201. Montagu A. A Scientist Looks at Love. The Phi Delta Kappan. 1970;51(9):463-7.

202. Berger B. The Social Roots of Prosperity. THE TWELFTH ANNUAL JOHN BONYTHON LECTURE; Sydney Australia: The Centre for Independant Studies; 1995.

203. Ross J, Fuertes J. Parental Attachment, Interparental Conflict, and Young Adults' Emotional Adjustment. The Counseling Psychologist. 2010;38(8):1050–77.

204. Anderson RE, Edwards L-J, Silver KE, Johnson DM. Intergenerational transmission of child abuse: Predictors of child abuse potential among racially diverse women residing in domestic violence shelters. Child Abuse & Neglect. 2018;85(80).

205. Royal Commission into Domestic, Family and Sexual Violence. In: Royal Commission into Domestic FaSV, editor. South Australia: Government of South Australia; 2025.

206. Crosson-Tower C. Extrafamilial Sexual Abuse, Misuse, and Exploitation. Understanding Child Abuse and Neglect. Boston, MA: Allyn & Bacon; 2005.

207. Xiao B, Liu J, Gong J, Luo X. Perceived parental rejection mediates the effects of previous maltreatment on emotional and behavioural outcomes in Chinese adolescents whereas mental illness has no moderating effect. South African Journal of Psychiatry. 2017;23.

208. Yoder JR, Leibowitz GS, Peterson L. Parental and Peer Attachment Characteristics: Differentiating Between Youth Sexual and Non-Sexual Offenders and Associations With Sexual Offense Profiles. Journal of Interpersonal Violence. 2018;33(17):2643–63.

209. Branden N. Valuing Love: www.nathanielbranden.com; 2013 [Available from: http://www.nathanielbranden.com/valuing-love.

210. Apostolou M, Christoforou C, Lajunen TJ. What are Romantic Relationships Good for? An Explorative Analysis of the Perceived Benefits of Being in a Relationship. Evolutionary Psychology. 2023;21(4).

211. Joel S, Eastwick PW, Allison CJ, Wolf S. Machine learning uncovers the most robust self-report predictors of relationship quality across 43 longitudinal couples studies. Psychological and Cognitive Sciences. 2020;117(32).

212. Bureau USC. Living arrangements of children under 18 years old: 1960 to present. . In: Bureau. USC, editor. Washington, D.C.2022.

213. The Father Absence Crisis in America2022.

214. Krause RRE. Cohabiting parents differ from married ones in three big ways: The Brookings Institution; 2017 [

215. Reeves JM, Griner SB, Jr KCJECJ, Shangani S. Exploring relationships between dating app use and sexual activity among young adult college students. Frontiers in Reproductive Health. 2024;6.

216. Borbón LRd. Psychology Finally Reveals the Answer to Finding Your Soulmate: The Gottman Institute; 2015 [Available from: https://www.gottman.com/blog/psychology-finally-reveals-the-answer-to-finding-your-soulmate/?mc_cid=13f52a1a4d&mc_eid=c3b69da93f.

217. Epsteina R, Robertsona RE, Smithb R, Vasconcellosc T, Laoc M. Which Relationship Skills Count Most? A Large-Scale Replication. JOURNAL OF COUPLE & RELATIONSHIP THERAPY. 2016;15(4):341-56.

218. Brittle Z. Turn Towards Instead of Away: The Gottman Institute; 2024 [Available from: https://www.gottman.com/blog/turn-toward-instead-of-away/.

219. Travers M. 2 Things That Partners Value Most In Relationships—By A Psychologist: Forbes; 2024 [Available from: https://www.forbes.com/sites/traversmark/2024/12/14/2-things-that-partners-value-most-in-relationships-by-a-psychologist/.

220. Sama JM. The Gentleman's Guide to Dating: How to Be a Man in a Sea of Boys: Sunstack; 2025 [Available from: https://substack.com/home/post/p-159109681.

221. Treas J, Giesen D. Sexual Infidelity Among Married and Cohabiting Americans. Journal of Marriage and Family. 2004;62(1).

222. 2020 International Day of Families "Families in Development: Copenhagen & Beijing+25: United Nations - Department of Economic and Social Affairs Family; 2020 [

223. Nyarks A, Hope MM. Impact of Effective Communication in a Marriage. International Journal of Research in Education, Sciences and Technology. 2022;4(2):33-40.

224. Adams M, Almonte A. First Time Mothers Definition of a 'Good'Mother. American Journal of Qualitative Research. 2022;6(2):195-206.

225. Melser NA. Soft skills for children: A guide for parents and teachers: Rowman & Littlefield Publishers; 2019.

226. Guillen CN. Protecting bonds for the years beyond today parenting program proposal: California State University, Sacramento; 2022.

227. Buehler CJ, Wells BL. Counseling the romantic. Family Relations. 2011;30(3):452-8.

228. Spears R, Postmes T, Lea M, Wolbert A. When are net effects gross products? Communication. Journal of Social Issues. 2002;58(1):91-107.

229. Victor WH. 9 Important Communication Skills for Every Relationship.2018. Available from: https://edis.ifas.ufl.edu

230. Uwom-Ajaegbu OO, Emmanuel O, Lekan Ajaegbu CP. An empirical study on the causes and effects of communication breakdown in marriages. Journal of Sound Islamic Thoughts. 2016;1(1):46-51.

231. Leuchtmann L, Milek A, Bernecker K, Nussbeck FW, Backes S, Martin M, et al. Temporal dynamics of couples' communication behaviors in conflict discussions: A longitudinal analysis. Journal of Social and Personal Relationships. 2019;36(9):2937-60.

232. Markman HJ, Rhoades GK, Stanley SM, Ragan EP, Whitton SW. The premarital communication roots of marital distress and divorce: the first five years of marriage. Journal of Family Psychology. 2010;24(3):289.

233. Ross JM, Karney BR, Nguyen TP, Bradbury TN. Communication that is maladaptive for middle-class couples is adaptive for socioeconomically disadvantaged couples. Journal of Personality and Social Psychology. 2019;116(4):582.

234. Nguyen TP, Karney BR, Bradbury TN. When poor communication does and does not matter: The moderating role of stress. Journal of Family Psychology. 2020;34(6):676.

235. Woodin EM. A two-dimensional approach to relationship conflict: meta-analytic findings. Journal of Family Psychology. 2011;25(3):325.

236. Wood P. Australia's porn problem Australia: ABC News Australia; 2019 [Available from: https://www.abc.net.au/news/2019-01-16/australias-porn-problem/10668940.

237. Warren D, Swami N. Growing Up in Australia: The Longitudinal Study of Australian Children (LSAC). In: Services DoS, Studies TAIoF, Statistics TABo, editors. Australia2020.

238. Papadopoulos L. Sexualisation of Young People Review. In: Office H, editor.: UK Government; 2010.

239. Martino SC, Collins RL, Elliott MN, Kanouse DE, Berry SH. It's Better on TV: Does Television Set Teenagers Up for Regret Following Sexual Initiation? Perspect Sex Reprod Health. 2009;41(2): 92–100.

240. Collins LM. As more couples use pornography, these challenges arise. Deseret News. 2021.

241. Harden KP. A Sex-Positive Framework for Research on Adolescent Sexuality. Perspectives on Psychological Science. 2014;9(5):455–69.

242. Wesche R, Kreager DA, Lefkowitz ES, Siennick SE. Early Sexual Initiation and Mental Health: A Fleeting Association or Enduring Change? Journal of research on adolescence : the official journal of the Society for Research on Adolescence. 2017;27(3):611-27.

243. Hahn CK, Hahn AM, Simons RM, Caraway SJ. Women's Perceived Likelihood to Engage in Sexual Risk Taking: Posttraumatic Stress Symptoms and Poor Behavioral Regulation. Journal of Interpersonal Violence. 2021;36(11-12):5872–83.

244. Pechansky F, Remy L, Surratt H, Kurtz Sp, Rocha TBM, Diemen LV, et al. Age of Sexual Initiation, Psychiatric Symptoms, and Sexual Risk Behavior among Ecstasy and LSD Users in Porto Alegre, Brazil: A Preliminary Analysis. Journal of Drug Issues. 2011;41(2):217-31.

245. Izdebski Z, Kozakiewicz A, Mazur J. The Age of Sexual Initiation Among Polish Youth: The Role of Individual and Social Factors. Sexes. 2025;6(1):5.

246. Li J, Li S, Yan H, Xu D, Xiao H, Cao Y, et al. Early Sex Initiation and Subsequent Unsafe Sexual Behaviors and Sex-Related Risks Among Female Undergraduates in Wuhan, China. Asia-Pacific Journal of Public Health. 2015;27(2S):21S–9S.

247. Schneider M, Hirsch JS. Comprehensive Sexuality Education as a Primary Prevention Strategy for Sexual Violence Perpetration. Trauma, Violence, & Abuse. 2018;21(3):439-55.

248. Sanderson CA. The Effectiveness of a Sexuality Education Newsletter in Influencing Teenagers' Knowledge and Attitudes About Sexual Involvement and Drug Use. Journal of Adolescent Research. 2000;15(6):674-81.

249. Steinberg L. A Social Neuroscience Perspective on Adolescent Risk-Taking. Developmental review : DR. 2008;28(1):78-106.

250. Norris AE, Pettigrew J, Miller-Day M, Hecht ML, Hutchison J, Campoe K. Resisting Pressure From Peers to Engage in Sexual Behavior: What Communication Strategies Do Early Adolescent Latino Girls Use? Journal of Early Adolescence. 2015;35(4):562–80.

251. Bongardt Dvd, Reitz E, Sandfort T, Deković M. A Meta-Analysis of the Relations Between Three Types of Peer Norms and Adolescent Sexual Behavior. Personality and Social Psychology Review. 2015;19(3):203–34.

252. Hart A. THE SEXUAL MAN: MASCULINITY WITHOUT GUILT. Dallas: WORD; 1994.

253. Manlove J, Papillio AR, Ikramullah E. Not Yet: Programs to Delay First Sex Among Teens. Washington, DC: THE NATIONAL CAMPAIGN TO PREVENT TEEN PREGNANCY; 2004.

254. Long-Term Benefits of Delaying First Sex Appear to Be Limited. Perspectives Sexual and Rproductive Health. 2008;40(2):121-2.

255. Ross MSI. ASSOCIATION OF PERCEIVED PARENTAL ATTITUDES TOWARDS PREMARTTAL SEX WITH INITIATION OF SEXUAL INTERCOURSE IN ADOLESCENCE Psychological Reports. 2002;91:781-4.

256. Steinberg L. A social neuroscience perspective on adolescent risk-taking. Developmental Review. 2008;28(1):78-106.

257. Fuller E. Influences on the sibling relationship: The relationship between attachment style and the sibling relationship, and the moderating effect of living in a household with an ill child: Tufts University; 2019.

258. Bryner J. Delaying Sex Makes Better Relationships, Study Finds: Life Science; 2010 [Available from: https://www.livescience.com/10935-delaying-sex-relationships-study-finds.html.

259. Seshadri KG. The neuroendocrinology of love. Indian journal of endocrinology and metabolism. 2016;20(4):558-63.

260. Förster J, Epstude K, Özelsel A. Why Love Has Wings and Sex Has Not: How Reminders of Love and Sex Influence Creative and Analytic Thinking. Personality and Social Psychology Bulletin. 2009;35(11):1479-91.

261. Comprehensive sexuality education: World Health Organisation; 2023 [Available from: https://www.who.int/news-room/questions-and-answers/item/comprehensive-sexuality-education.

262. Fileborn B. Let's talk about sex: Broaching sexual ethics with young people: Australian Institute of Family Studies; 2016 [Available from: https://aifs.gov.au/resources/short-articles/lets-talk-about-sex-broaching-sexual-ethics-young-people.

263. International technical guidance on sexuality education. Paris, France: United Nations Educational, Scientific and Cultural Organization (UNESCO); 2018.

264. Tatter G. Sex Education that Goes Beyond Sex - Why schools and families need to talk about relationships, caring, and consent as part of a comprehensive approach to sex ed: Harvard Graduate School of Education; 2018 [Available from: https://www.gse.harvard.edu/ideas/usable-knowledge/18/11/sex-education-goes-beyond-sex.

265. Goldfarb ES, Lieberman LD. Three Decades of Research: The Case for Comprehensive Sex Education. Adolescent Health. 2021;68(1):13-27.

266. Junkins T. An Education Model for Teaching Nonkilling. In: Swarup A, editor. Give Nonkilling a Chance. New Delhi: Konark Publishers Pvt. Ltd; 2019.

267. Haddad D. Attachment Styles Influence on Relationships2020.

268. Armsden GC, Greenberg MT. The inventory of parent and peer attachment: Individual differences and their relationship to psychological well-being in adolescence. Journal of Youth and Adolescence. 1987;16:427–54.

269. El-Sheikh M, Shimizu M, Erath SA, Philbrook LE, Hinnant JB. Dynamic patterns of marital conflict: Relations to trajectories of adolescent adjustment. Dev Psychol. 2019;55(8):1720-32.

270. Maya J, Fuentes I, Arcos-Romero AI, Jiménez L. Parental Attachment and Psychosocial Adjustment in Adolescents Exposed to Marital Conflict. Children. 2024;11(3):291.

271. Feinberg ME, Solmeyer AR, McHale SM. The Third Rail of Family Systems: Sibling Relationships, Mental and Behavioral Health, and Preventive Intervention in Childhood and Adolescence. Clinical child and family psychology review. 2012;15(1):43-57.

272. Why does child abuse happen? : Department of Child Safety, Youth and Women Queensland, Australia; 2020 [Available from: https://www.csyw.qld.gov.au/child-family/protecting-children/what-child-abuse/why-does-child-abuse-happen.

273. Darling N, Steinberg L. Parenting style as context: An integrative model. Interpersonal Development: Routledge; 2017. p. 161-70.

274. Kusterer KD. IMPACT OF PARENTING STYLES ON ACADEMIC ACHIEVEMENT: PARENTING STYLES, PARENTAL INVOLVEMENT, PERSONALITY FACTORS AND PEER ORIENTATION Ann Arbor, MI: Long Island University; 2009.

275. Sheh NO-M. Parenting styles and early childhood behavioural functioning: A comparison between self-reported and observed parenting styles. Alberta, Canada: University of Alberta; 2013.

276. Baumrind D. Child care practices anteceding three patterns of preschool behavior. Genetic Psychology Monographs. 1967.

277. Branden N. The Power of Self-Esteem. Deerfield Beach: Health Communications inc.; 1992.

278. Branden N. What Self-Esteem Is and Is Not 1997 [Available from: http://www.nathanielbranden.net/ess/exc04.html

279. Wang S, Hu BY, LoCasale-Crouch J, Li J. Supportive parenting and social and behavioral development: Does classroom emotional support moderate? Journal of Applied Developmental Psychology. 2021;77:101331.

280. Sahithya B, Raman V. Parenting style, parental personality, and child temperament in children with anxiety disorders—A clinical study from India. Indian Journal of Psychological Medicine. 2021;43(5):382-91.

281. Salavera C, Usán P, Quilez-Robres A. Exploring the effect of parental styles on social skills: The mediating role of affects. International Journal of Environmental Research and Public Health. 2022;19(6):3295.

282. Cox B, Calder M, Fien J. TEACHING AND LEARNING FOR A SUSTAINABLE FUTURE - a multimedia teacher education programme: UNESCO; 2010 [Available from: http://www.unesco.org/education/tlsf/mods/theme_d/mod22.html.

283. Bickley CS. Analysis of the relationship between parenting style and personal responsibility across generational cohorts: Indiana University of Pennsylvania; 2022.

284. Bi X, Yang Y, Li H, Wang M, Zhang W, Deater-Deckard K. Parenting styles and parent–adolescent relationships: The mediating roles of behavioral autonomy and parental authority. Frontiers in Psychology. 2018;9:2187.

285. Liu C, Rahman MNA. Relationships between parenting style and sibling conflicts: A meta-analysis. Frontiers in Psychology. 2022;13:936253.

286. Pastorelli C, Zuffianò A, Lansford JE, Thartori E, Bornstein MH, Chang L, et al. Positive youth development: Parental warmth, values, and prosocial behavior in 11 cultural groups. Journal of Youth Development: Bridging Research and Practice. 2021;16(2-3):379.

287. Putnick DL, Bornstein MH, Lansford JE, Chang L, Deater-Deckard K, Di Giunta L, et al. Parental acceptance–rejection and child prosocial behavior: Developmental transactions across the transition to adolescence in nine

countries, mothers and fathers, and girls and boys. Developmental Psychology. 2018;54(10):1881.

288. Xiao SX, Spinrad TL, Carter DB. Parental emotion regulation and preschoolers' prosocial behavior: The mediating roles of parental warmth and inductive discipline. The Journal of Genetic Psychology. 2018;179(5):246-55.

289. Zhou Z, Qu Y, Li X. Parental collectivism goals and Chinese adolescents' prosocial behaviors: The mediating role of authoritative parenting. Journal of Youth and Adolescence. 2022;51(4):766-79.

290. Guo Y, Zhang Y-Q, Wu C-A, Yin X-N, Zhang J-Y, Wu J-B, et al. Bidirectional associations between parenting styles and conduct problems in Chinese preschool children: the Shenzhen Longhua Child Cohort Study. Psychology, Health & Medicine. 2022;27(9):2007-20.

291. Li N, Peng J, Li Y. Effects and moderators of Triple P on the social, emotional, and behavioral problems of children: Systematic review and meta-analysis. Frontiers in Psychology. 2021;12:709851.

292. Delvecchio E, Germani A, Raspa V, Lis A, Mazzeschi C. Parenting styles and child's well-being: The mediating role of the perceived parental stress. Europe's Journal of Psychology. 2020;16(3):514.

293. Shengyao Y, Salarzadeh Jenatabadi H, Mengshi Y, Minqin C, Xuefen L, Mustafa Z. Academic resilience, self-efficacy, and motivation: The role of parenting style. Scientific Reports. 2024;14(1):5571.

294. Utomo P, Alawiyah I. Family-Based Character Education: The Role of Parenting as the Basic of Character Education for Elementary Children. JPE: Journal of Primary Education. 2022;2(1).

295. Doughty SE, McHale SM, Feinberg ME. SIBLING EXPERIENCES AS PREDICTORS OF ROMANTIC RELATIONSHIP QUALITIES IN ADOLESCENCE. J Fam Issues. 2015;36(5):589-608.

296. The benefits of chores for kids: Bright Horizons Family Solutions; 2025 [Available from: https://www.brighthorizons.com/article/parenting/benefits-of-chores#:~:text=Chores%20for%20kids%20not%20only,sense%20of%20responsibility%20that%20empowers.

297. Bahr T. 9 Tips to Help Teach Your Child the Benefit of Responsibility: Early Advantage Development Child Care Center LLC; 2024 [Available from: https://www.earlyadvantagedcc.com/early-advantage-parent-resou

rces/9-tips-to-help-teach-your-child-the-benefit-of-responsibility/#:~:text=Let%20Children%20Help%20Even%20If%20It%20Is%20More%20Work%20for%20You&text=Involving%20them%2C%20even%20in%20small,duty%20and%20boosts%20their%20confidence.

298. Sun Y. Among a Hundred Good Virtues, Filial Piety is the First: Contemporary Moral Discourses on Filial Piety in Urban China. Anthropological Quarterly. 2017;90(3):771–800,.

299. Transforming our world: the 2030 Agenda for Sustainable Development: Unitee Nations - Department of Economic and Social Affairs; [Available from: https://sdgs.un.org/2030agenda.

300. Guterres A. Secretary-General's address at Columbia University: "The State of the Planet": The United Nations; 2020 [

301. Education: United Nations; 2023 [Available from: https://sdgs.un.org/topics/education.

302. Morgan D. The Image of s Nonkilling Future. In: Swarup A, editor. Give Nonkilling a Chance. New Delhi: Konark Publishers Pvt. Ltd; 2019.

303. Marten GG. Human Ecology - Basic Concepts for Sustainable Development: Earthscan Publications; 2001.

304. Whitmee S, Haines A, Beyrer C, Boltz F, Capon AG, Dias BFdS, et al. Safeguarding human health in the Anthropocene epoch: report of The Rockefeller Foundation–Lancet Commission on planetary health. The Lancet Journal. 2015;386 (10007):1917-2028.

305. Patkar V. Mathematics for Building a Nonkilling Ethos. In: Swarup A, editor. Give Nonkilling a Chance. New Delhi: Konark Publishers Pvt. Ltd; 2019.

306. Feenberg A. Transforming Technology A Critical Theory Revesited. New York: Oxford University Press; 2002.

307. Floridi L. Information Ethics: On the philosophical Foundations of Computer Ethics. Ethics and Information Technology. 1999;1(1):33-52.

308. Sikka T. A critical theory of technology applied to the public discussion of geoengineering. Technology in Society. 2012;34(2):109-17.

309. Howes M, Wortley L, Potts R, Dedekorkut-Howes A, Serrao-Neumann S, Davidson J, et al. Environmental Sustainability: A Case of Policy Implementation Failure? Sustainability. 2017;9(2):165.

310. Kim JY. Why Investing in Poor Countries Helps All of Us: World Bank Blogs; 2014 [

311. Global Trends - Forced Displacement in 2019. United Nations High Commission for Refugees; 2019.

312. Dunlop N. Teaching and Learning with the Seventh Generation: The "Inward Bound" Experience Journal of Experiential Education. 2000;23(3):150-6.

313. Ku YJ. Is Environmental Authoritarianism a Desirable Environmental Governance Model? 2018.

314. Kumi E, Arhin AA, Yeboah T. Can post-2015 sustainable development goals survive neoliberalism? A critical examination of the sustainable development–neoliberalism nexus in developing countries. Environment, Development and Sustainability. 2014;16(3):539-54.

315. Díaz-Siefer P, Neaman A, Salgado E, Celis-Diez JL, Otto S. Human-Environment System Knowledge: A Correlate of Pro-Environmental Behavior Sustainability. 2015;7(11):15510-26.

316. Green Eco Tips for Sustainable Living: Global Stewards; 2020 [Available from: http://www.globalstewards.org/ecotips.htm.

317. Food: Too Good to Waste Implementation Guide and Toolkit: United States Environmental Protection Agency; 2020 [Available from: https://www.epa.gov/sustainable-management-food/food-too-good-waste-implementation-guide-and-toolkit.

318. Packaging and Recycling: McDonald's Restaurants; 2020 [Available from: https://corporate.mcdonalds.com/corpmcd/scale-for-good/packaging-and-recycling.html.

www.ingramcontent.com/pod-product-compliance
Lightning Source LLC
Chambersburg PA
CBHW081352070526
44583CB00020B/2533